Personal Best Running

COACH COOGAN'S STRATEGIES FOR THE MILE TO THE MARATHON

Mark Coogan

Scott Douglas

HUMAN KINETICS

Library of Congress Cataloging-in-Publication Data

Names: Coogan, Mark, 1966- author. | Douglas, Scott, 1964- author.
Title: Personal best running : Coach Coogan's strategies for the mile to
  the marathon / Mark Coogan, Scott Douglas.
Description: Champaign, IL : Human Kinetics, [2024] | Includes index.
Identifiers: LCCN 2022041751 (print) | LCCN 2022041752 (ebook) | ISBN
  9781718214712 (paperback) | ISBN 9781718214729 (epub) | ISBN
  9781718214736 (pdf)
Subjects: LCSH: Running--Training. | Running races--Training. | BISAC:
  SPORTS & RECREATION / Running & Jogging | SPORTS & RECREATION / Training
Classification: LCC GV1061.5 .C67 2024 (print) | LCC GV1061.5 (ebook) |
  DDC 796.42071--dc23/eng/20220917
LC record available at https://lccn.loc.gov/2022041751
LC ebook record available at https://lccn.loc.gov/2022041752

ISBN: 978-1-7182-1471-2 (print)

Senior Acquisitions Editor: Michelle Earle; **Managing Editor:** Kevin Matz; **Copyeditor:** E before I Editing; **Proofreader:** Leigh Keylock; **Indexer:** Andrea Hepner; **Permissions Manager:** Laurel Mitchell; **Graphic Designer:** Dawn Sills; **Cover Designer:** Keri Evans; **Cover Design Specialist:** Susan Rothermel Allen; **Photograph (cover):** Courtesy of Justin Britton; **Photographs (interior):** © Human Kinetics, unless otherwise noted; **Photo Production Specialist:** Amy M. Rose; **Photo Production Manager:** Jason Allen; **Printer:** Versa Press

We thank the TRACK at new balance in Boston, Massachusetts, for assistance in providing the location for the photo and video shoot for this book.

Human Kinetics books are available at special discounts for bulk purchase. Special editions or book excerpts can also be created to specification. For details, contact the Special Sales Manager at Human Kinetics.

Printed in the United States of America   10 9 8 7 6 5 4 3 2

The paper in this book is certified under a sustainable forestry program.

Human Kinetics
1607 N. Market Street
Champaign, IL 61820
USA

United States and International
Website: **US.HumanKinetics.com**
Email: info@hkusa.com
Phone: 1-800-747-4457

Canada
Website: **Canada.HumanKinetics.com**
Email: info@hkcanada.com

E8728

To every runner who has done a long run in the wind, rain, or snow and didn't complain—because they knew it was the best part of their day.

CONTENTS

ACCESSING THE ONLINE VIDEO

This book includes access to online video that includes 30 clips demonstrating strength, flexibility, and running form drills, as well as commentary from the author, Mark Coogan, discussing his training principles. Throughout the book, exercises and drills, as well as the author's commentary, marked with this play button icon indicate where the content is enhanced by online video clips: ▶

Take the following steps to access the video. If you need help at any point in the process, you can contact us via email at HKPropelCustSer@hkusa.com.
If it's your first time using HK*Propel*:

1. Visit HKPropel.HumanKinetics.com.
2. Click the "New user? Register here" link on the opening screen.
3. Follow the onscreen prompts to create your HK*Propel* account.
4. Enter the access code exactly as shown below, including hyphens. You will not need to re-enter this access code on subsequent visits.
5. After your first visit, simply log in to HKPropel.HumanKinetics.com to access your digital product.

If you already have an HK*Propel* account:

1. Visit HKPropel.HumanKinetics.com and log in with your username (email address) and password.
2. Once you are logged in, navigate to Account in the top right corner.
3. Under "Add Access Code" enter the access code exactly as shown below, including hyphens.

Access code: COOGAN1E-VXBA-VJKJ-H7NF
Once your code is redeemed, navigate to your Dashboard, then select the **Online Video** from the Library. You'll then see an Online Video page with information about the video. On the left side of the screen, you will see a list of links that correspond to the topics in the text that have accompanying video:

Coach Coogan's Training Principles

Staying Strong and Healthy

Using Your Mind to Run Faster

Following the Programs

Once you click on a topic, a player will appear. In the player, the clips for that topic will appear vertically along the right side. Select the video you would like to watch and view it in the main player window. You can use the buttons at the bottom of the main player window to view the video full screen, to turn captioning on and off, and to pause, fast-forward, or reverse the clip.

Your license to this online video will expire 7 years after the date you redeem the access code. You can check the expiration dates of all your HK*Propel* products at any time in My Account.

For technical support, contact us via email at HKPropelCustSer@hkusa.com. Helpful tip: You may reset your password from the log in screen at any time if you forget it.

ACKNOWLEDGMENTS

I would like to acknowledge that this book was made possible only because of the teammates, training partners, and coaches I've been lucky enough to learn and grow from over the last 40 years. So many miles with so many wonderful people.

To all my coaches and training partners, from the Attleboro YMCA to where I am today, coaching Olympians, national champions, and record holders for New Balance, a giant thank you!

I need to give a special thanks to Keith Gobin, Bob L'Homme, and my Bishop Feehan teammates. You introduced running to me, and you made it fun. To Charles Torpey and the University of Maryland team, you helped me grow and to see top-level NCAA running firsthand. To Bob Sevene, John Gregorek, Ray Treacy, and the entire Providence College teams of the 1980s and early '90s, you believed I could be an Olympian before I knew it myself. To Mark Plaatjes, Steve Jones, Arturo Barrios, Dan Reese, Chris Fox, and Mike Sandrock of Boulder, thank you for opening up your lives to me and helping me reach my potential. Boulder is where I learned I wanted to be a coach.

A special thank you to Barry Harwick at Dartmouth College. A big thank you to the colleges and universities that allowed me to coach and work with the most wonderful student-athletes you can imagine.

Thank you to my coauthor Scott, who put in countless hours working on this book. More importantly, working on this book rekindled a friendship that started in the '80s in Maryland.

Most importantly, to my family, you are the best, and I love you all. Katrina, Margaret, and William, you are everything to me!

—Mark Coogan

Thank you to editor Michelle Earle of Human Kinetics for her trust and gentle guidance.

Thanks to my coauthor Mark for asking me to do this project with him and for helping me to enjoy my training more. It's been great to reconnect more than 25 years after we went clubbing in Sweden.

Kudos to New Balance Boston members Heather MacLean and Drew Piazza for being the world's best (and fastest) exercise models.

Cheers to all of the current and former Coogan's Crew members who shared their stories for this book.

Once again, I'm grateful for Stacey Cramp's patience and support during a book writing crunch.

—Scott Douglas

FOREWORD

Mark Coogan started coaching me in the early summer of 2018, when I began my professional running career and joined his team training in Boston. I was young, fresh out of college, and quite naive to the entire professional scene. Since being coached by Mark, I've qualified for three world championships, won a silver medal in the World Athletics Indoor Championships, made an Olympic team, won two national titles, and set two national records. I say this in the most humble way possible and only because it's pertinent information for the purpose of this book. These accolades wouldn't have been possible without the exceptional coaching I've received from Mark.

The entire season leading up to my first world championships, when Mark and I decided I would focus on the 5K, he would tell me, "You just have to think about running 72 seconds for 12.5 laps." He said it over and over again, at practice or randomly at the end of a phone conversation. I would reply with a short and generally unamused comment like "Yup; thanks, Mark." But in reality this really helped me visualize and wrap my mind around the idea of running this pace for the distance I needed. At the 2019 world championships, I ran a personal best of 14:58–14:72 seconds a lap for 12.5 laps, just as Mark had said over and over again.

Mark has a way of simplifying the work that needs to be done. At the same time, he has the utmost belief in his athletes. He knows their capabilities and knows what they need to do. He has never asked me to do anything he knows I can't do. When talking about workouts, he more often than not presents them as if they're no big deal. When I first joined the team, the workouts were harder than I had been used to, so when Mark acted as if it was without question that I could complete his workouts, it came as sort of a shock. Soon I caught on and realized that I needed to change my frame of mind. Rarely does Mark make a big deal out of a workout, but when he says, "It's gonna hurt," you can bet it's gonna hurt.

I say that I caught on, but Mark might say otherwise. He knows I sometimes overreact about the difficulty of workouts before they happen, but he keeps his cool. One time in particular Mark knew this would be the case, so to make things go as smoothly as possible, he told me I was doing a hard 3,000 meters (under 9:00). That was all he said leading up to practice. Once I completed the 3K in 8:51, I asked if we were finishing the workout off with something else. He said, "Yes, you are gonna do that again in 10 minutes." I was in disbelief but had almost no time to react, so I just did it. I ran the second one in 8:53. I was shocked! He knew me too well—he knew what I could do, and he knew how I would react. It's just one example of his coaching expertise.

This book is filled with Mark's coaching experiences, strategies, and philosophies. Mark has been a part of the running world for quite some time, competing on the world stage as an athlete himself, raising his family around the sport, and coaching competitively at the NCAA and professional levels. He has done and seen a lot, and he is now widely acknowledged as an expert coach. He's also a huge fan of running—he's always watching races and can recite names and race times from years ago. Mark's knowledge base underlies his training programs that are so effective.

This book gives you access to all of Mark's wisdom about all aspects of running. He often says about our training group, "We don't have any secrets." Well, now we really don't, because everything he says to us at practice is within these pages and available for all the world to read. This book is a fantastic opportunity for new and experienced runners alike to learn from one of the very best.

—Elle St. Pierre

PREFACE

You're a busy person who wants to do well at running without it taking over your life. I can help you.

I've coached Olympians, national- and world-record holders, and national and NCAA champions. All of them had more important things in their lives than running. They reached the pinnacle of the sport while still meeting their other responsibilities, being great friends and family members, and enjoying life. In this book, I'll show you how to do the same. You'll learn how to be a happy, healthy runner who is also, as we say in Massachusetts, wicked fast.

This book brings together everything I've learned from more than 30 years at the highest levels of running as an athlete and coach. You'll benefit from the mistakes and lessons of my running career, where I went from not being a big college star to running in the Olympics. Along the way, I was ranked in the top 10 in the United States in every event from the mile to the marathon. As a college coach, and now as the head of an elite professional team, I've continued to refine my program. I'm really excited to share it with you.

What's in This Book

This book has two sections. In the first section, I'll describe the building blocks of good running. Chapter 1 explains my five main training principles. Chapter 2 shows why and how to build a healthy training environment. It's so important to enjoy your running no matter how ambitious you are. It's also important to be healthy and strong, so that you can train at the level you want. That's what we'll cover in chapter 3. In chapter 4, I'll share some simple psychological techniques that give you the mental strength to get the most out of your physical potential. In the final chapter of the first section, I'll explain how to make use of all the running information you encounter, including the data from your gadgets. A good coach sets people up so that they can do well on their own. These first five chapters will give you the why behind the how of my training programs.

The second section is all about the nitty-gritty of training and racing. As you probably know, good races don't just happen, no matter how fit you are. So the second section starts with a chapter on mastering the skill of racing. That's followed by chapter 7, a guide to following the training schedules that make up the remainder of the book. In it, I'll describe the main types of runs you'll encounter in the training schedules, including why and how to do them.

Then comes what you'll probably consider the main course. Chapters 8 through 12 have training schedules and event-specific racing advice for the most popular race distances: mile, 5K, 10K, 15K to half-marathon, and marathon. Each chapter has a shorter and longer schedule. Each of those options has three levels of weekly mileage to choose from. I've got you covered! (Chapter 7 describes how to choose the schedule with the proper length and mileage range for your situation.)

Chapters 13 and 14 are a little different from what you'll find in other running books. Chapter 13 is for the many runners who like to race frequently at a variety of nonmarathon distances (e.g., a 5K this weekend, a 10-miler the following weekend). First you'll get an eight-week schedule to prepare for an upcoming block of races. Then you'll find an eight-week schedule for the busy racing season itself. As with the previous chapters, the schedules have three weekly mileage ranges to choose from.

Finally, chapter 14 will show how to use the fitness you built for a half-marathon or marathon as the base for near-future success at a much shorter distance. The schedules will cover three such transitions—from the marathon to the 5K, from the marathon to the 10K, and from the 15K or half-marathon to the 5K or the mile. Again, there are three weekly mileage ranges in the schedules.

Throughout the book, you'll find short profiles of runners I've coached. I've highlighted parts of their stories that illustrate one or more of my coaching principles. I hope your overall takeaway is that they're happy, healthy, well-rounded people who also happen to be really fast. Do you want to be like them? Then let's get to work!

PART I

1

Coach Coogan's Training Principles

I don't have a one-paragraph coaching philosophy summary. I have something better—a handful of key principles that guide how I coach in person and that are the basis of the training schedules in the second half of this book. In this chapter, I'll explain what those principles are and why and how I use them. You'll also find sidebars about other important ideas specific to the running part of your training.

You should read this chapter carefully at some point if you're going to follow one of my training programs. It's always good to understand the "why" and "how" behind the "what" of your workouts.

Although the principles are numbered, that doesn't mean that, say, number two is more important than number four. They're like ingredients in a recipe that, when combined, amount to something better than the sum of its parts. As you read this chapter and follow one of the training programs, you'll see how these ideas intersect with and reinforce each other.

Principle 1: Be an Aerobic Monster

The training schedules in this book are for races that are almost entirely aerobic events. Yes, even the mile. To succeed at those distances, you need to be able to sustain a hard pace for several minutes, and often for more than an hour. You need to be an aerobic monster.

I like to explain this idea by talking about a common race goal. Many of the collegiate women I coached wanted to break 5:00 in the mile. I would ask, "Can you run 75 seconds for one lap of the track? Of course you can, pretty easily. How about 2:30 for two laps? Yes, but it's starting to get hard. How about 3:45 for three laps? Now that's getting really hard. Could you then run a fourth lap in less than 75 seconds? Almost certainly not right now."

My point was that a short segment at your desired race pace isn't a big deal. (If it is, you probably need a less ambitious goal.) If a reasonable goal for you is to break 20:00 for 5K, then running 400 meters in 1:36 or 800 meters in 3:12 won't be a major strain. You have the basic speed to run that pace comfortably. It's sustaining the pace that's the challenge. Being able to do that requires training that builds your high-end aerobic capacity. That's what I mean by being an aerobic monster.

What does this mean in practical terms? Mileage isn't everything, but most runners will become stronger aerobically by carefully and gradually increasing the volume of running they can handle. Increasing your mileage from year to year while still being able to hit your times in workouts and races will improve your $\dot{V}O_2$max (ability to pump a lot of blood to working muscles), lactate threshold (ability to clear lactate and therefore not have to slow), and running economy (amount of oxygen needed to hold a certain pace).

By "handle" mileage increases, I mean being able to run at something more than a crawl without getting hurt or worn down. A little extra soreness or tightness is common at a newly higher mileage. A sharp new pain, or soreness or tightness that doesn't go away once you're warmed up, is a warning sign. Similarly, if your goal is to run 6:00-per-mile pace for a 10K, but you're so tired from upping your mileage that you struggle to run a 6:00 mile in training, you're overdoing it. And if you're no longer a coherent person during the rest of your day, with no energy for your real-world responsibilities, you're definitely running too much (says the guy who in college studied standing up because he would fall asleep immediately if he read sitting down).

But there's more to being an aerobic monster than simply how much you run. Take two runners who average 40 miles per week. One might run almost the same distance every day at about the same medium-effort pace. He'll be a decent aerobic athlete. Another's week might include a long run, a tempo run, and some shorter recovery days. She'll be an aerobic monster.

I'll have a lot more to say about long runs and tempo runs in chapter 7. Here I just want to emphasize that they're key to building your ability to hold a strong pace. I'd much rather have you run 12 miles on Sunday and four miles on Monday than eight miles each day. Tempo runs are especially effective at raising your lactate threshold, the point at which your effort goes from aerobic to anaerobic, causing you to slow in the next few minutes if you tried to keep holding a given pace. A steady diet of tempo runs will make you able to run aerobically at a faster pace and will lengthen the time you can hold that faster pace. And a bonus: As you become more of an aerobic monster, your everyday runs will get faster at the same effort level, leading to that much more of a training effect.

The schedules later in this book—for all distances, from the mile to the marathon—are crafted primarily to maximize your aerobic development at a given mileage level. For now, I want to highlight some actual months of training by New Balance Boston member Heather MacLean, who made the 2021 U.S. Olympic team at 1,500 meters and was the 2022 national indoor champion at that distance.

These samples show only Heather's running; she also does regular strengthening and flexibility work of the sort I'll describe in chapter 3. On workout days, they show only the actual workout; assume that she also completed a two- to three-mile warm-up and one- to two-mile cool-down on those days.

Bear in mind that Heather's longest race lasts just four minutes. Yet much of her training before her peak racing season could be confused for that of a 5K or 10K specialist. You'll see she does a weekly long run and regular tempo workouts. Why? Because the same principle that was true for the collegiate runners who wanted to break 5:00 for the mile is true for Heather to break 4:00 for 1,500 meters. The average pace to do so—64 seconds per 400 meters—isn't a challenge for her to hold for one lap. What she needs is the ability to run the first three laps of the three-and-three-quarter-lap race aerobically, so that she can sprint against the best in the world in the final 300 meters. How did she get there? In large part, by steady work of the sort seen in these training samples.

The samples in table 1.1 are from the winter and spring of 2021. In the previous months, Heather's training looked even more like that of a 5K and 10K runner. By April, it starts to look more like what you might expect, with more miler-type workouts. With the Olympic Trials in late June and tune-up races starting in May, it was time for those types of workouts to become more prominent. But notice that, even then, she still did a good long run most weeks, and a good portion of her track sessions included longer repeats at more like 5K pace.

One other thing to notice is how Heather records some sessions in miles and others in minutes. This is a great example of someone concentrating on getting the proper work in without being overly precise about it. I'll have more to say on this idea in chapter 5.

You'll know you're becoming an aerobic monster when your training starts feeling more doable. You'll find you're finishing your long runs at a good pace, rather than hanging on and hoping they'll end soon. On hard sessions, you'll definitely be working hard, but you'll feel stronger while doing so, and you'll recover more quickly between repeats. You'll simply feel more capable than before; any given run won't seem to take as much out of you.

▶ Principle 2: 10 Weeks of B+ Workouts Are Better Than 4 Weeks of A+ Workouts

I'll illustrate this idea with some personal history.

Almost all of our workouts in college were super hard, nearly race-level efforts. Some guys on the team actually set personal bests in workouts. If you were grading our workouts, you'd give us an A+.

That might sound great, but we consistently underperformed in races. Then, dissatisfied with our results, we would try to run our next workout even harder. We'd arrive at our next race physically and mentally exhausted, and we'd again underperform. Then we would be back at it in practice a few days later, eager to prove to ourselves that we were better than our race results showed. And so on. A lot of guys had multiple injuries. I managed to stay injury-free but never raced like I thought I should. I graduated from college in 1988 without having qualified for the NCAA cross-country championship.

After college I was fortunate enough to join the Nike Boston club, coached by Bob Sevene. I did most of my workouts with that group while running most other days of the week with a bunch of pros in Providence, Rhode Island. I started realizing there was another way. Bob's workouts never had me going to the well. We might do 10 kilometers of fast running in a session, but under control. Workouts like three 2-mile repeats at around half-marathon pace, or lots of 800-meter repeats at around 10K pace, were typical. If you were grading these workouts, you'd give them a B+. I remember thinking, "This is too easy."

After about two months of this type of training in the winter of 1988/89, I ran an indoor 3,000-meter race as a tune-up before the U.S. qualifying race for the world cross-country championship. I battled Sydney Maree, an Olympian and former world-record holder, in that 3K. Although Sydney outkicked me, I ran a personal best by 10 seconds. I thought, "Wait, how did I just set this massive 3K PR after almost never running that fast in practice?"

TABLE 1.1 Heather MacLean Spring Training Log

	Sunday	Monday	Tuesday	Wednesday	Thursday	Friday	Saturday
January 2021						1 AM: Track workout: 2 × 200 meters; 600 meters hard (1:32); 400 meters in :60; 6 × 300 meters in :46-:48 PM: 20 minutes	2 30 minutes
	3 14 miles	4 8 miles, then strides	5 Altitude training in Flagstaff, Arizona AM: 60 minutes PM: 30 minutes	6 8 miles, then strides	7 AM: 60 minutes PM: 20 minutes	8 AM: 20:00 tempo, 4 × 1:00 hard/1:00 easy PM: 25 minutes	9 30 minutes
	10 90 minutes	11 AM: 8 miles, then strides PM: 20 minutes, then strides	12 AM: 6 × (1:30, 1 minute, 30 seconds) PM: 20 minutes	13 8 miles	14 AM: 8 miles, then strides PM: 3 miles	15 AM: 10 minutes PM: 2 × 800 meters, 6 × 400 meters in :66-:68, last one in :61	16 37 minutes
	17 14.5 miles	18 AM: 8 miles, then strides PM: 25 minutes	19 AM: 4-mile tempo run (splits of 5:45, 5:35, 5:25, 5:26) PM: 27 minutes	20 70 minutes	21 AM: 60 minutes, then strides PM: 30 minutes	22 AM: 10 minutes PM: 5 × 400 meters in :72, 6 × 300 meters in :48-:50	23 AM: 20 minutes
	24 90 minutes	25 AM: 60 minutes, then strides PM: 20 minutes	26 70 minutes	27 AM: 30 minutes PM: 6 (35 seconds hard, 1 minute easy)	28 AM: 60 minutes PM: 20 minutes	29 60 minutes, then fly to Arkansas	30 AM: 20 minutes PM: 10 minutes, strides, 5 minutes

(continued)

Table 1.1   Heather MacLean Spring Training Log (continued)

	Sunday	Monday	Tuesday	Wednesday	Thursday	Friday	Saturday
January 2021 (cont'd)	31 Indoor mile race, won in 4:27 with 30-second last 200 meters						
March 2021		1 AM: 8 miles, then strides PM: 25 minutes	2 50 minutes	3 60 minutes	4 4 miles	5 45 minutes	6 35 minutes
	7 10 miles	8 AM: 5 miles PM: 4 miles	9 10 miles, including 20-minute tempo run	10 8 miles	11 8 miles, then strides	12 AM: 9 × Heartbreak Hill repeats PM: 4 miles	13 4 miles
	14 90 minutes	15 AM: 9.5 miles, then strides PM: 20 minutes	16 AM: 7 × 800 meters (2:28-2:32) 7 × 300 meters (:46-:51) PM: 4 miles	17 8 miles	18 8 miles	19 4-mile progression run (splits of 5:50, 5:35, 5:40, 5:30)	20 5 miles
	21 14 miles	22 AM: 8 miles, then strides PM: 4 miles	23 AM: 10 × 300 meters in :47-:50 PM: 20 minutes	24 10 miles	25 AM: 8 miles, then strides PM: 4 miles	26 AM: 5 × 1 mile in 5:13-5:20, 4 × 200 meters in :29-:31	27 4 miles
	28 14 miles	29 AM: 8 miles, then strides PM: 4 miles	30 AM: 3 × 1 kilometer in 3:00-3:03; 3 × 400 meters in :63-:65; 2 × 200 meters in :28-:31 PM: 4 miles	31 8 miles			

April 2021	Sunday	Monday	Tuesday	Wednesday	Thursday	Friday	Saturday
					1 AM: 8 miles PM: 30 minutes	2 20-minute warm-up, SI joint bothersome, didn't start workout	3 Off
	4 Off	5 60 minutes	6 4 × 200 meters in :30-:31, 4 × 500 meters going through 400 meters in :66-:67, 4 × 200 meters in :28-:30	7 9 miles	8 AM: 8 miles PM: 35 minutes	9 2 × mile in 5:00, 4 × 800 meters in 2:17-2:23, 4 × 400 meters in :63, :62, :62, :58	10 8 miles
	11 13 miles	12 10 miles, then strides	13 8 × 400 meters in :65-:70	14 30 minutes	15 Altitude training in Flagstaff, Arizona AM: 60 minutes PM: 30 minutes	16 AM: 25 minutes PM: 8 × 200 meters in :30-:32	17 40 minutes
	18 10 miles	19 AM: 8 miles, then strides PM: 4 miles	20 AM: 15 minutes PM: 5 × 800 meters, 5 × 200 meters	21 10 miles	22 AM: 8 miles PM: 30 minutes	23 AM: 15 minutes PM: 8 × 400 meters in :63-:65	24 25 minutes
	25 12 miles	26 AM: 8 miles PM: 4 miles, then strides	27 AM: 8 × 1 kilometer cruise intervals (5:20/mile pace) PM: 20 minutes	28 AM: 10 miles	29 AM: 60 minutes, then strides	30 AM: 15 minutes PM: 1200 meters (laps of :75, :75, :67); 600 meters (1:42); 4 × 300 meters (:46, :44, :45, :42); 600 meters (1:36); 400 meters (:60); 4 × 200 meters (:29, :28, :28, :27)	

The 12K cross-country race was even more eye-opening. I finished third, behind Olympians Pat Porter and Ed Eyestone. I still can't believe that result—third in the country, behind two guys who were Olympians, even though less than a year earlier I hadn't even qualified for the collegiate cross-country championship. I proved that race wasn't a fluke a month later at the world meet, where I finished 39th and was again third American, beating people like a former 10K world-record holder. I thought, "You don't go from not making the NCAA meet to placing high at the world championship just because of one more year of maturity. It has to be the training."

My belief in the value of consistent B+ workouts only grew when I moved to Boulder, Colorado, in the early 1990s and started training with people like Arturo Barrios, who had set world records at 10K and the hour run. I couldn't believe how easy some of his workouts were for how good he was! I could match him stride for stride in them, and he was more than a minute faster than me at 10K. I also saw that marathoners like Mark Plaatjes and Rob de Castella, both world champions at the distance, and Steve Jones, who once held the marathon world record, almost never did the sort of A+ workouts we did in college. They went about their business week after week, stringing together B+ workout after B+ workout, while staying healthy, mentally fresh, and able to take on the best runners in the world.

I'm not completely opposed to A+ workouts. I prescribe them in some conditions, as you'll soon see. In general, though, I think almost all of your sessions should be at that B+ level. A+ workouts are really hard mentally. Just anticipating having to go to the well once or twice a week in training can be exhausting. If you're using all your fight in training, when you get to a race you're mentally worn out; you can't bear down and get the job done. See the sidebar "You Have Only So Much Willpower" for more on this.

The second big reason I favor regular B+ workouts is that A+ workouts take a greater physical toll. It's a lot easier to pull a muscle or tweak a tendon or get really sore from all-out workouts. As I write this, we haven't had a major injury on my team in more than a year. It's rare for someone to miss even one workout because they're nursing a niggle or are otherwise too beat up from training. It doesn't matter how big a fitness boost you get from a workout if you can't make it to the starting line healthy.

Think of A+ and B+ workouts as the difference between what you can do and what you should do. Say you can run 40:00 for 10K. On a really good day, you could probably do a workout of 20 400-meter repeats in 90 seconds with a 200-meter jog between. But it would be a major effort. You'd almost always be better off breaking that workout into two sets of 10 repeats, running 95 seconds per repeat in the first set, taking a five-minute break, and then running 92 or 93 seconds per repeat in the second set. The B+ version will have you walking away feeling good about yourself and eager for your next workout. The A+ version might really beat you up and lead to the beginning of an injury a couple of days later. And that assumes you finish the workout. You might wind up exhausted after 16 repeats, and then get down on yourself for slowing or cutting the workout short.

Immediately after a B+ workout, you'll feel tired, and you'll know you've worked hard, but you'll feel like you could have done one or two more repeats at the same pace without killing yourself. I love it when my team says, "Really, that's it? I could do more." That tells me I have them working in that sweet spot. If they say they can't complete the workout, or if they're rolling around on the ground after, I asked too much of them.

▶ You Have Only So Much Willpower

Abbey Cooper (then D'Agostino) turned me on to this idea when I was coaching her at Dartmouth. The fact that we all have limited mental capital to spend was really pertinent to the Ivy League student-athletes I worked with. It's also relevant to most readers of this book, who try to balance ambitious running with work, family, and other responsibilities.

The main takeaway here is that it's really important to understand and account for other stressors in your life that are more important than running and that affect how you feel in a given workout. When you're mentally tired, you're just not going to be able to bear down in an interval session like you can when you're psychologically fresh. Those times are an example of needing to be okay with bumps and setbacks in your training program. Remind yourself that even though a given workout didn't go how you wanted, there was an obvious explanation, and that you still got fitter. Tell yourself that when your goal race is coming up, you might be able to reduce your outside stressors and regain your mental strength.

Training partners are especially valuable when you're in one of these periods. Lean on them to pull you along, or even to get you out the door. You can usually rally when there's someone to share the work with.

If you mostly train by yourself, give yourself visual reminders to help you through a mentally draining time. Post your performance goals on your refrigerator or desk; seeing them should help you get going on a workout that might not be perfect, but that's better than one that you didn't do.

Courtesy of Justin Britton.

Lean on training partners to pull you along when other life stressors are wearing you out.

On the day after a B+ workout, it's okay to be a little tired, but you shouldn't be super sore. You shouldn't be dreading that day's run because you're physically and mentally exhausted. You should feel like saying, "I'm happy to take it easy today, but I'm also happy to run." One of the signs that you're doing too many A+ workouts is that you're not looking forward to training. After all, most of us run because we love it.

You'll see this principle of B+ workouts building on one another in this book's training schedules. Few of the hard sessions should cause you to shudder or wonder if you can complete them. You'll instead see a steady progression of hard-enough workouts that will advance your fitness week by week while leaving you fresh enough to absorb and enjoy your training.

The schedules do contain the occasional A+ workout. For example, week 9 of the 12-week 10K schedules calls for either a tune-up race or a workout of three miles continuous at 10K pace. The latter is hard! That's the first half of a 10K, on your own, while deep in serious training. Similarly, you'll see this on the Tuesday workout in the penultimate week of the mile schedules. It includes two 800-meter repeats at your mile race pace. If that's not an A+ workout, I don't know what is.

Doing a workout that hard once in a great while steels you mentally for racing. I most often have runners do them as an important race approaches, especially if they haven't raced for a while. For example, in January 2022, Elle St. Pierre and Heather MacLean were scheduled to race the mile at the Millrose Games. It was to be their first race since the Tokyo Olympics five months earlier. I wanted them to experience some of the stress and strain of racing before the big stage of Millrose. Eight days before the meet, I had them start a workout with a 1-kilometer time trial. They both ran 2:34, which is fast enough to win most races at the distance. The following week, Elle won her second consecutive Millrose mile title.

I think there will be some innovation in this area because of "super shoes"—the plated, higher-stack models with next-generation midsole cushioning. They allow you to run faster while not incurring as much muscle damage. So there might be more frequent A+ workouts in my runners' future. But there's still the toll of hammering all of your workouts and being flat mentally when it's time to race. It can be tempting to post epic workouts on Strava or elsewhere online. Just remember that they give out medals for races, not workouts.

Principle 3: Train and Race at a Wide Variety of Paces and Distances

Consider all of the running you did last week. What was the fastest and slowest you ran? How long was your longest day, and how short was your shortest day?

Now consider an average week for Drew Piazza, an 800-meter specialist I coach. On a Sunday, he might run 10 to 12 miles at an average pace of 6:30 per mile. Two days later, he might do 200-meter repeats at well under 4:00 per mile pace. The day after that workout, he might run for an hour at no faster than 7:30 per mile. On the Friday of that week, he might do a tempo run a little slower than 5:00 per mile.

How does Drew's range of paces and distances compare to yours?

If you're like a lot of runners, you do much of your running within a pretty narrow band. Your everyday pace might be within a minute per mile of your tempo run pace, and you probably don't run your recovery runs three minutes per mile slower than your fastest workouts, in contrast to Drew. In terms of distance, you might not vary greatly from day to day.

That's fine if you want to be in decent racing shape. But to be at your best, you need to work at a greater range of paces and distances. It's important to touch on all your different energy systems. Short, fast repeats, like Drew's 200-meter intervals or the postrun strides I advocate, strengthen your tendons and muscles. They also recruit fast-twitch muscle fibers that you need to be able to call on in the last part of a race to finish strongly. Tempo runs at a "comfortably hard" effort build your ability to hold a strong aerobic pace for a long time. Repeats at around 5K race pace boost your ability to pump and deliver blood to your working muscles. At the other end of the effort spectrum, true recovery runs, done at a gentle, nontaxing effort that feels like you're holding back, allow you to absorb the benefits of your hard workouts and be fresher for the next one.

As for distance, Elle St. Pierre is an Olympian at 1,500 meters, which is shorter than a mile. She does long runs of up to 18 miles. As I said earlier, I'd rather have you run 12 miles one day and four the next than eight miles both days. The training schedules in this book reflect the value of longer long days and shorter short days than a lot of recreational runners do in a typical training week.

So if you follow one of my training programs, you'll be working at a lot of different paces and distances. I want to reemphasize my earlier point about making the days after hard workouts true recovery days. The athletes I coach are better-trained than most readers of this book. They could probably get away with running faster on their recovery days. But they don't. They know they worked hard the previous day, and that they'll be doing so again. They know that striving to hit a certain pace on what should be recovery days will make them a little more tired, and maybe a little more sore or tight, when it's time to go fast again. They know that being fresh enough to have the hard workout they're capable of will give them a bigger fitness boost than running 30 seconds per mile faster on the days leading up to it and starting the workout a little more run-down.

I like to see runners take that same broader-spectrum approach to race distances. I'm really proud of having been top-ten ranked in the United States in every distance from the mile to the marathon. One time, I ran a mile race on Friday and the Bay to Breakers 12K on Sunday. The range of distances within a year and over the course of my career kept me more enthusiastic than if I'd focused on the 5K or marathon year after year. Racing is fun, and you can't run some longer events all that often. Also, the different training warranted for different distances will keep you physically and mentally fresh. I created the training schedules in the final two chapters to help and encourage more readers to race a lot of distances.

Having said all that, I want to make an important point: You should mostly train and race to your strengths. If (after enough experience) you know you're really good at tempo runs and struggle to keep with up others on 200-meter repeats, you probably won't enjoy always training like a miler. You'll probably be most motivated by racing at the distances you're best suited for.

But variety is still important here. Lots of adults who didn't run in school automatically gravitate toward long road races, because they think they're not fast but can keep going. Odds are that many people in marathons are more genetically suited to shorter races. You won't know if you don't try.

A Proper Warm-Up
Is Necessary for Peak Performance

In chapter 3, I'll describe some key prerun exercises for everyday training. Here I want to highlight what goes into a good warm-up for hard workouts and races.

Whatever the specifics, I think it's crucial that you do the same warm-up for both situations. Having a set routine means you know exactly what you're going to do once you get to a race's start area. That familiarity will take away some race-day stress. And on the training side, a solid preworkout routine will have you ready to hit the right pace from the start of your first repeat.

In my pro career, I used the same warm-up for workouts and races. It just wasn't a very good warm-up. The standard then was to do our two- or three-mile warm-up jog, put on our racing shoes, do a few strides soon before starting the workout or race, and then rip right into fast running. If we felt tight or had a little extra time, we might throw our legs up on a bench to stretch our hamstrings.

That's not how my group, or other top runners, do it now. Their warm-up is a longer, systematic process that prepares their cardiorespiratory and muscular systems to operate at

Courtesy of Justin Britton.

A proper warm-up is essential for a good workout.

a higher level from the first step of a workout or race. I'm convinced that my performances back in the day would have been better if I'd done the sort of warm-up that's typical today.

I'll start by describing the preworkout and prerace warm-up the runners I coach do. Then I'll show how best to condense it when you're pressed for time.

Let's say we meet at a track for an interval session. The runners start with some elastic band exercises to engage their hips and glutes. They might use a lacrosse ball or massage gun on their glutes or feet or any other particularly sore or tight spot. Once they feel comfortable and ready to run with good form, they'll do a warm-up jog of 20 or so minutes. (For them, that's closer to three miles than two miles.) If it's really hot, they might jog a little less; if it's really cold, they might jog a little more. After their warm-up run, they do a series of running form drills and other dynamic movements, such as leg swings. Finally, they'll do six to eight 100-meter strides. Barring any last-minute bathroom trips, it's now time to start the workout.

That's the ideal. I should mention it takes about an hour to do. What's a reasonable shorter version that's still better than my old routine? Before starting your warm-up jog, make time for a few exercises to loosen your hips and lower back and get your glutes firing. Mild bounding and high knee lifts are good here, too. All of these shouldn't take more than a few minutes. Then do your warm-up jog. Afterward, take a few minutes to either repeat what you did prejog, or to do a few form drills. Then do at least four 100-meter strides.

If you're really pressed for time, such as if you're rushing to a group track workout after work, I'd rather have you do one less repeat in your workout and devote a few extra minutes to a better warm-up. You'll have a better overall workout and a lower injury risk.

On race day, make sure you give yourself the time for a full warm-up. Aim to be at the start area no less than an hour before race time. That's better than getting caught in traffic or in the portable toilet line or other logistical hassles. Races are special. You owe it to yourself after all the training to set yourself up to do the best you can.

Whatever version of this routine you settle on, see chapter 3 for descriptions of the form drills and other warm-up exercises I recommend.

Even if you know what distances you're best suited for, don't be afraid to mix things up. Doing the same thing all the time gets boring. Focusing on what is, for you, an outlier event for a season can mean returning refreshed to your favorite distances. You might also find that at different points in your running life some types of races interest you more than others. Trust those instincts.

Principle 4: Get the Work In

A phrase you'll hear a lot at New Balance Boston practices is "we're getting the work in." I love hearing that, because it means team members have internalized a really important idea.

"Get the work in" starts from the premise that running is something we love and have chosen. So when the weather is bad, or you face other challenges, don't turn running into a negative. Just get out the door, don't feel sorry for yourself, and do the day's training the best you can.

In practical terms, this usually means not getting hung up on what pace you're running. If it's cold and windy, or really hot and humid, a 10-mile run that my team would usually do in 65 minutes might take 70 minutes. And that's okay. They're still advancing their fitness. Your body knows effort much more than it does precise paces.

The same thing is true on workout days. You're just not going to be able hit the same times on the track in challenging weather as you do in mild conditions. Again, that's okay. Everything doesn't always have to be perfect. Training is cumulative over six months, a year, three years. Any one session isn't going to make or break your program. So just get the work in. With experience, you know what 5K race effort, or half-marathon effort, or regular run effort feels like. Trust yourself that you're working hard enough, regardless of what your watch might tell you.

Find Something Positive in Every Run

People tell me I find something positive in every situation. On tough weather days I have told my training partners we would have been flying if it hadn't been so windy, or cold, or hot, or something. They used to joke that if I didn't run the times I wanted in an interval workout, I'd tell myself the track was long.

I've always had that kind of attitude in all aspects of my life. I recognize it doesn't come as naturally to some people. But it's definitely worth cultivating this mindset. Running is hard, and it's easy to feel defeated by it. Finding something good to say about the day's training counters that negative takeaway. It reminds you the day wasn't a complete waste, and it makes you eager to get out there the next day.

My college coach, Charles Torpey, looked us in the eyes and shook our hand after every hard workout. It was a way to end things on a high note. I've incorporated that into my coaching—I high-five people, tell them they did a good job, things like that. If I say "That was great" after what they consider a terrible workout, they might not believe me right away. But later that day they might think about why they had a tough day and start to reframe things.

We don't train in a laboratory. Every workout isn't going to be perfect. So many things can get in the way of even feeling halfway decent. Don't get down on yourself after one of these tougher days. If you don't hit your goal times in a workout, look for reasons rather than have as your default conclusion that you suck. Maybe work has been stressful, you didn't sleep well, the weather was challenging, or your stomach was off. Or maybe all of them were true!

Of course, you still need to heed what your body is telling you. If you don't get the results you think you should in a workout, take that into account on subsequent days. Do the shorter end of the range of miles prescribed before your next hard session. More is definitely not better in this situation.

An option when the weather or logistics are challenging is to do hard workouts by time on an unmarked course. If your program says to do six 800-meter repeats at 5K pace but the wind is howling or it's raining hard or it's 90 degrees, do the workout on the roads or a bike path. Run at 5K effort for how long your 800s would take in good conditions, and jog for the amount of time it would take you to do the prescribed recovery between repeats. You'll probably stay more positive and engaged during the workout and be pumped about your accomplishment afterward.

Another aspect of "get the work in" is that there are many ways to get fit. When I was training in Boulder in the 1990s, people were really good about compromising and working together. A lot of us were on the same basic weekly schedule and often showed up at the track at the same time. Someone might want to do three 2-mile repeats, another person might want to do six 1-mile repeats, and another might have planned 25 400-meter repeats. We usually landed on a workout that worked for everyone, such as 10 1-kilometer repeats. It was almost always better to not be so precise and rigid and instead have the company on the workout. Sometimes I wound up running a little slower than I planned, and sometimes I wound up running a little faster. I figured it all evened out over time. If you're following one of the schedules in this book but can have company by altering a workout while maintaining its essence, go for it.

Courtesy of Justin Britton.

Get the work in. When the weather is bad, or you face other challenges, just get out the door and do the day's training the best you can.

The exception here is if you're coming up on a big race. Two weeks before a goal 10K, I'd rather have you stick to the schedule and do what's 100 percent right for your training. (You could always try to talk others into joining you.) Similarly, for something like a key long run before a marathon, I'd rather have you switch training days around if the weather is soon going to change dramatically and enable you to really nail that run before or after you originally planned to do it. But for the most part, especially when you're further out from your goal race, just get the work in.

Principle 5: Consistency Is King

None of these things really matter if you're inconsistent with your training.

Overall consistency is the big-picture equivalent of 10 weeks of B+ workouts being better than four weeks of A+ workouts. You're better off regularly running five or six days a week with some quality than fluctuating between nailing a few weeks of great training and barely running the next few weeks.

Think of building fitness like making small but regular investments that compound over time. That doesn't necessarily mean running every day. In my pro career, I probably never went more than three months without taking a day off. I often took off the day after a big race, even a 5K, partly to mark the end of one phase, and partly because it was time to let loose a bit and celebrate. After a marathon, I might take the next two weeks off, depending on how beat up I was. I encourage the runners I coach to take downtime after their season is over, even if their longest race is a mile. They've sacrificed a lot in other parts of their lives. A little time off gives them the opportunity to indulge in activities and interests they may have put aside during intense training and racing.

During a prerace buildup, I occasionally took a day off if I'd put together a solid month of training and could honestly tell myself, "I'm good, I'm just going to take tomorrow off." The days I missed were usually what would have been a short recovery run. Making a few of them a year into no-run days gave me a little mental recharge for the next block of training.

So what I mean by consistency is following your training program the best you can and not taking days off unless they're scheduled, you're injured or sick, or a personal emergency or extreme weather is a true impediment to running that day. You'll see this principle reflected in the training schedules in the second half of the book. Especially in the higher-mileage programs, I don't prescribe a lot of off days. I assume you've committed to training more seriously for the six or 12 or 16 weeks of the schedule you're following. Sticking to the schedule the best you can means that if some brief interruption does arise, you'll feel okay with skipping a day if need be. One missed workout or long run isn't going to ruin your race. (But if you blow off most of your long runs, we have a problem. "I didn't feel like it" doesn't count as a personal emergency.)

Consistency during a prerace buildup also means taking extra care of yourself—regularly getting enough sleep, eating well, and doing your supplementary exercises. These were the periods where I would most often treat myself to sports massage. Being a little more dedicated about tending to your body means you'll feel better running, and that makes it easier to train consistently.

The biggest benefit from training consistently is improved race performance. There are others. You might look at some of the recovery days in your training schedule and think, "Two to four miles—why bother? Won't I be better able to consistently do the really important workouts with a little more rest?" With enough experience, most runners find the opposite to be true. Say you did a long run on Sunday and have an interval session coming up on Tuesday. A few easy miles on Monday will help you feel better on Tuesday. Almost nobody feels better on a hard workout if they didn't run at least a little the day before. That's why in the marathon schedules, you'll see I advise an optional day off two days before the race but a short jog the day before.

Overall, if you've never gotten into a routine of running almost every day, you might not realize that once you hit that rhythm, most runs feel better than when you're more sporadic. Consistency also takes away some of the mental stress of training. If you know you're going to run most days, you don't waste energy deciding whether to go on any given day; you just have to figure out when and where.

I also recommend being consistent with your running even when you're not pointing toward a specific race. Many runners have great swings in mileage and intensity as they shift from maintenance running to gearing up for a big race. That's a bigger stress on your body than starting a dedicated training block from a baseline of decent fitness. If you never feel out of shape, then you can get race-ready surprisingly quickly. That idea underlies the shorter schedules, such as the six-week 5K schedules, later in this book.

My team used this benefit of never starting from scratch during the Covid pandemic. When it became obvious that most of the 2020 racing schedule would be canceled, we switched to sustainable basic training—long runs, tempo runs, and occasional shorter, faster repeats. We trained consistently like this for more than a year. We had short notice late in 2020 that a few indoor track meets would be held. We were able to sharpen up quickly, highlighted by Elle St. Pierre setting the U.S. indoor record for two miles in February 2021.

2

Building a Good Training Environment

Would you like to join the team I coach? Let's go over the basic requirements.

You need to be pretty fast, as in having the potential to qualify for the Olympic Trials, and you need to be sponsored by New Balance.

Those are the easy ones. Here's the real filter: We won't have anybody on the team unless the whole team wants that person. It doesn't matter if you're a superstar who can set a world record. We'd rather have a woman who can run a 4:30 mile and who's a good fit than a 4:20 miler who's an egomaniac. We're like a family looking out for each other, and unlike your birth family, here we get to choose who's part of the family.

Mine isn't a universal approach. Some coaches focus on winning at all costs. Running history is full of examples of athletes who were briefly world beaters and then either quickly faded or simply disappeared. A main reason is that some of them were in unhealthy training environments. For a season or two, they could put up with things and post great results. But their situation was unsustainable. Maybe there was toxic sexism, emotional abuse, or unrealistic performance requirements. Or maybe they just weren't enjoying themselves. Sooner, rather than later, their running tanked. More importantly, their mental health suffered.

The most important thing I can do as a coach is create a healthy training environment for my runners. It's one in which they feel safe, supported, happy, and respected. That trumps any workouts I (or any other coach) might prescribe. In that sort of setting, people can be their best selves, they can continually find joy in their running, and they'll reach their long-term potential. They'll be better people and better runners. That's a win-win that beats winning at all costs!

This is as true for a middle-aged man who trains alone as it is for a young woman on a college team. You'll run your best when you're happiest. In this chapter, I'll describe how to surround yourself with training partners and others whose support will enable peak performance. I'll also tell you about three runners I've coached whose stories demonstrate my overall points.

What's a Healthy Training Environment?

I started thinking like this when my three children began playing sports. The most important thing for me was that their coaches treated them the way I treated them at home—with the care and support that freed them to be their best. If a coach didn't treat my kids that way, I didn't care how well they performed.

I tried to implement that idea when I started coaching college runners. Then, as now, I wanted the people on my team to know I cared more about them as a person than how fast they were. Their well-being was my top priority. I wanted to put them in the best position they could be to run well, which eventually leads to running fast. That was just as important for the slowest people on the team as it was for someone like Abbey Cooper, a seven-time NCAA champion during my time at Dartmouth.

In practical terms, this means I find out how everyone on the team is doing every day at practice. Not just how their hamstring feels, or what they think about the day's training, but how they're doing as people. If they're having a bad workout, I talk to them during it to see why things aren't going well. Depending on what they tell me, I might try to get them reengaged in the workout, or I might tell them that's good enough for today. After every hard workout, I high-five them or shake their hand or pat them on the back while looking them in the eye. I let them know I know what they just went through. And, like I said in the previous chapter, I try to help them find something positive from the day's work no matter how it went.

Supported, Not Coddled

Keep in mind the difference between being supported and being spoiled. The idea of training-group-as-family applies here. My kids know how much I love them. But I didn't spoil them. They had their chores, and it wasn't my job to make sure they never encountered setbacks. In a good training group, you have responsibilities to others. There's an expectation that you'll pull your weight. And, like in a family, sometimes people need to be told their current approach and attitude isn't helping anyone.

Some adversity makes you a better athlete. When I was coaching at Dartmouth, I read *The Little Book of Talent*, by Daniel Coyne, which includes the idea of choosing sparse settings over luxurious ones. Coyne tells how some of the best mathematicians in the world come from a South Korean school that's basically concrete blocks. In the running world, the greatest men's marathoner in history, Eliud Kipchoge, chooses to live most of the year in a no-frills training camp where he helps to clean the toilets. The athletic facilities at Dartmouth were nothing compared to those at the University of Oregon or other big NCAA Division I schools. I tried to get my runners to see this as a positive rather than something that was holding them back. You're always better off keeping running simple and not thinking that things have to be just so for you to do your best.

Treating everyone as humans first and runners second can mean different setups for different people. Elle St. Pierre values family more than running. She's a homebody who is most comfortable with her husband on their dairy farm in rural Vermont. For much of the year, Elle splits her time between training solo there and doing regular team practices in Boston, four hours away. She might—emphasis on *might*—run a little faster for a season or two in a more traditional setup. But she would be miserable. Joining the group for key weekday workouts and altitude-training camps and doing the rest of her running solo in Vermont

Coogan's Crew: Drew Piazza

Personal Bests: 1:45 800 meters; 3:56 mile

Career Highlights: Olympic Trials qualifier; three-time All-American

Years With Coach Coogan: 2021-

Courtesy of Justin Britton.

Drew joined New Balance Boston at the beginning of 2021. A Massachusetts native, he struggled after college as a pro based in Oregon. The emphasis there was almost entirely on results, and when Drew didn't perform up to his and others' expectations, his mental health suffered.

"When the results didn't start coming, I thought, 'Okay, what's wrong? Let's figure this out,'" he says. "When I didn't figure it out in the timeline I thought I would, I was like, 'Crap, what do I do?' In my head, performance was the only thing that mattered."

Drew looked for things outside of running to find fulfillment and pleasure from. But he felt isolated while far away from his family and friends. "It becomes like a loop," Drew says. "You start performing poorly and you need positive things outside of running that will release your stress and make you feel better. But when all you have is running and it's going poorly, then you spend too much time thinking about it, and then you have another bad workout and think, 'Oh no, this is all I have.'"

Running was no longer fun for Drew. He had trouble sleeping; sometimes he would wake at three a.m. and go for a run just to clear his head. In the spring of 2020, realizing that he was physically and mentally exhausted, he returned home to the Boston area.

Toward the end of that year, he and I started talking about him joining our team. I told him it was up to the other members of the team, not me. I also told him we really are a team—a group that supports and cares for each other, not just fellow fast people to train with.

"I didn't have the year I wanted," Drew says about 2021. Although he qualified for the Olympic Trials, he didn't make the 800-meter final, which was a big goal.

"But," Drew says, "it didn't sting as much as other years because I had a lot of fun. I really enjoyed myself with the team. Everyone really did have each other's back. We're friends, talking about things other than track, rather than always talking about running like that's all there is to life. It released the burden of thinking track is the only thing I have."

"I still get worked up about how my season is going," Drew says, "but I'm not freaking out as much as I used to. Now, if I have a race that's not how I think it should be, I think about what I need to do to get to where I want to be. And if I can't get to that point for some weird reason, that's okay, too—it's not the end of the world. I'm glad I've gotten further away from that all-or-nothing, freaking-out mindset."

If that was Drew's main takeaway from an Olympic year, then I did my job as his coach.

is what's best long term for Elle. It allows her to spend lots of time with both her family and her teammates. And it has allowed accomplishments like winning a world silver medal, making an Olympic final, and setting U.S. records.

Grounding my coaching in the human element is more important than something like having a PhD in exercise science. You need to know the science and training theory, of course, but you don't have to be an expert in it. The best coaches are experts in people and treating people the right way. I treat my team like grown-ups, like I would want to be treated, like I want my kids to be treated. It helps that my daughter Katrina is on the team. She's a constant check that I am indeed treating everyone like family.

Get a Good Training Group

You're probably not part of a formal training group with a coach and set daily practices. You can still benefit from applying this people-first-runners-second framework to whatever setup you have for training with others.

Coogan's Crew: Sam Chelanga

Personal Bests: 13:04 5,000 meters; 27:08 10,000 meters; 1:00:37 half-marathon

Career Highlights: NCAA 10,000-meter record holder; four-time NCAA champion

Years With Coach Coogan: 2013-14

Michael Dodge/Getty Images

Sam is one of the most talented runners I've had the honor of working with. A native of Kenya, he came to the United States in 2006 to attend college, first at Fairleigh Dickinson University, then at Liberty University. While at Liberty, he won four NCAA titles (two in cross-country, one each in indoor and outdoor track) and, in 2010, he set the NCAA record for 10,000 meters.

After graduating from Liberty in 2011, Sam joined a professional training group in Oregon. He struggled to match his college success. More importantly, he struggled to enjoy his running.

"I felt like someone going to work—clock in, clock out," Sam says. "It felt like a chore. When it came to competing, I just wasn't there mentally. Sports is about more—the mental aspect, the emotional aspect, everything that goes into being your best."

Sam felt added stress because he was a new father and was trying to become a naturalized U.S. citizen. He started looking for alternatives. His wife is from Plymouth, Massachusetts, so he thought about relocating to New England. But he needed someone to train with. At the time, I was coaching Ben True, an ace

For most of my pro career, I was part of a loose confederation of runners, rather than a member of a formal team. I like running with others a lot more than by myself. Wherever I lived, I was always trying to get people together for both regular runs and workouts. Those conversational-pace 10-milers are so much more fun when you're, well, conversing with others. Workouts are easier, physically and mentally, when you can lean on others.

The groups I was part of were always welcoming. In Boulder, Colorado, there were a lot of guys who could run around 2:20 in the marathon. They could do almost all of the training of the faster guys I ran with—the ones who'd run 2:10 or better in the marathon or sub-29:00 for 10K. Only on hard workouts or if we got rolling at the end of a long run would the 2:20-type guys not be able to keep up. They were such a great addition. Most of them worked full-time. It was inspiring to hear their stories about balancing their jobs and ambitious running. They were a great reality check for us pro runners about how fortunate we were to pursue running without their constraints. (It was also nice to have such easy access to an insurance agent or a loan officer.)

---

on the track and roads and in cross-country who lived in Hanover, New Hampshire, which is also where I lived because of coaching at Dartmouth. Sam made the move in 2013 to work with Ben and me.

"I got to Hanover and it was like I'd found the missing link," Sam says. "Ben True had my back—I knew I could trust him. And Coogan was always there for us. That's what I'd experienced in college—someone who supports you and helps you reach your goals. Being treated with respect and getting the support I needed enabled me to tap into my potential."

Sam's new mental freshness led to some of the best running of his life. In October 2013 he ran what was then his half-marathon PR. On Thanksgiving that year, he won the fabled Manchester Road Race in Connecticut. The following month, he won the prestigious Zatopek 10,000 meters on the track in Australia. Then in January, he set a 5,000-meter personal best of 13:04 at an indoor meet in Boston.

"I felt like for the first time I was a pro," Sam says. "Before that I felt like I couldn't compete with the pros, that these guys were in a different league above me. In Oregon, I'd been throwing up before races because I was so nervous."

Sam also benefited from being reminded how talented he is. Sometimes he would say a workout I recommended was too fast. I would tell him not to overthink it, to just get in there with Ben and start the session and see how it went. I'm flattered now to hear Sam say, "Coogan got me to think that I could do things that I didn't think I could do."

When I left Dartmouth in 2014 to start coaching New Balance Boston, I had to stop working with Sam, who was sponsored by Nike. That's simply a fact of professional running. Sam and I both wish we'd had more time together. We remain good friends, and I've enjoyed seeing him continue to race well, such as placing 11th overall and first American at the 2017 World Cross Country Championships and lowering his half-marathon best in 2018. I hope that Sam, who is now in the U.S. Army, continues to find himself in healthy, happy training environments for many years to come.

Keep this in mind when you think about finding people to run with. You can look beyond people who are right at your race times. Maybe that means connecting with faster runners for some of your regular runs, like the 2:20 guys in Boulder did. Or maybe it means reaching out to slower runners for your easy runs and the first part of your long runs. This is an especially good idea if you tend to push the pace when you're supposed to be doing a recovery run. You can even run "with" others who are a different speed than you on workout days by agreeing to show up at the track or bike path at the same time and doing separate workouts. You'll still draw energy from each other and benefit from the camaraderie.

Gathering a group like this is also beneficial emotionally. Cast a wide enough net and you'll meet people of different backgrounds and ages and outlooks. The miles together will quickly bond you and give you a support network that a lot of adults lack. It's hard to overstate how important that is for your mental health.

Coogan's Crew: Alexi Pappas

Personal Bests: 31:36 10,000 meters; 53:10 10 miles

Career Highlights: Olympian, Greek national-record holder at 10,000 meters

Years With Coach Coogan: 2010-12

Hyosub Shin/Atlanta Journal-Constitution via AP

I had the pleasure of coaching Alexi in her final two years at Dartmouth. She's a great example of how you can thrive in running while living a full life outside of running. That's probably your reality—pursuing ambitious running in conjunction with personal and professional responsibilities and other interests. Alexi graduated magna cum laude in 2012 while being a two-time All-American, an Ivy League champion, and almost certainly the only one on the starting line who was submitting entries to film festivals.

When I got to Dartmouth in 2010, I could tell that Alexi could be a much better runner. I could also tell how important her other interests were to her. It's so healthy for runners at any level to have more in their lives than training and racing. So I didn't want Alexi to give up those interests. I just wanted her to rethink her relationship with running.

"Mark told me I could take my running dreams more seriously," Alexi says. "Hearing that made it easier to give myself permission to take those steps. It made me see my running as a choice, rather than a sacrifice. I started to make choices towards my running goals, such as sleeping more, drinking less, and

The first thing I always looked for in a training partner was reliability. If you agree to meet someone early in the morning before work and they often cancel on you, that's disheartening. I wouldn't keep trying to cultivate that relationship.

The other main thing was simply whether I enjoyed the person's company. I loved laughing with and learning from others on the run. You probably know how, a few miles into a run, you start talking more freely than you might in other situations. Even we pros wound up talking about things other than running most of the time. Training partners who become your friends are a reminder that your well-being is more important than how fast you can run.

It's okay if you don't click with everyone. In Boulder there was a fast marathoner that we eased out of the group. He was competitive all the time, which is something I think you should avoid in a group, no matter how loosely defined it is. He also one-stepped us—he was always at the front, just slightly ahead, trying

---

doing the little things that would allow me to handle the 50 to 60 miles a week that we were running with composure.

"I didn't really change any of my activities," Alexi says about her filmmaking and other passions. "Those all served to help me, and Mark was really encouraging of me being that well-rounded person. It was a bigger mental shift than a physical shift."

Alexi had athletic eligibility left when she graduated from Dartmouth. She went to the University of Oregon to get her masters in creative writing. While there, she earned three more All-American honors and helped Oregon win the 2012 NCAA cross-country title. While at Oregon, and then as a pro runner, she continued to seriously pursue filmmaking and writing. She wrote, directed, and starred in movies, including *Tracktown* and *Olympic Dreams*, that played at prestigious festivals and had widespread release. Her memoir, *Bravey*, was published in 2021 to widespread acclaim. All that occurred while, competing for Greece, she ran the 10K in the 2016 Rio Olympics and competed well on the roads, including a 2:34 marathon PR in 2020.

"I never had the thought [that] that would make me better," Alexi says about setting her other interests aside to concentrate solely on running. "I think for the athletes who are so focused on just running, it's challenging for them to not put those results on a pedestal and not need the success. You have to be a thriving person to do well in athletics.

"My time went to running first," Alexi says. "I think the misconception is that I was doing many things at once. The truth is that there was a priority list and running was the priority. I was running 125 miles a week before Rio. I was doing it as much as you can do it. I was just using the time in between differently than many athletes."

One really important film Alexi made is only five and a half minutes long. She created an autobiographical video for the *New York Times* about her post-Olympic depression, when she found herself wondering what to do next athletically. Feeling adrift like that led to her overtraining and ignoring signs of injury. In her *Times* video, Alexi made the case that athletes should be as vigilant about monitoring and treating their mental health as they are their physical health. That's a great message for everyone, not just runners.

to put his stamp on the run rather than tucking into the group and relaxing. One day, when this guy was pushing the pace as we climbed a hill, former marathon world-record holder Steve Jones started talking about how hard the hill after our current one was. Then Steve put up his hands to get the rest of us to slow. The one-stepper kept going hard and turned to start the second hill, while the rest of us kept going on our usual route, downhill into town. We didn't hear from him again. However it's manifested, rudeness doesn't make for a healthy or enjoyable environment.

Solo and Supported

It's still important to build a supportive training environment if, by choice or necessity, you do almost all of your running alone.

Share your running goals with the people close to you. Explain why running is important to you. Even if they're not physically out there with you logging miles and doing workouts, they'll be with you emotionally. You'll still get the accountability to others that's such a big part of a good training partner or group.

Inviting others to be part of your running will likely lead to stronger relationships with them. They'll see the effort you put in and will be inspired by your dedication. You might get home from an early morning track session and find that someone has made you breakfast before you have to rush off to work. You'll likely then want to show your appreciation for their support and return a kind gesture. Suddenly, this running thing that some people make out to be so lonely becomes a way to further bonds with your loved ones.

Another crucial part of a healthy environment is keeping running in perspective. Even pros shouldn't make it their be-all and end-all. You shouldn't regularly neglect other important parts of your life because you're running, or recovering from running, or thinking about running. Ideally, running is something that adds meaning to your life, not something that keeps you from finding meaning elsewhere in life. As Alexi Pappas puts it, think about running in terms of choices, not sacrifices. It's okay during a short-term buildup for a goal race to choose to lessen involvement with other aspects of your life. But that shouldn't be your default simply because you're a runner. That will likely result in focusing on running more than is physically and mentally healthy.

Like I said, I always liked training with others more than by myself. That's just my makeup. The opposite take is equally valid. If training by yourself clears your head and makes the rest of your day better, that's a huge positive. Just being out in the fresh air, away from screens and sitting, is going to improve your well-being. That will then make you a better friend, partner, parent, sibling, and colleague. You're a person first, a runner second. If running by yourself makes you a better person, embrace it.

3

Staying Strong and Healthy

The best way to improve as a runner is to follow a good training program. There's no substitute for the right mix of long runs, hard workouts, recovery days, and everyday runs.

But the best training program in the world doesn't matter if you're frequently injured, worn out, or sick. There are many nonrunning activities and lifestyle practices that can bolster your running. Targeted strength, flexibility, mobility, and technique exercises will improve your running form, allow you to hold that form better when you tire, and reduce your injury risk. Good dietary, sleep, and recovery habits will allow you to consistently train hard without feeling run down, mentally shot, or ill. In this chapter, I'll describe the why and how of some best practices in all of these areas.

Don't worry, I'm not about to recommend things that are going to add hours to your weekly training load. These are simple, do-almost-anywhere exercises that you can do just before or after running. Think of the small amount of time they take as an investment in getting the full benefit from the running you do. And bear in mind that, although I have them grouped by type, there are crossover benefits. For example, band walks are great as part of a dynamic warm-up but they also strengthen you, lunges build strength but also improve your range of motion, and so on. There's really a lot of payoff from what I'll recommend in the rest of this chapter.

Strength

I was told in college or early in my pro career that if you could bench press your body weight, you were strong enough for running and didn't need to lift weights. I don't know where that came from. Presumably it was made up by someone who could do it and didn't want to lift. I weighed 140 and could bench press 150, so I happily played along and did no strength training for many years. Later in my career, I wised up and was very dedicated to core strengthening and other exercises I could do using only my body weight.

Now, almost all elite runners strength train two or three times a week. My team does so for three main reasons: They can run more, they get injured less often, and they can recruit secondary muscles to hold good form when they tire and be able to sprint at the end of a race. If you look at photos of Olympians Heather MacLean and Elle St. Pierre, you'll notice that their form looks the same when they're a few meters from the finish line as when they're in the first 400 meters of a race. That's not true for many recreational runners.

The strength training we do and what I recommend isn't designed to pile on muscle or help people look good at the beach. It's running-specific. And it's convenient—you can do almost all of these exercises with just your body weight. Do this routine twice a week. My team does their strength training on the same days as their two hardest workouts of the week. This is in line with the principle of making their hard days hard and keeping their easy days easy. If you don't have the time to strength train directly after your hard sessions, later on those days is good. If that doesn't work, the days before your hard workouts are fine. I'd rather you consistently do the work whenever you can than not strength train because you think you should do so only on certain days. The main caution here is to leave at least two days between strength training sessions.

PUSH-UP

Why to Do It

Push-ups strengthen your deltoids, pectorals, triceps, forearms, and biceps. They can help strengthen your abs and lower back because they're done in a plank position. This will help support and balance your body.

How to Do It

Get on all fours, positioning your hands a little wider than your shoulders. Don't lock out the elbows; try to keep them slightly bent. Extend your legs back so you're balanced on your hands and toes with your feet hip-width apart. Contract your abs and tighten your core by pulling your belly button toward your spine. Keep a tight core throughout the entire exercise and maintain a straight line from head to toe without sagging in the middle or arching your back.

Slowly bend your elbows and lower yourself to the floor until your elbows are at a 90-degree angle. Keep contracting your chest muscles and pushing back up through your hands to return to the start position. Do two sets of 10 to 25 reps.

CRUNCH

Why to Do It

The crunch strengthens your abdominal muscles, which help you maintain good running form. Crunches are safer than the traditional sit-up.

How to Do It

Lie on the floor with your back flat and your knees at an approximately 60-degree angle. Keeping your feet flat on the floor, cross your wrists over your chest. This is the starting position. Bring your upper body up so that your shoulder blades are just off the floor and your body forms a "C." Exhale as you do so and hold the contraction for one second. Slowly return to the starting position. Inhale as you do so. Do 15 to 20 reps.

▶ SINGLE-LEG ROMANIAN DEADLIFT (RDL)

Why to Do It

When you run, one leg at a time supports the rest of your body. Single-leg RDLs do many things that improve your single-leg mechanics, making this exercise more pertinent to running than standard RDLs: They increase endurance in the hamstrings and glutes; they activate your hamstrings and limit the amount of lumbar extension that can occur when running; and they improve balance, intrinsic foot coordination and strength, ankle and knee stability, and hip function.

How to Do It

Learn the movement before adding weight. Shift all your weight to your right foot. Make sure you knee isn't locked. Hinging at the hips, push your butt back to bend forward at the waist. As your left hand slides down, your left leg raises up in the air. Keep your right arm parallel to your body, unless you need to extend it to maintain your balance.

Once you can do the movement 10 times on each leg with good form, add weight with a dumbbell or kettlebell. Use just enough weight to make the exercise more challenging. Don't sacrifice proper form for more weight. Do 5 to 10 reps on your right foot, then 5 to 10 reps on your left foot.

LUNGE SERIES

Why to Do It

Lunges are an easy and efficient exercise to build strength in your quadriceps, glutes, hamstrings, calves, and core, all of which will help your running form and performance. They also improve your balance, increase your hip flexibility, develop better coordination, build muscle size and strength, improve spine health, and enhance your core stability. Lunges are relatively safe to do and require no special equipment to complete.

▶ STANDING LUNGE

How to Do It

Stand with your feet shoulder-width apart and your weight on your heels. Bring your right leg forward and bend both knees to drop down to the bottom of a lunge. At the bottom, both knees should be at a 90-degree angle. Drive through your right heel to return to a standing position. The knee should always be right over the ankle. Do 10 to 15 reps. Repeat on the other side.

▶ REVERSE LUNGE

How to Do It

Stand with your feet shoulder-width apart and your weight on your heels. Hinge forward at the hips; bring your right leg behind your body and drop your knee into the bottom of a lunge. Driving through the left front heel, return to a standing position. The knee should always be right over the ankle. Do 10 to 15 reps. Repeat on the other side.

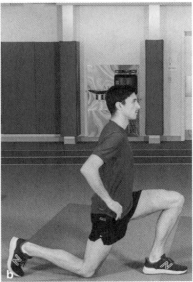

LUNGE SERIES

▶ AROUND-THE-WORLD LUNGE

How to Do It

This is similar to the standing lunge but you do four lunges in each direction. The first movement is the forward lunge (basically, the standing lunge from earlier). Then do a standing lunge to the right at three o'clock, then a reverse lunge to the back at six o'clock, and then a lunge to the left at nine o'clock. Keep your hips forward while lunging to the right and left. Do four or five reps. Repeat on the other side.

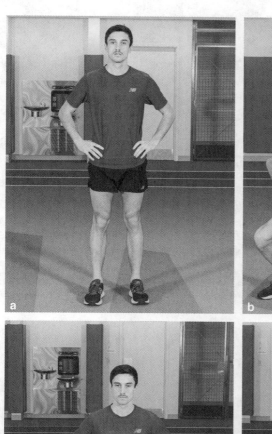

LUNGE SERIES

▶ WALKING LUNGE

How to Do It

Stand with your feet hip distance apart. You should be upright and tall, with your core engaged, shoulders back, and chin lifted. Look straight ahead.

Take a wide step forward with your right foot and plant it approximately 24 inches in front of you, allowing your left heel to lift naturally as you step forward. Try to let your arms swing naturally, with the elbows bent at 90 degrees. Keep your

core engaged and upright. Bend both knees and lower your back knee toward the ground. Stop just before it touches the ground. Breathe in during the lowering part of the exercise.

Press firmly through your right heel and extend your right knee to rise to stand as you lift your left foot from the ground, swinging your left foot forward to plant it about 24 inches ahead of your right foot. Avoid leaning your torso forward from your hips as you take this step. Breathe out as you rise to stand. Continue stepping forward with each lunge, alternating sides as you do. Do two sets of about 15 to 20 meters, or four to five on each leg.

▶ LUNGE OFF THE BENCH

How to Do It

The bench lunge is an advanced variation of the regular lunge. You increase the intensity by lunging with the top of your back foot resting on a bench instead of being flat on the floor. Raising your back foot will put more weight on your front leg and increase the work of your quadriceps. Your knee should always be directly over your ankle, even when using a bench. Do 10 to 15 reps. Repeat on the other side.

▶ HIP THRUST

Why to Do It

This is another exercise to help strengthen the glutes and make sure they're firing. They go a long way in keeping you injury-free and making your core strong.

How to Do It

Sit on the floor with your back against the long edge of a gym bench or some other support, such as a couch or chair, and your feet flat on the floor. The bench's pad should be positioned just under your shoulder blades. Engage your core, then push through your heels to lift your hips toward the ceiling, keeping your chin tucked to prevent your back from arching excessively. At the top of the lift, squeeze your glutes very hard, and then slowly lower your butt to within a few inches of the floor. Do 10 to 15 reps.

If you don't have a bench, do glute bridges. This is a hip thrust with your shoulders on the floor. Perform the same movement. At the top, you should have a straight line from your shoulders to your knees. Do 10 to 15 reps.

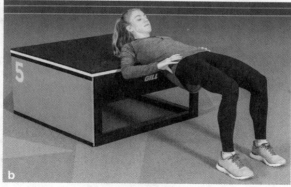

PLANK SERIES

Why to Do It

The plank is possibly the best core exercise for strength and stability. Besides your core, it works your shoulders, back, chest, arms, legs, and butt. There are many plank variations; a few of my favorites follow. You can get a total body workout in with just planks, thanks to all the variations.

FOREARM PLANK

How to Do It

Position yourself to face the floor, balanced on your toes and forearms, with your weight resting on your forearms. Tighten your abs, clench your glutes, and keep your body straight from head to toes. Hold for 30 to 60 seconds.

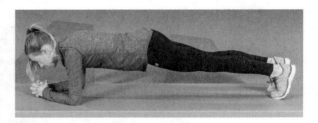

FOREARM SIDE PLANK

How to Do It

Start in a traditional forearm plank. Then lean onto your right forearm and rotate your left hip a quarter turn to the right. Keep your hips and shoulders aligned. Your left side should be facing the sky and your right side facing the ground. Keep your core engaged throughout the exercise. Tighten your abs, clench your butt, and keep your body straight from head to toes. Hold for 30 to 60 seconds. Repeat on your left arm.

PLANK SERIES

FOREARM PLANK WITH WEIGHT

How to Do It

Get in the position for a standard forearm plank. Once you're set, have someone put a weighted plate on your back to make holding the plank position more difficult. The weight should only be heavy enough to make the exercise harder. If it causes your back to buckle, it's too heavy. Hold for 30 to 60 seconds.

▶ PLANK ON PHYSIO BALL

How to Do It

Get in the position for a standard forearm plank, except place your forearms on top of a physio ball, with most of your weight on your forearms. Tighten your abs, clench your glutes, and keep your body straight from head to toes. The ability for the ball to move makes holding this plank more difficult. Hold for 30 to 60 seconds.

DOLPHIN PLANK

How to Do It

This version of the plank is great for mobility and strength in the hips and shoulders. Start in a regular forearm plank position. Inhale while lifting your hips toward the ceiling to form an inverted V. Hold for 15 to 30 seconds, and then slowly return to starting position with an exhale. Do 5 to 10 repetitions.

▶ CATERPILLAR

Why to Do It

These are great for lower back and core stability and mobility. They're also a great warm-up exercise before training.

How to Do It

Standing, start by putting both feet on the floor slightly farther than shoulder-width apart. Engage your core by drawing your pubic bone to your belly button. Looking straight ahead, bend at both the hips and knees, and place your hands on the floor directly in front of your feet. Without moving your feet, walk your hands forward. Continue walking your hands forward until you are in a push-up position with both legs extended behind you. Try to rest on the balls of your feet. Without moving your feet, walk your hands back toward your feet. Stand up to return to the starting position. Do 5 to 10 reps.

▶ CLAMSHELL

Why to Do It

If you sit a lot, your hips can get tight and your glutes can lose strength. This exercise addresses both of those problems. Clamshells can help strengthen your external hip rotators, which improves your stability. As a result, you'll be less likely to suffer injuries in the hips, knees, and ankles, as well as pain in the lower back.

How to Do It

Lie on your right side with your legs on top of each other. Bend your knees to a 45-degree angle. Make sure your hips are stacked one on top of the other. Use your right arm to prop up your head so it's not on the ground. Use your left arm to stabilize your upper body by placing your left hand on your left hip. Engage your abs by tucking in your belly button.

Keeping your feet together, move your left knee up (toward the sky) as high as you can, opening your legs. Make sure your pelvis and hips don't move. Pause, but don't hold, with your left knee lifted, then return your left leg to the starting position. Do 10 to 15 reps. Flip over and repeat on the other side.

▶ FIRE HYDRANT

Why to Do It

This exercise helps strengthen and activate your glutes and increases hip mobility.

How to Do It

Begin this exercise on all fours, on your hands and knees with your back straight. Draw in your belly button to engage your abdominal muscles. Keeping your hips level and keeping your left leg bent at 90 degrees, lift your left knee out to the side and up, away from your body. This will help open your left hip. Hold for one second. Then return your left knee to the floor. Make sure you keep your core engaged and elbows locked the entire time.

Do 10 to 20 reps, then repeat on the other leg.

Flexibility and Mobility

Here's another area where I could have done things better back in the day. Most of my friends and I were from the touch-your-toes-and-go school of heading out to run. We used the first mile of our runs to loosen up, and then got going at more like our normal pace. I was a rarity in that I seldom got injured. Most others got injured pretty often. I think one reason was our lack of prerun prep.

Now we know better. My team does a short but comprehensive set of exercises before every run. The goal is to increase blood flow and muscle activation so that they're ready to run with good form from the first step. That should lower their injury risk, because they're not compromising their gait, and it simply feels better. They can also run the first mile a little faster at the same effort level rather than sort of wasting it as a warm-up stumble.

I was better in this regard after runs. It just felt good to stretch my hamstrings, hips, quads, and lower back after an hour or more on the roads. People who are against stretching will tell you there's no evidence that it prevents injury. I don't disagree with that. But it sure makes you feel better the rest of the day and when starting the following day's run, compared to finishing and quickly transitioning to everyday life.

The exercises that follow improve your flexibility and mobility. In technical terms, flexibility has to do with lengthening soft tissue like muscle. Mobility has to do with soft tissue and joints being able to move freely. In practical terms, we're talking about the ability to move easily through a full range of motion. Having good flexibility and mobility allows your running form to be the best it can be. That helps you run faster at the same effort level than if you have soft-tissue or joint restrictions.

One set of exercises is a dynamic warm-up you can do inside before heading out on your run. The rope stretches are good before and after. Doing the dynamic warm-up before and the rope stretching after you run is a powerful combination. Try to do at least a few of these exercises before and after every run. This will take only a few minutes. After hard sessions and long runs, try to find the time for a full postrun stretch. You'll feel so much better the next day.

Prerun Dynamic Warm-Up

▶ **KNEE TO CHEST TO LEG BEHIND QUAD STRETCH**

Why to Do It

This exercise improves your flexibility and warms up your muscles. When you pull your knee toward your chest, you're stretching your hamstrings, adductors, and the muscles around your hips and butt. When you do the quad pull, you're stretching the front of your leg, the quads. This stretch allows you to run more smoothly.

How to Do It

Take a couple of steps, and then take one knee with both hands and pull it toward your chest. You should feel a good stretch at the top of your hamstrings. Then let the leg go back to the ground, take another step, and grab the same leg at the ankle with the same side hand, and pull it back toward your butt to get a good quad stretch. Your knee should be pointing toward the ground. Your opposite arm can reach toward the sky to increase the stretch.

Stay tall; don't bend too much in any direction and try to have good posture. Keep your core engaged during the entire exercise. Once you've done the knee to the chest and the quad stretch, take another step and continue the exercise with the opposite leg. Do two to four sets for 20 meters (about five to six reps) each.

▶ FORWARD AND BACKWARD LEG SWING

Why to Do It

This a great exercise to loosen the front of your legs as well as your glutes and hamstrings. Many runners have very tight hip flexors.

How to Do It

Have a support on your left side, such as a chair or a wall, for your left hand. Keep your hips and shoulders facing squarely forward. Pick up your left leg, slightly bend it at the knee, and draw your knee up as high as you can. Then swing your leg backward to full extension behind you. You want to really draw the leg back with some effort to mimic your running stride, but exaggerate the motion to get the full stretch at each end of your flexibility spectrum. Do two sets of 10 for each leg.

▶ CROSSBODY LEG SWING

Why to Do It

This exercise increases range of motion in your adductors, hips, and iliotibial band.

How to Do It

Face a wall or have a support in front of you, about an arm's length away. Grasp or press both hands into the support in front of you, keeping your shoulders and hips square. Start with your right leg extended, knee slightly bent. Swing your leg out to the right as high as you're able, and then back in and across your body as much as you're able. Keep a normal range of motion, not straining on either end of the exercise or torquing your hips too much as you swing the leg across. Do two sets of 10 for each leg.

▶ SIDE BAND WALK

Why to Do It

Helps develop hip stability and strengthen the abductors. Side band walks really get your glutes firing.

How to Do It

Place a small band around both ankles. Position your feet hip-width apart. The band should be stiff, but not overly stretched. Bend your knees slightly and move into a half-squat position to activate your glutes. Keep your feet in line with your hips and look forward, with your body weight evenly distributed over both feet.

In the half-squat position, move your weight over one leg and take a step sideways with the other leg. Keep your hips level during the exercise. Try to keep a low, forward-facing posture. Your back should be straight, not rounded. You should really feel this exercise in the hips.

Take 10 steps leading with the right leg, then lead with the left leg for 10 steps.

Pre- and Postrun Rope Stretching

This form of stretching is technically known as active isolated stretching. In contrast to traditional static stretching, in which you hold stretches for up to a minute, this is a dynamic form of stretching, with each stretch lasting only a few seconds. The idea is that you engage the opposing muscle to the one that you want to stretch, thereby letting the target muscle relax and lengthen. For example, to stretch your hamstrings, you engage their opposing muscle group, the quadriceps. I think you'll find you'll feel looser after dynamic stretching compared to static stretching.

In these stretches, you use a rope to get a full range of motion. (A rolled-up towel also works.) For most of the stretch, use the rope only to guide the motion; don't tug on the rope to move your leg. As you near the end of each motion, slightly extend the stretch by gently pulling the rope.

ROPE HAMSTRING STRETCH SERIES

Why to Do It

Having strong, healthy hamstrings helps prevent them tearing or straining when you run. Lengthening your hamstrings can also help prevent knee pain and pelvic rotation, which can lead to many running injuries.

▶ STRAIGHT LEG HAMSTRING STRETCH

How to Do It

Lie on your back with one knee bent and the foot flat on the ground. Make a loop with the rope and place it around the bottom of the straight leg's foot. Use your quads to lift your leg as far as you can; your foot should aim toward the sky. Take the ends of the rope with both hands and climb the rope with both hands while keeping tension on the rope. Use the rope for some gentle assistance at the end of the stretch. Return the straight leg to the ground to complete one rep. Each rep should take only a few seconds. Do 10 reps on each leg.

ROPE HAMSTRING STRETCH SERIES

▶ OUTER HAMSTRING STRETCH

How to Do It

Start the same as the straight leg hamstring stretch, except once you have a loop around your foot, wrap the rope around your leg so it turns your foot inward. Now do the same motion as the straight leg stretch with your foot pointing inward. Do 10 reps on each leg.

▶ INNER HAMSTRING STRETCH—MEDIAL (INSIDE)

How to Do It

Start the same as the straight leg hamstring stretch, except once you have a loop around your foot, wrap the rope around your leg so it turns your foot outward. Now do the same motion as the straight leg stretch with your foot pointing outward. Do 10 reps on each leg.

▶ QUADRICEPS STRETCH

Why to Do It

Your quads are some of the largest muscles in your body. Increasing their range of motion will help you to run smoother and faster.

How to Do It

Lie on your side with your knees curled up next to your chest. Put your bottom arm under the thigh of your bottom leg, and place that hand around the outside of your foot or use the rope to go around your bottom foot. With your upper hand, grasp the ankle of your upper foot. Keep your knee bent and your leg parallel to the surface that you're lying on.

Contact your hamstrings and butt muscles and move the upper leg back as far as you can, using your hand to assist at the end of the stretch. Do 10 to 20 reps on each side.

▶ ADDUCTORS STRETCH

Why to Do It

Adductors are muscles on the inside of your thigh that bring your leg toward the center of your body. Strong and healthy adductors stabilize your pelvis. You use your adductors more as you run faster or up and down hills.

How to Do It

Lie on your back with both legs extended straight out. Loop the rope around the inside of the left ankle, then under the left foot. The ends of the rope are on the outside of the left leg. Lock the left knee and rotate the left leg inward slightly.

Using the muscles on the outside of your left hip, extend your left leg out from the side of your body, leading with your heel. Keep some tension on the rope and use it for some gentle assistance at the end of the stretch. Do 10 reps, then switch to the other leg.

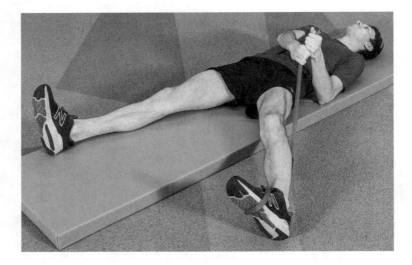

▶ CALF STRETCH

Why to Do It

Stretching these muscles will prevent injury to the lower leg, foot, and ankle. Stretching your calf can also help stabilize the ankle and help prevent Achilles issues.

How to Do It

Sit with both legs straight out in front of you. Loop the rope around the foot of the leg you want to stretch. From your heel, flex your foot back toward your ankle. Use the rope to gently assist at the end of the movement. Do two sets of 10 on each leg.

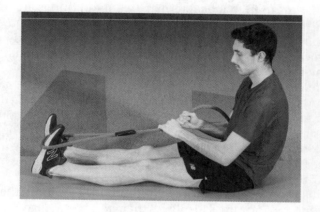

Running Form

Some coaches never talk about running form. The idea captured by the phrase "just run, baby!" is that your body will automatically and naturally find its best form. Other coaches tinker with the smallest element of form, such as how to hold your thumbs, even with people who are already Olympians.

I'm between those extremes. It's true that experienced runners usually have better running form than beginners. And it's true that even some elite runners could be faster with improved form. If you want to run your best, you need to pay attention to your form. But it's not something to obsess over; you can do more harm than good by trying to make big changes in your form.

What does that mean in practical terms? Two main things are important here. First, I think all runners should regularly do form drills. Second, I like to have runners focus on good form when doing strides and to do body checks during workouts and races. But let's back up a bit and briefly look at what good running form is and why it matters.

You'll see different running styles among the top finishers in pro races. Still, most recreational runners watching would think, in general, "I wish I looked like that when I run." Even the supposed exceptions, such as former marathon world-record holder Paula Radcliffe, are very efficient from the waist down. Everyone is light on their feet rather than looking like they're putting on the brakes or pounding into the ground with every step. Their gait has an almost circular motion, with the back of the foot coming up near their butt. (Marathoners generally have less of this back kick, but there's still a fullness in their stride.) These common elements mean their movement is almost entirely directed forward. This allows them to cover a huge amount of ground with every stride. Combine that with a quick cadence, and the result is fast running.

One reason the top runners are top runners is that their natural form is efficient. Yet these runners still regularly work on their form, via technique drills, strengthening exercises, and cues they repeat to themselves. If they think improved running form is worth some of their time, you probably should spend time on it, too.

What follows are a few technique drills that will go a long way in helping you run with your best form. I'm also a big fan of bodily awareness as a way to improve form. When we tire, our form tends to get a little worse. I tell my runners to visualize running smoothly. During workouts and races, if I yell "body check!" they know to quickly scan head to toe to check for areas of tightness they weren't aware of. Is their head in line with their shoulders, or is it thrust out? Are their shoulders low and even? Are their arms and hands relaxed? Are they running with a slight lean from the ankles rather than bent over at the waist? Are they landing lightly under their center of mass instead of overstriding and hitting the ground hard?

Postrun strides are a great time to work on your form. On each stride, concentrate on one element of good form. I also like the idea of implanting an image of good form when you're doing intervals. I'll tell my runners something like "this next repeat, smooth and fast, no fighting" or "let's see how easily we can run a 400 in 64 seconds." You can make these cues even more effective by having a friend take video of you when you're running fast. It can be really helpful to know what you look like and then think about evening out any kinks you see.

Finally, you can improve your form simply by taking better care of your body. The strengthening and flexibility exercises in this chapter will help to reduce imbalances and restrictions that detract from good form. Taking regular breaks from sitting, such as moving about for a minute every hour during the workday, will also contribute to having a body better able to have and hold good running form.

RUNNING FORM DRILLS

Ideally, you'll do these drills as part of your warm-up before workouts. If that's not possible, do them two other days each week. My recommendation in that scenario is postrun on the day after a workout (Wednesdays and Saturdays if you're following the schedules as presented in chapters 8 through 14).

▶ BUTT KICK

Why to Do It

Butt kicks help you learn to run on the balls of your feet and spend less time on the ground with each foot strike, which will increase your speed when running. Doing this drill helps you engage the hamstrings and loosen up the quadriceps.

How to Do It

Start with your feet about shoulder-width apart, your body straight, and your head looking straight ahead. As you do the drill, don't lose your good posture, and don't lean forward or backward.

While on the ball of your right foot, lift your left knee slightly, then pull the heel of your left foot toward your butt and slightly under it. You aren't trying to kick your butt. As your left foot comes back down under your center of gravity, it should land on its ball, while you pull your right heel toward your butt and do the same action the left foot just made.

Continue doing this as you move slowly along the ground. The movement is quick, but your forward movement isn't fast. Do for 20 meters two or three times, jogging back to your starting point between.

RUNNING FORM DRILLS

 A-SKIP

Why to Do It

This is a great running drill for your hamstrings and glutes. It will improve your form and agility.

How to Do It

This A-skip is a skip in which you drive the knee up high, above your hip, and then bring it down quickly. When you're driving your knee up, keep your foot dorsiflexed (toes pointing toward your shin). Then land and use a slight pawing as you pull backward while the opposite knee is driven up. Push off on the front third of your foot.

Maintain good form by keeping your head up and looking straight ahead. You can lean very slightly forward, leading with your chest. Drive your arms forward the same as you would when running. Do for 20 meters two or three times, jogging back to your starting point between.

RUNNING FORM DRILLS

▶ B-SKIP

Why to Do It

Like A-skips, B-skips work your hamstrings and glutes and improve your form and agility.

How to Do It

The B-skip mimics the A-skip until the knee drive is at its highest. At that point, extend your leg out in front of you as far as you can. Claw the ground with the front third of your foot as it hits the ground. You get a lot more pawing motion in B-skips compared to A-skips because of extending your leg in front of you.

Use your arms as if you're running, and keep good form by keeping your head up and your gaze straight ahead. You can lean very slightly forward, leading with your chest, as you do the drill. Do for 20 meters two or three times, jogging back to your starting point between.

RUNNING FORM DRILLS

▶ BOUNDING

Why to Do It

Bounding is a much higher-intensity running drill than A- and B-skips. Bounding improves the power and efficiency of your stride.

How to Do It

The idea behind bounding is to have an exaggerated run in which you try to get a lot of vertical and horizontal distance with each stride. Try to launch yourself forward off your left leg, driving your right knee up to waist level while keeping your left leg straight. Be in the air for a second before landing softly on the ball of your right foot. When the foot hits the ground, launch yourself forward.

Use your arms like you're running. The arm opposite your lead leg should swing forward for more momentum. If you have a hard time immediately getting into the bounding motion, try jogging for a few meters and then launch into the drill. Do for 20 meters two or three times, jogging back to your starting point between.

One important thing to remember about A-skips, B-skips, and bounding is that they're plyometric exercises that focus on minimizing the amount of contact time with the ground. You hit the ground with a lot of force when doing these drills. Don't do more than recommended—you want to get their form-improving benefits without increasing your risk of injury.

RUNNING FORM DRILLS

▶ CARIOCA

Why to Do It

This is a cross-stepping drill that moves the body laterally. It can help with knee lift and the hips' range of motion. It's a great drill for runners with tight hips. The carioca also really works the stabilizing muscles that help you maintain good form; activates your glutes, hamstrings, and hip flexors; and helps your core muscles stay engaged to maintain stability.

How to Do It

Stand in a good athletic stance, with more weight on the balls of your feet. Start by stepping your right foot across your body and over your left foot, allowing your hips to rotate to the left. Then step to the left with your left foot while your right foot is still on the ground. You're now back in the starting position. Cross your right leg behind you. Now, with your left foot on the ground, step with your right foot behind your body. This allows your hips to open to the right. Keep contact with the ground on your right foot and step to the left with your left foot. This uncrosses the legs and returns you to the beginning stance. Pump your arms as if you're running.

Move sideways along the ground as you cross one leg over the front of your other leg and then behind. Once you've figured out the drill, go in the opposite direction by reversing the steps. Do two to four sets for 20 meters in each direction.

Running Shoes

It makes sense to briefly discuss running shoes here, in part because your shoes can affect your form.

I like to keep running simple. That includes shoes. I think most runners should be in the simplest shoe that works well for them that doesn't have too many bells and whistles. By that I mean you feel like the shoe works as an extension of your body rather than impeding or otherwise changing your natural stride. One of the best things you can say about your running shoes is that you don't really think about them while you're running.

That recommendation has to do with everyday runs. Most competitive runners like to wear a lighter training shoe or racing shoe for workouts. The athletes on my team wear spikes for some key track sessions. Marathoners do some long runs, especially ones with miles at race pace, in the high-stack, special-foam, plated models known as super shoes.

I'm in favor of this approach—viewing shoes as tools, with different models being the most appropriate tool depending on the day's run. I'm not in favor of wearing super shoes for all of your runs. It might be tempting to think, "I run 10 seconds a mile faster in them when I race, so if I always train in them, then I'll get a lot fitter." I don't think it works that way, any more than doing all of your runs on a slightly downhill course with a tailwind will make you faster than training in normal conditions.

Let me put it this way: The runners on my team get their shoes for free. They could run in the most deluxe models every day and not have to worry if they blow through a pair in 100 miles. But that's not what they do. On most runs, they wear basic training shoes. They save the lighter, faster shoes for workouts and races. Physics aside, it's motivating to lace up those models only occasionally. It's a way of telling yourself it's time to do something special, and you have just the right tool for the job.

Diet

Eating well is really important for running your best. It's also pretty straightforward. Runners should have the same well-rounded diet as everyone else. My team eats lots of fruits and vegetables, whole grains, lean proteins, and healthy fats. They try to buy seasonal, local, organic foods as their budgets allow. They don't purposefully avoid types of food—donuts occasionally appear at practice—but they don't eat a lot of junk food or processed food.

I didn't always eat like this in my early competitive days. It was common back then to think that you could eat whatever you wanted as long as you ran enough. And you could, if all you cared about was calories in and calories out. But with experience and exposure to elite runners with long careers, I realized the quality of the fuel going into the furnace mattered as much as the quantity. Now it's pretty rare to find consistently successful runners who, like I used to, think that Cap'n Crunch is the breakfast of champions. The way my team eats is the norm among modern elites.

Eating better means you're going to be more healthy overall, which means your immune system will work better, which means you'll recover more quickly and get fewer colds. You're also less likely to have on-the-run digestive problems. For a great guide to eating for both health and performance, I recommend *Endurance Sports Nutrition*, by Suzanne Girard Eberle, a sport dietitian and former elite runner.

One area where I was a little ahead of the curve was purposefully taking in calories soon after finishing running. I learned about this in the early 1990s from training partner Arturo Barrios, who at one point held the world record for 10,000 meters and the hour run. After every run—and I mean every run—Arturo ate a banana almost as soon as we finished. He explained to me that immediately after running, your muscles will reload their fuel stores at up to three times the rate they normally do. So if you get some calories in during the first hour postrun, your muscles will recover more quickly, and you'll feel better the next day. If you've ever finished a long run with an upset stomach and didn't feel like eating or got busy with something else and forgot to eat for a few hours and then found yourself dragging for the rest of that day and the following day, you know the downside of waiting to refuel.

Sport nutrition experts like Suzanne Girard Eberle advise a 3:1 or 4:1 ratio of carbohydrates to protein in your postrun drink or food. One of my runners, Olympian Elle St. Pierre, likes chocolate milk for this purpose. (Yes, she's the one who grew up on a dairy farm.) Most runners find it easier to get in a few hundred calories of carbs and protein soon after a workout from a drink than solid food.

Although Arturo did this after every run, you'll probably be okay being dedicated to the practice only after your hard workouts and long runs. Arturo was running more than 100 miles a week and usually ran twice a day. He needed to stay on top of recovery more than someone running five miles on a recovery day.

The only other thing I want to touch on in the realm of diet is weight.

I never had a scale in my house when I was competing. I would weigh myself occasionally at the gym out of curiosity, but I didn't do anything differently based on the number I saw. (I mean, come on, I ate Cap'n Crunch for breakfast!) None of the runners I now coach weigh themselves regularly. If you saw them running together, you'd say they look fit, healthy, muscular, and athletic. In my experience, it's the runners who obsess over their weight, restrict calories, and omit food groups (without being advised to do so by a registered dietitian) who most often fail to reach their potential. They might be super light and run well for a season or two at a time, but they can't seem to sustain it. They get injured a lot (especially bone injuries), they catch a lot of colds, and eventually they just can't train well.

I'm not saying weight has no effect on performance. But I'd rather you be healthy and happy and have a good relationship with food, and maybe weigh a little more, than have a restrictive diet for the sake of weighing as little as possible. With experience, you'll know when you're at a good running weight. You'll have a feeling of ease and comfort on most runs. When it's time to run fast, you'll feel light but strong and capable.

Sleep

When I coached college runners, the nonrunning thing I most emphasized was getting enough sleep. The head coach I worked under at the Massachusetts Institute of Technology had a rule that athletes couldn't come to practice if they got less than four hours of sleep the previous night. They also had to miss practice if they hadn't gotten a total of 11 hours of sleep in the previous two nights.

Obviously, we weren't in dorm rooms with sleep trackers to enforce these rules. But you get the idea: You can run intervals all day and train your butt off, but if you're not sleeping enough, you're just going to stay where you are, athletically. It's while you're sleeping that the training effect takes place: Your muscles and bones repair themselves, you make new red blood cells, and your body builds back a little stronger, a little better at holding a strong pace for a long time. You also refresh psychologically, so that you're pumped to take on the next day's training.

Your situation may be similar to that of college runners; you're trying to run ambitiously while having lots of other responsibilities and demands on your time. It's normal to think, "I'll stay up a little later so that I can get a head start on all I have to do tomorrow."

The thing is, if you've pegged an upcoming race as so important that you've committed to a formal training program for it, you owe it to yourself to make your training a priority. And that's going to mean regularly getting enough sleep. I can't offer universally applicable advice about how to do so. But, if you're like me and most adults I know, you could probably be better about time management. Do you really need to scroll through social media or watch another episode of a meh show soon before bedtime? Is feeling a little less sharp on the following day's run worth it?

Stepping away from your phone and other screens in the hour before bedtime should help you fall asleep sooner. (The light from screens interferes with your body's sleep-inducing hormones.) Doing so will also help you go to bed more relaxed—you'll be less likely to lie there and stew over a work message or an upsetting social media post.

There weren't as many of these temptations when I was competing. I still always made a conscious decision to go to bed early on days when I'd done a workout or long run. I didn't drink alcohol on those days because I knew it interfered with my sleep.

Try this approach most nights during the weeks that you follow one of my training schedules. I bet you'll soon notice you're sleeping better and feeling a little more lively and eager on your runs.

Other Aspects of Recovery

I've already described the importance of getting in fluids and some calories soon after your longest and hardest runs. Getting in that habit and stretching your tightest areas postrun will make a big difference in how well you recover between sessions.

You can enhance your recovery with a few other practices as your schedule allows. After hard workouts at Dartmouth, we would gather in a circle and stretch and talk about the session runners had just done and what was going on in their lives. It was a way for me to know they were ending practice on a good note. It was like a continuation of their cool-down, helping them to transition from the hard work back to normal.

I encourage you to take a little time for a similar decompression after your hardest runs. Rushing in the door after a workout and then immediately going into frantic everyday-life mode will catch up with you later in the day. You'll feel a little more on edge and a little more beat up or tight. Just a few minutes of light stretching, yoga, or meditation will calm your body and mind and make your workout a little more effective. As a pro, I tried to plan things so that I wouldn't be too busy or running around like crazy after a long run or hard workout. See if you can implement some of that approach. If you're doing a long run on Sunday, maybe you can knock out most of your weekend errands on Saturday so that there's time to relax on Sunday. Maybe you could even sneak in a nap!

Recovery devices like foam rollers and massage guns weren't a thing when I was competing. I mostly lazed around as time allowed, with my feet propped up on the sofa or my legs up against a wall. These days, there are tons of self-massage tools. The athletes on my team use them a lot while watching television or just sitting around. Even if they're getting only a placebo effect, if they like it and feel like it's doing something, it's probably helping them.

4

Using Your Mind to Run Faster

There's a story about Percy Cerutty, a famously eccentric Australian coach, that goes like this. On the morning of the 1960 Olympic 1,500-meter final, Cerutty and his star athlete, Herb Elliott, were at the practice track. Cerutty, then in his 60s, had Elliott watch while he ran a 1,500-meter time trial. Cerutty collapsed on the infield after and, with spit and sweat covering his weathered face, called Elliott over. "You may run faster than me," Cerutty told Elliott, "but you will not run harder." Elliott went on to win the Olympic title that evening in a world record.

I loved that story when I was a young runner. (I still love it!) In high school and college, I had a Cerutty quote on my bedroom wall that read, "The thing that marks the super athlete is his *capacity to suffer,* and stand up to continued suffering."

That was the prevailing attitude toward the mental side of running at the time. As a Massachusetts native, I knew all about how another Bay Stater, Alberto Salazar, once pushed himself so hard at the Falmouth Road Race that he was administered last rites. It was all about "suck it up," "run through the wall," and "wimps let go" (except that we used a crude anatomical word instead of "wimps"). Mental toughness meant mind over matter, and I thought I was tougher than anyone. As a kid, nobody was going to hold their breath underwater longer than me. Later, if someone challenged me, I'd hold a plank until everyone else quit.

My views on the topic started to expand when I became a professional runner. They've continued to evolve during my coaching career. You certainly need a good bit of that never-say-die attitude, but there's a lot more to the mental side of running than continually thrashing yourself. I now use another Cerutty quote—"while a man is racing, he must hate himself and his competitors"—mostly to explain to runners why I disagree with it.

In this chapter, I'll describe a more nuanced take on successful sport psychology and share some simple techniques to help your mind get the most out of your body.

Psychological Strength Versus Mental Toughness

What images come to mind when you think about mental toughness? If you're like most runners, you probably see someone gritting her teeth and pushing herself to her absolute limits. You might also see someone who runs through pain, who never cuts a workout short, who sticks with the day's plan regardless of weather, fatigue, injury, or illness.

It's hard to think beyond those types of clichés. So I'm going to suggest dropping the phrase "mental toughness" and instead thinking about psychological strength. I've learned over the years that psychological strength in running is about a lot more than sprinting through every wall you encounter. Being psychologically strong is a healthier perspective that says you can try to be your best without running controlling your life, and that you can enjoy the process of discovering how good you can be.

One of the first eye-openers for me was a group workout in Boston soon after I graduated college in 1988. Among the people at the track was Bill Rodgers, the four-time Boston Marathon champion, whom I'd idolized growing up. Anyone who knew running would say that Bill was mentally tough.

But one thing I realized during that workout was how at ease he was with himself and everyone else. He wasn't threatened by me, a speedy newcomer, or anyone else in the group. He had a self-confidence that had nothing to do with running others into the ground. He knew what he could do and that he would give it his best when it really mattered.

I recognized that same trait in the world-class guys I trained with in Providence, Rhode Island, at the time, like Olympic marathon medalist and world cross-country champion John Treacy. When I moved to Boulder, Colorado, a few years later, I was again struck by the kinder, gentler version of self-confidence I saw in people like world marathon champion Mark Plaatjes and former marathon world-record holder Steve Jones. They were all self-secure enough to welcome others and help them along. It was a lot different from a warrior mentality.

Another big insight came from a different Boulder training partner, Arturo Barrios. I remember thinking about how hard Arturo's track sessions must be. After all, he had set world records at 10,000 meters and the hour run on the track. So I was amazed when Arturo did workouts like 20 400-meter repeats in 64 seconds with a minute's rest between repeats. Without context, that might sound like a killer workout, but a 64-second 400 was his 10K race pace. Most decently fit runners can do that workout at their race pace. Heck, I could do that exact workout with Arturo, and I was more than a minute slower than him at 10K. He would say, "That's enough for today. We'll be back at it in a few days. Let's not dig a hole."

It finally started to sink in that the best runners in the world rarely went to the well in workouts. I touched on this idea in chapter 1, when describing why it's better to have 10 consecutive weeks of B+ workouts than sporadic race-effort sessions. This principle also relates to the mental side of the sport because of how it shifts what true "mental toughness" is. In terms of training, it's not so much your ability to push yourself once a week to the point of puking; it's more the dedication to the day-to-day routine of consistent work that might not look stunning in isolation but builds to something big.

I also talked in chapter 1 about each of us having finite willpower. Part of being psychologically strong is rationing out your willpower over the course of a training block or racing season. That's almost always going to work out better than giving it your all for three weeks and then finding yourself mentally depleted when it's time for the most important workouts and races.

A key part of this broader version is Arturo's approach of "that's enough for today." Runners are driven people. It sometimes takes more discipline to know when to say enough is enough. That can mean not running everything as hard as possible or doing as much volume as possible. It can even mean not running at all on a given day.

Like most pro runners, you might need someone to hold you back more often than you need a Cerutty-esque kick in the pants. I often cut a runner's workout short if I see them struggling during a workout they should be able to complete. At the other end of the spectrum, if someone is really nailing a workout and says they want to do more, it's usually my job as their coach to say, "Let's not get greedy. That's enough for today." Continuing to push on when a workout isn't going as it should and adding to a workout because it's going well are both great ways to get hurt or overly fatigued. Then your subsequent training is compromised, and you ultimately don't race as well as you would if you'd had the discipline to know when to stop.

Let me point out one more problem with the old-school view of mental toughness. On race day, if you're not honest with yourself about your abilities, your performance is going to suffer. The best runner in the world during most of my pro years was Haile Gebrselassie, who won two Olympic 10K titles and set dozens of world records. It wouldn't have mattered how much I told myself to "just suck it up and hang with Haile today." It just wasn't going to happen, no matter how "tough" I was. Being a hard-ass like that isn't going to make you better. It's just going to ruin your race.

Characteristics of Psychological Strength

As part of getting my master's degree in sports science, I wrote a research paper on mental toughness, or what I'm here calling psychological strength. I identified four traits in athletes who excel in this area: unshakable self-belief, inner arrogance, the ability to overcome obstacles, and the belief that desire will ultimately lead to fulfilling potential. Let's look briefly at what these mean in practical terms.

Unshakable Self-Belief

At the elite level, this is a runner's conviction that she has qualities and abilities greater than those of her opponents. That might sound odd. If there are 12 runners on the start line of an Olympic Trials final, and all 12 think they're better than everyone else in the field, most of them are wrong. Only three of them will make the Olympic team.

The thing is, even at that level, they don't all think that way. Some will be thinking about how their buildup hasn't gone well. Others don't really believe in their heart of hearts that they can place in the top three and make the team. At most, very few of the people who make an Olympic team think after the race "Oh my God, I can't believe I did this." They almost all truly believed they could make the team.

I speak from personal experience here. At my first Olympic Trials in 1988, I was happy just to be there. I had no sense that I deserved a spot on the team. Four years later, I thought I could make the steeplechase team. But I tore my hamstring two weeks before the meet, and my self-belief tanked. I ran horribly in the final because I'd lost that mental edge of "I got this." Finally, in 1996, I stood on the line of the Olympic Marathon Trials with the feeling that one of the team spots belonged to me, and that nobody was going to deny me it.

The elites who have unshakable self-belief that they're one of the best in the country or world base that belief on their training and racing. They know what it took to get to that level and how to perform at that level. It just happens to be the case that their level puts them at the pinnacle of the sport. This attribute applies to all runners, because it really has to do with performing up to your potential. Drawing strength from your training is key here. The more you nail challenging workouts and meet your targets, the more confident you should be. You learn to trust that you can set a goal for yourself and reach it, despite inner voices that might tell you otherwise.

Inner Arrogance

Maybe "arrogance" has a negative connotation for you. So think "swagger." It's a belief that if you set your mind to something you can do it. This obviously goes hand-in-hand with self-belief. In this case, there's an element of others picking up on your self-belief, even though you don't go around telling people you're going to beat them.

When I started coaching at Dartmouth, the team had a history of underperforming at big races like the conference cross-country championship. It seemed like a lot of the Dartmouth runners had put themselves in what they thought should be their place before the race even started—if the team finished fifth in the conference last year, well, why would they think they could do better this year? I was able to shift some of that thinking. Drawing confidence from training was again key. I told them they'd run such and such times in workouts, and that meant they were able to run certain times in races, and if they ran those times, the team should finish near the top. Once they started to perform up to their potential, they carried themselves a little differently. There was an air of "look out; here comes the Dartmouth team."

One of my current runners, Elle St. Pierre, has this quality. When she does prerace strides in front of her competitors, she's all business. She just looks like a champion. She probably mentally defeats a couple of her competitors in the warm-up area.

Of course, it's not true that you'll achieve something just because you set your mind to it. Few people become astronauts or Nobel prize winners or elite marathoners. You need to have ambitious but realistic goals. Then work toward those goals like you know you can accomplish them.

Ability to Overcome Obstacles

One of my former training partners, Mark Plaatjes, is one of the least outwardly arrogant people you'll ever meet. Inside, though, he just knew he could be a world champion in the marathon, even though there were dozens of people faster than him. Mark got himself and his family out of apartheid South Africa, became a U.S. citizen, and won the world title in 1993. Despite the obstacles put up by his place of birth and skin color, as well as logistics and legalities, Mark never stopped believing in or working toward his goal.

Coogan's Crew: Heather MacLean

Personal Bests: 1:59 800 meters; 3:58 1,500 meters

Career Highlights: 2021 Olympian at 1,500 meters; 2022 U.S. indoor 1,500-meter champion

Years With Coach Coogan: 2018-

Courtesy of Justin Britton.

If you sometimes struggle to be a confident runner, then you should get to know Heather MacLean.

Heather has rapidly progressed since becoming a pro in 2018. At the beginning of 2021, she and I were among a handful of people who thought she could make the Olympic team at 1,500 meters. At the Olympic Trials, Heather followed our race plan perfectly and placed third—in a personal best—to make the Olympic team. She carried that momentum into 2022, winning the national indoor title at 1,500 meters in March, breaking 4:00 for 1,500 meters during the summer, and finishing the year with a top-10 world ranking.

So it might surprise you to hear Heather say, "I definitely struggle with imposter syndrome in all aspects of my life. Running's my job, so particularly there. I started the sport late compared to others, and in college I didn't progress linearly. Every time I'd get to a certain level, I'd be shut back down and have to start from scratch. It made me feel like I'm not good enough to be where I'm at."

Heather knew she needed to learn how to be more confident to reach her potential. One way she does that is leaning on running's objective nature. "If

Successful runners are also good at handling more immediate obstacles. If weather or their schedule presents a challenge, they find a way to get their training in. Maybe they get up extra early to do a long run before traveling. Maybe they buy a day pass at a gym and work out on a treadmill during a snowstorm. In races, they're able to roll with the punches. Missing a water stop, developing a blister, even getting knocked over doesn't derail them. They might not run as fast as they'd hoped, but they don't give up just because things haven't played out perfectly.

Because you know what? They seldom do. At a big indoor meet in college, the traveling crew was just me, a hurdler named William Skinner, and our coach, Charles Torpey. Charles wasn't allowed in the warm-up area; he sat in the top row of the stands to get a good view. As my race neared, he said, "Grab your spikes, go warm up, and I'll see you after the race." I did my warm-up, reached in my bag to put on my spikes, and discovered I'd grabbed William's spikes. He wore size 13, I wore size 9. I tried to get Charles' attention, frantically waving to somehow communicate about the spike snafu. Charles thought I was just being affable me,

I'm training well and hitting the times I'm supposed to in workouts, that builds confidence," she says. "I tell myself, 'If I can do that in a workout, imagine what I can do in a race.'" Heather also draws strength from telling herself that if she can train with U.S. record holder Elle St. Pierre, then she should be able to race with her. "When people would say Elle's a no-brainer for the Olympic team, I'd think, 'I train with her every day, I stay with her in workouts, so why isn't this a possibility for me?'" No matter how much you doubt yourself, you should be able to look at your training objectively and accurately predict what you're capable of in races.

As a college runner, "I had always been afraid to set goals, because I was afraid if I didn't meet them, it would confirm that I shouldn't be doing what I'm doing," Heather says. But starting in 2020, rather than being frightened by setting the goal of making the Olympic team, she used it to remind herself she belonged. She set an image of the Tokyo stadium as her LinkedIn background. She put a sticky note reading "I'm an Olympian" on her mirror. "It was a little reminder every day," Heather says. "It's not that if you don't make it, it's the end of the world, but you have to believe that you're capable of making it."

Heather says she'll always be a work in progress in this area. She frequently uses the phrase "facts over feeling" to boost her self-confidence. As she explains it, "Fact: I have run these times and won these races, versus feeling that everybody is so much faster and that that means I can't compete against them. And it's a fact that your times can improve."

Leading up to a big race, Heather seeks out activities and practices that bring her peace and confidence, such as meditating, watching favorite movies like *Shrek*, being in nature, and getting plenty of sleep. "These are ways to stay calm and quiet that negative inner voice," she says. "They're all about not counting myself out."

and simply waved back. A friend who ran for Boston College got the attention of the University of Massachusetts coach, who grabbed somebody's size 9.5 spikes and threw them to me. I laced up and hit the track. I didn't win, but I did okay, and that itself felt like a victory.

Successful runners also don't create obstacles. In day-to-day life, they plan things so that they won't get cut short on time and have to curtail or skip training. On race day, they don't obsess about things they can't control. Maybe you've timed your warm-up to be ready to race at the advertised start time, but the race starts 20 minutes later, and you have to find a way to keep your heart rate up while standing in a corral. Maybe it's windy, which might keep you from setting a personal best. But it will be windy (or cold, or hot, or rainy, or whatever) for everyone. You can still run to the best of your ability for that day in those conditions. In fact, you can probably outperform many people who will be thrown off by things they can't control. As I used to tell my college teams, 20 percent of runners will screw up their race before they ever step on the line.

Belief That Desire Will Result in Reaching Potential

Think of this as the long-term culmination of the previous three traits. It's having strong enough self-belief that you know you can eventually do something, despite the inevitable obstacles, that you currently can't. This might be something so ambitious that it doesn't even count as a next-year goal. It's a dream of yours, such as qualifying for the Boston Marathon, that you're willing to work over a long time to achieve, and that you believe you will achieve if you do that work.

In my running, it was during my time training with a large group of world-class guys in Providence that I started to get the feeling I could make the Olympic team. Once again, for me this belief stemmed largely from training. These guys made national teams and set records. I kept up with them almost every day. On great days, I sometimes led them in workouts. Seeing that they were human, with the same challenges and setbacks I had, I started thinking, "Why not me?" It took several more years for my Olympic dream to come true, but I always believed I could do it.

Techniques for Being Psychologically Strong

So far in this chapter, I've explained what psychological strength is and how it differs from traditional takes on mental toughness, and I've described the main qualities of a psychologically strong runner. Now I want to share some specific things you can do to be a psychologically successful runner.

As with fitness, psychological strength isn't something you either have or don't have—it's something you have to work on. And that's good news! It means that you can learn and fine-tune ways to become the best version of yourself mentally, just like the right training builds the best physical version of yourself. Here are five techniques to have on hand. They're key to prepping for and thriving when running gets challenging. They're useful in both training (especially hard workouts and long runs) and racing. I think you'll find there's a lot of interplay among them; getting good at one makes it easier to employ the others.

Goal Setting

Good goals are great motivators. They get you out the door and keep you working hard once you're out there. When you hit that ultimate point of despair in a race—"Why am I doing this?!"—good goals reground you. Thinking about why you set your sights on this race and what doing well in it will mean to you should get you back on track.

So, part of a good goal is that it's personally meaningful to you. It should be something that fires you up when you think about it. Feeling like you "should" do something, like run a marathon because people keep asking you when you're going to, isn't what we're after here. It has to be meaningful to you.

Another key part of a good goal is that it's a good balance of stretching yourself and being realistic. It's not all that motivating to set a goal of running 10 seconds faster for a 5K than you did last season (unless you're one of the best in the world, in which case every second is a major accomplishment). But it's probably not realistic to set a goal of running two minutes faster for a 5K than you did last season. Shooting for the moon isn't necessarily more motivating. You'll probably be continually frustrated in your training if you overreach. Being honest with yourself will lead to being more successful.

With some experience as a runner, you have some idea of what's possible. You know what it took to run your recent race times. Say your most recent marathon was 3:05. You'll probably start thinking about breaking 3:00. You'll get ideas about what you can do differently in training and racing. You'll probably realize you need to put in more work than you did to run 3:05 and that you'll need a great pacing and fueling plan on race day. If those ideas feel a little scary but also get you pumped, you've probably found yourself a good goal.

I have goal meetings with all of my runners after each season. First, we review the racing season that just ended. Did you meet your goals? Were they too hard? Too easy? Then we look ahead. Based on how this season went, what are good goals moving forward? We generally work six months to a year out. You can have longer-term goals than that. But you need stepping-stones to them. For my runners, we're usually targeting national championships and, ideally, the world championships and Olympics that the top finishers at the national championships compete in. Then we work backward to see what we should be doing to be in peak fitness for the season's ultimate goal. We slot in tune-up races both to see where we are and to have shorter-term goals that keep things more exciting.

We always put our goals on paper. Seeing them in that concrete form adds accountability to yourself. I also recommend you share your goals with people you care about and who care for you. That adds more accountability. If you start to slack off, someone who wants to see you happy will say some version of "Look, you've been talking about this race for four months. Don't screw it up now!"

▶ Visualization

I thought about Bob Kempainen when I went to bed every night in early 1996. Let me explain.

Bob was the favorite to win the 1996 Olympic Marathon Trials, held in February in Charlotte, North Carolina. The most likely scenario for how the race would play out was gradual attrition of the lead pack through 16 or 18 miles, then Bob pushing past 20 miles to leave no more than two guys near him. I knew my best shot at making the three-man team was to relax early on and then be ready when Bob made his move.

My hunch proved correct. When Bob surged with five miles to go, I committed to covering the move. Keith Brantly was the only one who went with me. Keith and I worked together to try to catch up with Bob, but he was too strong for us that day. (And that was with him vomiting while pulling away.) When it became obvious Bob wasn't coming back to us, and that nobody would catch us, I told Keith, "We're on the team." Keith and I ran together until half a mile to go, and then I surged to claim second place. I was an Olympian!

Handling Prerace Nerves

Almost everyone gets nervous before a race. Your race is important to you, you've put in a lot of work toward it, and you want to do well. It's natural to worry about things like whether the race will fall on one of those off days for your body or mind. When we want to do well, we tend to become hypersensitive. I had races where during my warm-up I thought, "Why are my quads so heavy? What does this mean for how I'll feel a few miles in?"

With enough experience, you'll learn these little bodily twinges are almost always meaningless. If instead of racing I were doing a normal run with friends on those days, I probably wouldn't have even thought my legs felt heavy. And if I had, I wouldn't have worried what that would mean 45 minutes later. I know it's easier said than done, but try to ignore these supposed signals your body sends in the hours before a race. They're usually just noise that will disappear once the race starts.

Experience should also teach you the right amount of prerace arousal for your personality. If you're more of a worrier, you don't need to get fired up. You're probably already thinking about the race too much. You need to find a prerace routine that calms and centers you. Listen to relaxing music, practice progressive muscle relaxation, meditate, and so forth. Other people need a little jolt to get their head truly in the game. Their prerace music is faster and more driving. With time, you'll find that sweet spot of eager-but-calm that has you thinking "bring it on."

One reason I met that lifetime goal is that I visualized the race for weeks. Creating a mental image of how I wanted a race to play out is something I'd done for years at that point. I picked up the practice as a young runner when I read a book by Marty Liquori, a top American miler and 5K runner of the 1960s and '70s. Marty talked about running a race a hundred times in your head before you run it on the track.

I was fortunate to sort of stumble on this practice that I later learned is backed by science. Studies have shown that when you visualize something like a race, your body partially responds as if you're actually doing it—your heart rate and blood pressure increase, for example. Your brain gets wired to run the race how you've visualized it. Come race day, some of the mental work is already done. You've already made some of the decisions about how you'll run. When Bob started to pull away that morning in 1996, I didn't have to think, "Should I go with him?" I already had many times in my head and knew the answer was yes. I was relaxed and simply did what I'd prepared myself to do both physically and mentally.

I encourage all of my runners to visualize important races. I tell them, "Start thinking about it. What do you think is going to happen? How do you want to race it?" I want them to visualize best-case scenarios. I think that's a lot better than imagining all the things that can go wrong. Of course, races don't always go as planned. But they're always going to be hard, and there will always be decisions to make. When those crunch times come, having thought about them will help, even if the details are a little different on race day.

A great time is when you first lie down in bed. Spend 10 to 15 minutes running the race in your head. Make the details as vivid as possible. (If you'll be running an unfamiliar course, see if you can find a course-tour video online.) Pretend you're running the first mile, getting out well but staying in control. See yourself settling into a good rhythm and feeling relaxed and upbeat. Spend a little extra time visualizing making the tough decisions—maybe it's running strongly up a big hill at halfway, or latching on to another runner who passes you with a mile to go. Picture yourself nearing the finish, running strongly through the line and getting everything out of yourself.

Usually I recommend starting these bedtime visualizations a week or two before the race. When I coached college runners, I didn't want to overload their minds; a Dartmouth student has enough to think about without me telling them to start imagining something that's three months away. That's probably similar to your situation if you're fitting in your running around a busy professional and personal life.

If you have the mental bandwidth, you might benefit from longer-range visualization for really important races. Elle St. Pierre usually starts visualizing races two weeks out. For something like the Wanamaker Mile at the Millrose Games, which she has won twice, she'll ask me a couple of weekends beforehand what I think her race strategy should be. Then she'll run that race in her head every night leading up to the meet. That's plenty for a race that's important but not the focus of her year.

In 2021, however, Elle started visualizing the Olympic Trials 1,500-meter final in February, four months before the race. We figured that Elle's best shot at making the team was in a fast race, because a quick pace would require most of the other women in the race to run a personal best just to stay near her. And we figured that it would be up to Elle to ensure the race started fast and stayed that way.

So almost every night for months, Elle built a vision of getting out fast and feeling strong while not letting up. She visualized herself running in the front, hard, over the last three laps. She saw herself free of other runners as she crossed the line to make her first Olympic team. We incorporated this race strategy into her training leading up to the Trials. We regularly finished track workouts with Elle running a hard 800 meters by herself. Those workouts reinforced the benefits of her visualizations, and vice versa.

In the Trials final, Elle took the lead in the first 300 meters and held it to the end, winning in a meet record and personal best.

Chunking and Focusing on the Process

You probably already do what sport psychologists call "chunking." That's breaking what could be an overwhelming task into manageable pieces. Ideally, you then focus on the chunk you're currently engaged in, and the completed chunks add up to completing the larger task.

Let's say you're following the medium-mileage 12-week 10K schedule found in chapter 10. Week 7 of that schedule includes a workout of four or five 1-mile repeats at 10K pace with a 400-meter jog between repeats. That's a tough workout! It would be understandable if you spent your warm-up trying to wrap your head around what you're about to do. If you found the pace challenging early in the

Coogan's Crew: Elle St. Pierre

Personal Bests: 3:58 1,500 meters; 9:10 2 miles (indoor); 14:58 5,000 meters

Career Highlights: 2nd, 2022 world indoor championship 3,000 meters; 2021 Olympian at 1,500 meters; U.S. indoor records at 1 mile and 2 miles

Years With Coach Coogan: 2018-

Courtesy of Justin Britton.

Elle St. Pierre is one of the most psychologically strong runners I've coached. She's also one of the most accomplished. Coincidence?

A lot has been made about Elle growing up on a dairy farm in Vermont. She tends to downplay her upbringing affecting her running. I think there's something to it that we can all learn from. Elle knows what hard work is, and with her husband, Jamie also being a dairy farmer, she gets regular reminders. Long days on the farm seven days a week—cows don't take weekends off—is harder work than most of us are used to. Elle is able to draw on her background to keep running in perspective. There will be discomfort in training and racing, along with times we don't feel like doing it. But we've chosen to run. We don't help ourselves by feeling sorry for ourselves or complaining about it.

More specifically, Elle is great at many of the psychological tools I describe in this chapter. Instead of getting overwhelmed by a hard-sounding workout, she chunks it. "Once I'm in the workout, I'm thinking about only the rep I'm on," Elle says. "The next rep is in the future. I worry about it only when it's time for that one." During each interval, Elle uses process goals. "On whatever the current rep is, I focus on hitting the splits I want," she says. "If I'm being paced, I just look at the back of their legs or shoulders and take it one lap at a time."

Elle has honed these skills over time. "I used to count to pass the time, but now I know that just makes it go by slower," she says. She now uses mostly second-person self-talk, such as telling herself between intervals, "Elle, you can do this." In line with research on the topic, she uses first-person self-talk more often "if I'm feeling sorry for myself," she says. There's always room for improvement in this area. (I'll describe the different types of self-talk in detail later in this chapter.)

Elle is also resilient. She bounces back quickly from setbacks, which all runners will have at some point. At the 2022 U.S. indoor championships, Elle got nipped at the finish line of the 1,500 meters and placed third. Only the top two finishers made the team for the world indoor championships. After the race, I told her, "Jamie still loves you, your family still loves you, and you still have the farm at home." Despite being upset about finishing third in a race she thought she should win, Elle regrouped. The following day, she won the 3,000 meters to qualify for the event at the world championships. At that meet featuring the world's best runners, she finished second, earning her first, but probably not her last, global medal.

second repeat, you might start to think, "It's early in the workout and I'm already tired. I can't possibly finish this."

Chunking the workout would have you thinking differently. You would take it one 1-mile repeat at a time. You would do your best to hit the right pace on that repeat and not think about how you might feel on the next hard mile. It's normal to subchunk your chunks in this situation, such as taking each repeat one lap at a time and focusing on running that lap at the right pace as easily as possible.

As you jog between repeats, you would tell yourself how much of the workout you've completed, and then start thinking about the next one. You would continue this process until you found yourself jogging before the final repeat and telling yourself "just one more." And then pretty soon, the workout would be over. This approach is also helpful for long runs and long races, when the thought of running for two or more hours might be almost incapacitating.

What are known as process goals go hand in hand with chunking. Process goals are step-by-step actions you take to help meet an ambitious target. That target is what's often called an outcome goal—the result you're trying to achieve. It would seem that thinking about your outcome goal should be motivating. But it's usually too abstract to guide what you should be doing. Thinking about it can make you worry ("Am I going to succeed?"), which usually has the perverse effect of interfering with the very thing you're trying to do well. In contrast, process goals give you something tangible to do. They keep you more engaged. Like chunking, completing a series of process goals adds up to meeting your overall goal.

For example, I usually had a really bad headache after marathons because I had buckled down mentally for more than two hours. I was constantly executing process goals. At every mile mark, I would note my time and do some quick math to see if I should stay steady, pick it up, or slow. I also did a body check every mile. (More on that shortly.) The fluid stations were usually every 5K, so as I approached them I would make sure I was on the correct side of the road and in position to efficiently grab my bottle. Then I would concentrate on getting in four to six ounces of fluid, spread over one or two minutes. Other actions such as monitoring moves by others and going up and down hills efficiently kept me busy mentally. Each thing I did contributed to running my best while also taking my mind off the totality of racing 26.2 miles.

Body Checks and Focused Thinking

You may have struggled to come up with a short answer to the question of "what do you think about when you run?" Your thoughts on a 10-miler with friends or a solo trail run are probably a lot different than when you're doing a workout or racing.

On easy runs, hopefully you're mostly thinking about whatever you feel like thinking about. On harder runs, you're probably more focused on how your body is feeling than, say, how pretty the fall foliage is. This is known as attentional focus. That's paying attention to the things that will help you reach your goal for the task you're doing. Cues from your body, such as how hard you're breathing, provide information on how to proceed in your workout or race.

The thing is, you don't want to pay too much attention to physical sensations like breathing or whether your legs feel heavy. Getting uptight about staying relaxed isn't good. If you're constantly thinking, "Yup, still breathing hard," your observations will become self-fulfilling. You'll think, "No wonder I'm so tired!"

Quick but regular body checks are the solution here. Like I said, in marathons I did a brief one every mile. I scanned head to toe to make sure I wasn't too tense anywhere. If there was surging going on, I'd take a deep breath and tell myself to relax and stay calm. Then I would return my attention to something else pertinent, like an upcoming turn in the road.

The runners I coach know exactly what I mean when they hear me yell "body check!" They do that same whole-body scan. They drop their shoulders, shake out their arms, check their legs to make sure they're not overstriding. They might try to kick their butt with their heels for a couple strides. This takes just a few seconds but has huge benefits. It helps them to run a little more efficiently, which directly translates into either running faster at the same effort or having the same pace feel easier. It can also wake them up mentally. Having this helpful thing to focus on, even for a short time, can get them out of a bad patch and refocus them on competing.

Plan to do these body checks on your own. On a long run, check in every few miles. During a race, try one each mile. In a hard workout, do one on each repeat after the first repeat.

Positive Self-Talk

We all talk to ourselves when we run. The self-talk of successful runners is almost entirely positive. It motivates them to keep working hard and increases their self-confidence. Phrases such as "good job; keep it going" or "you've done this before; you can do it now" will lead to much better performance than their opposites.

It's not that good runners don't have negative thoughts when a workout or race gets hard. Everybody does. What people who are good at self-talk do is instantly counter those negative thoughts with positive, motivational phrases. On the fourth of six 800-meter repeats, you might think, "This is getting really hard. I don't know if I can do three more at this pace." Good self-talkers will acknowledge that thought but immediately reply to themselves with something like "I'm tired, but I can keep going, just like I did in last week's workout." It's good to experiment with your positive self-talk and find a few phrases that work best for you. Mine were pretty simple, like "you're good, Mark" or "stay on it, you're fine."

You may have noticed that in my examples, I called myself by my name or "you." There's research from a lot of types of undertakings, including endurance sports, showing that second-person self-talk can be more effective than first-person ("I") self-talk. The performance improvements in these studies are usually small, on the order of 1 or 2 percent. But that's a massive difference in the real world—a 40:00 10K runner who goes 2 percent faster will run 39:12!

Second-person self-talk is thought to be more effective because it creates a distance between you and what you're telling yourself. It removes some of the emotional involvement. Some people tend to use first-person self-talk more when they're feeling sorry for themselves, like "Why do I have to be out here in the rain doing a workout?" The second-person perspective is more like hearing from a coach. And I would never say to one of my runners "this is pointless; drop out" or "you're tired; it's okay if you slow down for the final mile." Talking to yourself as a motivating coach might seem strange. But we do lots of odd things to run better. Few of them will be as effective as mastering positive self-talk.

Self-Talk After a Disappointing Race

Apply the idea of second-person self-talk to postrace analysis, especially when things didn't go like you wanted. A lot of people are their own worst critics. If they can step outside themselves and view their performance as they might that of a friend or family member, they might be able to be kinder to themselves and have a more positive take on how things went.

One of the hardest marathons I ever ran was New York City in 1997. I trained too hard and was a little cooked going into the race. I lost contact with the lead pack two miles in. I ran solo for more than the next 20 miles. I tried every trick in the book to stay positive and keep myself going. I would count to 100, trying not to miss any numbers, then start counting again. When it started to rain, I told myself I like rain and that others would tighten up and come back to me. And so on. I finished a well-beaten 18th in 2:20:41, more than seven minutes slower than the PR I'd set just a year and a half earlier.

Once I was over the "that sucked!" emotions of the moment, I thought about the race like a coach might. I recognized that I practiced effective self-talk. I congratulated myself for not dropping out when doing so would have been understandable and easy. (After you cross the Queensboro Bridge to enter Manhattan in the 17th mile, it's a short run up 59th Street to get to the finish.) I told myself it's pretty impressive to run 2:20 by myself in a race I overtrained for.

Try this approach on yourself. Pretend you're talking to someone close to you. Look for positives and lessons. Then carry all of that into your next race.

5

Being a Student of the Sport

Gather 'round, modern runners, and let the old guy tell you how it used to be.

In the early 1980s, running information was hard to come by. I had access to a few monthly magazines and a handful of books. I graduated high school with little knowledge of how good runners trained. I learned a little more in college, thanks to finding more books to read and talking with other runners and hearing stories from my coach. Still, I was hungry for every tidbit of potentially useful running information I could find.

Runners of all ages have the opposite problem today. We're overloaded with information about all aspects of running—how much to run, how fast to run, what to eat and drink, what to wear, how (or whether) to stretch, and on and on and on. It's probably harder to be truly knowledgeable about running now than 30 years ago. How do you know who's worth listening to and what's really relevant when anyone can claim to be an expert?

In this chapter, I'll explain why it's worth being a student of the sport and how to become knowledgeable about running. I'll also describe how to best use one of the main sources of information overload—all the data from your smart watch.

My Running Education

When I graduated college in 1988, my interest in running was much greater than my knowledge of it. I loved my time training under Charles Torpey at the University of Maryland. Charles was a great motivator and really cared about us as people. But he didn't explain much of the "why" behind what we did, and I wasn't about to interrogate him on the topic.

That didn't really concern me. I knew I wouldn't be coaching myself as a young pro. I certainly didn't think I'd one day be coaching others. What I knew about training came from talking with others and the books and magazines I mentioned. Even that reading was more like a collection of snapshots than a comprehensive explainer. You might see a week or two of someone's training but not know what they did the rest of the year. (And, come on, we all know runners who exaggerate their training.)

After college I moved back home to Attleboro, Massachusetts. I got in touch with Nike Boston, an elite training group, and was invited to join. Saying I was a "young pro" is stretching things a little, because while I was young, I wasn't getting paid. I got some gear and support for traveling to a few meets, and some fast new teammates. I also got a great coach, Bob Sevene, who had helped guide the training of runners like 1984 Olympic Marathon champion Joan Benoit. I worked afternoons at a running store and was psyched to have an opportunity to keep running.

Another great thing happened around then: A steeplechase time from my junior year of college qualified me for the 1988 Olympic Trials. I got reenergized hanging out at the meet for a week and meeting lots of great runners. One of them was John Gregorek. John had made the 1980 and 1984 Olympic teams and was the sort of runner I aspired to be. He seemed to always be in great shape and was competitive at a huge range of distances. (Late in his career, John, who had been a world-class miler, steeplechaser, and 5K runner, qualified for the 1996 Olympic Marathon Trials.) John was training with a group of top runners in Providence, Rhode Island, and invited me to join them when I wanted. So starting in the fall of 1988, I worked out once or twice a week with Nike Boston and did most of my regular runs with John's group.

I learned more about running in the Providence College locker room than anywhere else. Much of what I learned there is reflected in the training principles I described in chapter 1—consistency, working in that sweet spot of hard but not too hard, focusing on high-end aerobic work, enjoying your running, and more. When I moved to Boulder, Colorado, and started training with a large, loose group of world-class track and road runners, the Providence lessons were reinforced. Everyone had their little tweaks and preferences, but at its core, the fundamentals of how people trained were remarkably similar. I'll return to this point in a bit.

My education continued as I transitioned from being an athlete to being a coach. I studied training theory more systematically while getting a master's degree in sports science. I regularly traded ideas with other coaches and read exercise science and sport nutrition research. Equally important, I observed and

Listening to coaches and other runners is one aspect of becoming a student of the sport.

Courtesy of Justin Britton.

listened to the runners I coached to see how principles worked out in real life. Being a student of the sport is an ongoing process. How I coach now is different from how I coached 10 years ago, and how I coach in another 10 years will likely look different than how I do now.

Who Should You Listen To?

I was incredibly fortunate as a young pro runner. I got to train with and learn directly from Olympians, world champions, and world-record holders. That's probably not your situation. Also, unlike when I was soaking up all this knowledge pre-Internet, you can find, in seconds, a million suggestions on every aspect of running. So how do you go about deciding what's good advice?

My story is relevant here. The people who were giving me advice had results worth emulating. One member of the Providence group was John Treacy, an Olympic silver medalist in the marathon and two-time world cross-country champion. When he told 22-year-old me that I should run 90 miles a week, not 70, you better believe I believed him. Mick O'Shea, another Providence training partner, told me I didn't have to live like a hermit to be a world-class runner. But, Mick said, you do need to be in bed at a decent hour and get good sleep to allow the training effect to occur. Or when Bob Sevene prescribed workouts that were different than what I was used to from high school and college, I did them. I would have been an idiot not to, given the large number of champion runners he'd coached.

Bob's recommendations carried even more weight because his explanations simply made sense. He had us do a tempo run once a week in the fall. This was a new type of workout for me. One day I worked up the nerve to ask why we did tempo runs. He said, "If we can bring your threshold up a bit, then running 4:30 mile pace will only be running at 80 percent of your max, not 90 percent. These tempos are the quickest, most efficient way to build your threshold."

The track and road runners in Providence and the marathoners I trained with in Boulder didn't just have the results to back up what they advocated. I saw them doing exactly what they said I should do. I think that's another important standard for deciding who to listen to. For example, if someone tells you that weekly mileage doesn't matter as long as you do your hard workouts, but he himself consistently runs a lot, it's worth questioning his advice. Similarly, if you hear a coach advocating one way of training but you find that her runners train pretty differently than that, be skeptical. (I hope by now you see that what I recommend in this book is in line with how I coach in person.)

Another thing to consider is that none of the people who gave the young me advice were selling me something or otherwise had a vested interest in my doing what they said. If anything, they would have been better off misleading me, so that I wouldn't improve and perhaps beat them. There's nothing inherently wrong with selling something—I'd love it if you bought 10 copies of this book!—but if the person doing so doesn't also have the results and lived experience, be skeptical.

Becoming a Student of the Sport

If you're relatively new to running, your best bet is to use the broad standards I've discussed to pick a training program, then execute it the best you can. There's a lot to be said for this approach. One reason that so many elite runners have a coach is that they can off-load thinking about their workouts to someone they trust. Then they can devote all their mental energy to training and racing.

Most experienced recreational runners don't have a coach. They need to decide how to train. There's nothing wrong with these runners also selecting a solid training program and sticking with it. But a lot of these runners get more interested in running. They start to read about training and listen to podcasts with accomplished runners and coaches and less-accomplished but equally vocal runners and coaches. It's at this point they might encounter information overload and not know how to determine what's valid.

This is when being a student of the sport comes in handy. In any field, it makes sense to study what the most successful people in that field do. If you read and hear about the training of top runners and study what successful coaches prescribe, you'll have the same realization I did when I had direct contact with all those good runners and coaches: The training of most top runners looks similar. Most do regular long runs, tempo runs, longer repeats at around 3K to 10K race pace, and shorter repeats at around mile race pace, all interspersed with easy recovery runs and moderate-pace getting-in-the-miles runs. And most do get in the miles—the top distance runners who don't do fairly high volume are the exceptions.

This is an incredibly helpful base of knowledge. If you hear someone recommending something counter to this general approach, especially if they say they have a "secret workout" or claim special knowledge, break out your BS meter. Trust me, if something other than what most elites do were the key to running faster, top runners would have been the first ones to try it. And if it worked, then most other top runners would have immediately adopted it, and it would already have become commonplace. As I said in chapter 3, when I was a pro, few of us did regular strengthening exercises. Now almost everyone does nonrunning work to stay healthy. Why? Because enough people experimented with this work and realized it helps reduce their injury risk, which leads to more consistent training, which leads to running faster. That's how advances in training happen.

Use the same standard when weighing claims about other aspects of running. Top runners put in a lot of time to get a fraction of a percent faster. Some even risk their health and livelihood by doping to get an edge. If some special, unconventional diet really were the key to running faster, then top runners would already be on it. The same goes for running barefoot or purposefully running with a certain foot strike or taking walking breaks or any of the other unconventional claims that come up again and again.

When you're studying how others train, it's really helpful to put the common elements in context. Compare the times you see for various types of workouts to the person's race times. In the abstract, someone doing a workout of six to eight 800-meter repeats in 2:20 might sound impossibly fast. But if you do the math, you'll probably realize that's close to her 5K race pace. You can then translate that workout to an equivalent at your 5K race pace, and better understand it as a tough but doable session. Or consider seeing that someone does a 20-mile long run at 6:00-per-mile pace. That also sounds crazy fast until you realize it's more than a minute per mile slower than his marathon race pace, and that you also can do long runs at that effort level. One of the best things you can do in this vein is compare elites' recovery-run pace to their race pace. It's probably a greater differential than you run on your nonworkout days. Take that lesson to heart.

Coogan's Crew: Jacqui Wentz

Personal Bests: 10:04 3,000-meter steeplechase; 17:05 5,000 meters

Career Highlights: NCAA Division III steeplechase champion; five-time All-American

Years With Coach Coogan: 2007-2009

I was an assistant coach at the Massachusetts Institute of Technology from the fall of 2007 through the spring of 2009. I worked with the distance runners during indoor and outdoor track.

The students at MIT were the smartest people I've ever been around. Everything else at MIT was so intense that running was like a refuge for them. I tried to keep things simple and not too intense so that they would always look forward to coming to practice. Not that they, and I, didn't take their running seriously. MIT runners were hard workers in every area of their lives, and they were used to succeeding.

The head coach, Halston Taylor, let me take over some of the distance runners' training. I appreciated Halston's trust and the opportunity to change some aspects of the athletes' training when I thought that was warranted.

One runner I really enjoyed working with was Jacqui Wentz. She was a sophomore when I arrived. She had barely competed her freshman year because of injuries. Although she says she continued to struggle with injuries throughout college, we were able to keep her healthy enough to race regularly during the two years we worked together.

"My training under Mark was more individualized," Jacqui says. "Before, we all did basically the same workout, usually something like 12 400s. With Mark it was more [like] 'this is the right workout for you today.'"

Because of Jacqui's injury history, I kept her mileage lower and tried to make sure her hard workouts really counted. Jacqui remembers her sessions as "exciting workouts at race pace with longer rest and slightly less distance." One staple I had her do was 1,600 meters, 1,200 meters, 800 meters, and 400 meters, getting progressively faster to steel her physically and mentally for racing.

Jacqui's results went in the right direction with this guidance. She started winning races and became a top runner among NCAA Division III colleges. She won numerous conference championships, and she had great range, running everything from a leg on the four-by-400-meter relay up to 5,000 meters. Her lifetime 5K best came during one of our indoor seasons together. The year after I left MIT, she won the Division III NCAA steeplechase title. I like to think I played a role in setting her up for that accomplishment.

Jacqui is a good example of not being afraid to change your training if what you've been doing isn't getting the results you want. Remember, though, that we're talking appropriate adjustments more than full-scale makeovers. With Jacqui, the right approach was to emphasize quality over volume. For you, it might be the opposite, but always within the framework of an overall sound program.

These days, Jacqui is doing postdoctoral work in aerospace engineering at the University of Colorado in Boulder. She no longer competes but is still a runner. If I had any role in her continuing to run, that means a lot to me. I always thought when I was coaching collegians that if they still loved to run when they graduated, I had done something right.

Once you have this base of knowledge, you can better decide how and whether to change your training. If you feel like you've plateaued for a few years without an obvious explanation, it might be time to try something new. But not 10 new things. Add one new element that's a part of many good runners' programs—such as short hill repeats, longer long runs, or regular form drills—and see if you notice any difference after a month. Or maybe just change where you do some of your runs. Switch from the flat bike path to a hilly road loop, or vice versa, for example. Remember, there are many ways to get fit. As a student of the sport, you can feel confident that you're not going to ruin everything with a tweak or two. It's like being a knowledgeable baker: You have this great recipe for chocolate chip cookies, but one day you don't have enough white sugar. So you put in some other sweetener, and the cookies are still fabulous.

Another really helpful thing is reading biographies of great runners and following online those who regularly post their training (not just their A+ workouts). You'll learn about their struggles and setbacks, which will probably be similar to yours, and about their mental approach to the sport. Maybe most importantly, you'll be reminded that everything doesn't have to be perfect to run your best.

At some point, enough is enough. There's so much information out there that it can overwhelm you. One of my main points as a coach is that you don't have to obsess over every detail. Remember that most good programs are pretty similar. Find a good training program and trust that it will work. That's a much better approach than picking and choosing like you're at a training cafeteria. Save your mental energy for the running. Don't suffer paralysis through overanalysis.

Which leads me to smart watches.

Dealing With a Data Deluge: Using a GPS Watch

Everyone I coach runs with a GPS watch. They all use them a little differently. My main message is the same, regardless of how they use their watches: The watch is telling you how fast you ran. It shouldn't be telling you how fast to run.

A lot of runners, especially those without coaches, do otherwise. They check their splits every mile, or more often, and if the watch says they're going slower than they think they should be, they pick up the pace, regardless of how they feel. Similarly, once they hit a certain pace on a run, they try not to go slower the rest of the run, whether or not maintaining that pace is the right effort for the day, or they're going uphill, or they've hit a headwind, or any of the many other things that will naturally cause your pace to vary throughout a run.

That's not a smart way to train, no matter how smart the watch is. (Which might not be as smart as you think. All the obsession with precise numbers assumes your watch is 100 percent accurate all the time. It's not.) Remember the get-the-work-in principle from chapter 1. Your body knows effort. It doesn't know what a mile or a minute is. I always tell my team they know what a certain pace in perfect conditions feels like. If they're at that effort level, I don't care what the actual pace is. It's fine to look at your watch to see what a certain effort feels like in different conditions. That can be helpful information for situations like racing on a hilly course or varied weather. That's an entirely different approach than straining to maintain a certain pace up a hill because you don't want your watch to tell you that you slowed during that mile.

Another good use is to check the data after your run to see how your fitness is progressing. Maybe you ran the same time for a five-mile loop as you did a month ago but at a lower heart rate. Or maybe you ran the loop faster at the same heart rate. Again, though, look at this data after your run. If you look during, don't change what you're doing just because of what the watch says.

In general, think of your smart watch as a training companion or coach. You wouldn't keep running with somebody, or being coached by somebody, if during and after most runs that person made you feel bad about your running or didn't help you improve. Have the same relationship with your watch. Make it a positive, not a negative. If that's not possible, like if you constantly check your splits and run too fast on recovery days, or if you regularly think "I suck" because of the data even though you felt like you had a good run, it's time to get an old-school GPS-free watch.

Trust your body over your watch when it comes to recovery. I've had athletes tell me things like "I slept great, but my watch says I'm not recovered" or "I didn't wake up once in eight hours, but the watch says I didn't get enough sleep." And then they'll wonder if they should stick with their planned training for the day, even though they feel fine. That's the opposite of getting something positive from the watch and using its data intelligently.

Look again at Olympian and national champion Heather MacLean's training log excerpts in chapter 1. Some days she records her training in time, other days in distance. Heather knows that units like a minute or a mile are arbitrary. You'll never see Heather run another 38 seconds past her apartment until her watch says she's done exactly 10.00 miles and that she's therefore allowed to stop. This is someone with the proper perspective on what matters.

PART II

6

Racing Is a Skill You Can Master

Let's say you haven't raced in a while. You go to a 5K and run as hard as you can. One week later, you do another 5K and run much faster.

How is that possible? It's unlikely that you got significantly fitter in the intervening seven days. A more likely explanation is that you needed to relearn how to race. Racing is a skill. It comes more naturally to some runners than others. But, as with most skills, even the best can't set it aside indefinitely without losing some prowess.

You can find distance-specific racing tips in the training schedule chapters. In this chapter, I'll share some general thoughts on how to race, including why two equally fit runners can have vastly different race results.

Racing Is the Reward

Let me start with a seemingly obvious statement, but one that some runners seem to forget: We don't train to get good at training. We train to race.

I loved to race. As I said elsewhere, one weekend I raced a mile on Friday and the Bay to Breakers 12K on Sunday. Don't get me wrong—I also loved getting together with friends and talking and joking through workaday 10-mile runs. That time together was usually the highlight of my day. But racing? That was often the highlight of my month. I loved the challenge and sense of accomplishment that even the hardest workout can't bring.

Most pro runners race less often than was the case when I was competing. There are a few reasons, including greater use of altitude training. If you go to a high altitude, you want to stay there for four or five weeks to get a big boost in red blood cell count. Do that twice a year, and right there you've removed at least two months of potential races out of your calendar.

Another reason some pros race infrequently is psychological. As a pro, you usually don't want to get beaten by people who shouldn't beat you. So why show up when you're at 50 percent and give someone the idea that they're better than you? I tell people on my team that they're not going to race until they're ready to put in a decent performance. The main exception is something like the Olympic Trials, where what's at stake is so important that I want them there even if they're not fully ready.

Your racing schedule probably isn't affected by altitude training and your place in the professional pecking order. That's good! It means more opportunities for you to hone your racing skills and enjoy the unique treat of competition. I'm not saying you have to race a lot. But if you like racing, have at it. Put your training toward its intended purpose.

Of course, if you race every weekend you're probably not going to perform up to your potential. You'll spend too much time being sore and recovering physically and mentally to advance your fitness. The schedules in chapter 13 will prepare you for regular racing at a range of distances and show you how best to balance training and racing once you start a block of frequent competition.

What Makes a Good Racer?

Two people can do the same training, perhaps even as training partners, and seem to be equally fit. Yet odds are that one will consistently beat the other. Why is that?

One reason is that one of the pair might be overdoing it in training. If the two are training partners, those 800-meter repeats they do together might be at 80 percent effort for one but 90 percent effort for the other. The one who's regularly working a little too hard in training is going to enter races tired, while the one whose overall training is at the right effort level will absorb her training and enter races fresh and eager. The training schedules later in this book aim to have you be that fit-but-fresh runner on race day.

A second reason is that one of the two is a better race tactician. Running too fast the first mile—or even the first quarter-mile—is the most common and harmful mistake here. I don't care how fit you are, if you blast off the line at a pace that's substantially faster than you can hold for the distance, you're not going to run what you're capable of. In each of the training schedule chapters, I have racing advice specific to that chapter's distance. But for all of them, the number one counsel is "Don't run stupidly early on."

Consistently good racers have a strategy that takes into account their fitness, the course and weather, and potential surprises. They'll know what their outcome goal for the race is, and they'll have process goals that help them achieve that outcome. They'll also have backup goals to keep themselves motivated and

---

A Few General Racing Tips

- Wait until the week before a goal race to really think about how fast you should aim to run. Don't base pacing decisions on how tired you feel during heavy training.
- Always take into account race-day weather and course difficulty.
- Remember that you have limited willpower. Account for any unusual mental stress in the week before your race.
- Know the course the best you can. If you haven't been able to preview it, try to do your warm-up near the finish area to mentally prepare for nailing the last section. Pick a spot or landmark near the finish and tell yourself, "From there, I'm going to run like my life depends on it."
- Run the tangents!

working hard if it becomes obvious they're not going to hit their main goal. For example, if a good racer realizes at mile 18 of a marathon he's not going to set a personal best that day, he doesn't just step off the course or jog to the finish.

Part of any good strategy is knowing and preparing for the fact that, at some point, things are going to get really hard. You're going to have to decide to keep riding the red line or back off. That's why I'm such a big advocate of prerace visualization. Running the race in your head helps you make that decision to stick with it before the race even happens. Then, in the race, you don't really have to think about it. You just do it.

Those decision points don't necessarily mean things are going to keep getting worse the rest of the race. Maybe a key spot comes on a hill in the fifth mile of a 10K. You might need to push hard up that hill to stay on target, but you might also be able to tell yourself there's a gentle downgrade after the hill where you can recover a bit while still staying on pace.

Coogan's Crew: Abbey Cooper

Personal Best: 14:52 5,000 meters

Career Highlights: 2016 Olympian at 5,000 meters; seven-time NCAA champion; 5th, 2016 World Indoor Championships 3,000 meters

Years With Coach Coogan: 2010-2017

Courtesy of Justin Britton.

Working with Abbey Cooper (then D'Agostino) was one of the highlights of my time coaching at Dartmouth. I learned a lot from her, and hopefully she learned a few things from me.

One insight I had thanks to Abbey is something I still use today. My standard schedule for college runners called for a meet on Saturday, a long run on Sunday, and a workout on Tuesday. Abbey would often not run as well as I thought she could on those Tuesday workouts. I realized that she's someone who gets 100 percent out of herself in races. She's so talented and so driven that races took more out of her than most of her teammates. So to follow that with a long run the next day and a hard session three days later was too much. Because of being able to dig so deep in races, she needed more recovery time after. Once we adjusted her postrace schedule to allow for that recovery, she excelled and wound up winning seven NCAA titles in her four years at Dartmouth. I now build in that extra recovery for the pros I coach.

Abbey is modest and says about her racing prowess, "When you're the person doing it, you don't think about it a lot." She also says that she wasn't always the fearless competitor she is now. "When I was young, I would hold back in elementary school gym class because I was afraid if I ran too hard I'd puke at the end," she says. "I'm naturally risk-averse, so this has been an arena where I've learned to press my boundaries and explore what happens."

She really came into her own at Dartmouth as early successes built on each other. "A lot of my motivation came from learning that I have this untapped talent that I didn't know was there," she says. Abbey enthusiastically pursued my recommendation of prerace visualizing and imagery. "It allows me to go through the event and anticipate different situations," she says. "Obviously you never know exactly what's going to happen, but it eases some of the surprise element and gives me the ability to reshift my attention in the midst of chaos happening in the middle of the race." Abbey still does guided prerace visualization with the help of her husband, Jacob, a sports psychologist.

Once in a race, Abbey practices some of the techniques I described in chapter 4.

"I've learned the difference between awareness and attention," she says. "When I start to worry about things like if the pace is too much for me, I focus on keeping my form relaxed, shifting to something tangible in my body that allows me to focus on the task and be present. That might be a word, like 'stay,' or something as simple as keeping my elbows square."

In her qualifying heat at the 2016 Olympics, Abbey tripped over Nikki Hamball of New Zealand, who had fallen in front of her. You probably recall the moving images of Abbey stopping to help Nikki up, and then immediately wincing when she tried to resume running. In the mishap, Abbey had torn her ACL and meniscus. She had surgery later that year, and she didn't race again until the fall of 2017. Her take on resuming racing after such a setback is instructive for any runner in that situation.

"The idea of going out and racing myself into shape was uncomfortable," Abbey says. "I really wrestled for a long time with balancing the physical aspect and my expectations. I felt like I had so much untapped potential but I was so far from where I had been one year before. I needed to learn how to manage my expectations and channel them in a way that's helpful, not limiting."

Abbey kept faith that her best running days were still ahead of her. She produced one of the most impressive performances I saw at the 2021 Olympic Trials. You may have missed it, because it happened in her qualifying round, not the final. Abbey entered the meet lacking the 5,000-meter Olympic standard and was unlikely to achieve it in the final because a heat wave was forecast to arrive by then. So even if she finished in the top three in the final, she would be left off the Olympic team because she didn't yet have the Olympic standard. What did Abbey do? Three days before the final, in more favorable conditions, she took the lead a few laps into her qualifying round and soloed to a 15:07 win, under the Olympic standard and just four seconds slower than what was then her personal best. Her run was a great example of taking advantage of opportunities as they present themselves. Two months later, she joined the select group of American women who have broken 15:00 for 5K with a 14:52 PR.

I'll let Abbey have the last word on her remarkable resurgence and psychological skills.

"Now, more of my confidence comes from what I've been through," she says. "There's a freedom that comes from knowing that my identity does not lie in my performance. To actually believe that and then step out and race and still have to be vulnerable, there's a different kind of freedom—the freedom to fail."

A third reason two equally fit runners race differently is that people simply have different mental makeups. The psychological tools I described in chapter 4 will help you be the best you that's possible. But your training partner might just naturally be more competitive. Some people are content to know they gave their best. That's a completely valid approach. Others, however, thrive on competition. They try to do their best, but also really care about beating the people around them.

To see what I'm talking about, watch the women's 3,000-meter race at the 2022 World Indoor Championships. I like to say that if Elle St. Pierre wants to be in third place on the second lap, she's going to be in third place. She's not going to let others push her around. She has that extra natural competitiveness, a little bit more of a killer instinct than even most of the other world-class women she races.

What I said about Elle being where she wants to be is exactly how the race played out. Elle wanted to be near the front to be able to react to any moves and stay out of trouble in a big field on a small track. The race was close for all 15 laps, and the pace varied throughout. But Elle was a constant presence near the front. Others moved back and forth through the field, wasting energy. Elle was well-positioned when the kicking began and was rewarded with her first global medal.

You Should Never Have a Bad Race

One thing I constantly tell my team is that they shouldn't have any bad races. In fact, I tell them, they should never even have a bad workout.

You're probably thinking, "Wait, what? I've had lots of bad races." You might even look at my competitive record and think there's a stinker or two. What do I mean by saying you should never have a bad race?

Think about being in school. If you put in the work, you're not going to get an F. You would never do all your assignments all semester and then head into an exam thinking, "I have no idea how I'm going to do today."

The same reasoning applies to racing. If you've trained well and crafted a sound race strategy, how you're going to do shouldn't be a complete mystery. If you usually run around 20:00 for 5K, you're not going to run 28:00, unless you're injured or ill or take a fall during the race. You might not run the time you want because of weather or other variables, but you're going to be close to what you expected to run, and that should be a positive experience.

Of course, some races are going to be a lot more difficult than you think they should be. Some days you're just off. I had to dig deeper in most of my slower marathons than I did when I set my PR. You might find half a mile into a 5K you just don't have the fight you usually do. That happens. But physiologically, the fitness you've built is still there.

In these instances, you need to dip further into the bag of psychological tools I described in chapter 4. Break the remaining part of the race into chunks, come up with a goal for each chunk, and think about only that part of the race. In a 10K you might tell yourself, "I'm going to really push it from four to five miles and see what happens." Eight miles into a half-marathon you might say, "I'm going to latch on to the next person who passes me and see how long I can hang on." Toward the end of a 5K it could be, "As soon as I see the finish, I'm going to kick like I never have before." These little games will keep you engaged, distract you from the overall "I suck" narrative, and perhaps give you some techniques to use in future races.

Do a postrace analysis the day after a not-great result. (Don't do it that day—let your emotions cool off some.) Ask yourself where things went wrong. Did you charge up a hill and pass 20 people but exhaust yourself, so that those 20 and others passed you in the next mile? Did you run the first mile 15 seconds faster than your goal pace? Try to find the places where you made a mistake that threw off the rest of your race.

If you can get something out of a race that didn't go like you wanted, then it wasn't a bad race because you learned something. The key is to not make the mistake again. Don't be like the person who apologizes for being late 12 times in a row without changing his ways. Really learn from your mistake and don't repeat it.

Benefits of Tune-up Races

Three weeks before I placed second at the 1996 Olympic Marathon Trials, I ran an indoor 5K. I ran under control and won in 13:49.

Although the time was 27 seconds slower than my best for the distance, the race gave me confidence that I was ready for the Trials. I ran it coming off a 100-mile week and had been training for a marathon, not a 5K, the previous few months. So to run a decent time and not really feel tired afterward was encouraging. I felt like if I had rested for a few days before the 5K I would have been close to my PR. I told myself that probably nobody else in the Trials field could run that fast for 5K right then. I also told myself that I'd easily be able to handle the probable pace at the Trials, 5:00 to 5:10 per mile. That meant I could just hang out in the lead pack and still be comfortable when the real racing started late in the race. I doubled down on visualizing that race scenario. Things played out that way at the Trials, and I made the Olympic team.

That's a lot of benefit for less than 14 minutes of running!

Most runners will do better in their goal races if they've run one to three tune-up races. You can train as hard as you want but there's still something unique about race day. Veteran pros who are natural competitors and have years of experience against the best in the world maybe don't need tune-up races. This is most often the case with elite marathoners. The rest of us, however, probably need tune-ups. Like I said earlier, racing is a skill that rewards practice.

Tune-up races are helpful beyond giving you a chance to hone your tactics. Getting ready for a race is a lot different than getting ready even for an A+ workout. Going as hard as you can, dealing with nerves and logistics, having to be ready to start when someone else says "go"—these are all things you can't adequately simulate in training. There's a lot of value in experiencing them before your goal race.

Tune-up races can also give you the psychological boost I got from that pre-Trials 5K. If you run a fast 5K a few weeks before your goal 10K, you'll be pumped. It will give you a little bit of extra confidence you might not have if you just kept training. And if a tune-up race doesn't go as well as you'd like, it's still a positive. You should be able to find valid reasons, such as you're in the midst of hard training and it's not at the distance you're focused on. You know that once you rest up, you'll feel much fresher in your goal race. Plus, you still got practice at dealing with prerace nerves and the mental strain of racing.

So, yeah, I'm a big fan of tune-up races. I've incorporated them into most of the longer training schedules. As you'll see in the next chapter, I'm also okay if you add one or two more if that will keep you motivated.

Race Well and the Times Will Come

Many non-elite runners go into races focused solely on time. That's understandable. Times give you an objective measure of how you did. And unlike pro runners, non-elites often don't know whether there will be one or 100 people at a race who are around their level.

Yet there are still things to learn from the pros here. Most of my PRs came in races that I won or placed highly in. I was focused on competing and doing the very best I could that day, and that resulted in fast times on those days. I'm more proud of having finished second in U.S. championships at 5K and the marathon than I am of running a 3:58 mile, which didn't put me among the best milers in the country.

Or consider Elle St. Pierre's 1,500-meter Olympic Trials record and personal best of 3:58.03. Elle did what she had to do that day to win. That meant setting a strong pace from the start and grinding it out the whole way to deny anyone the chance to get close enough to outkick her. Racing like that resulted in running the Trials record. But setting that mark wasn't her focus. Winning the race was. Competing hard led to a great time. (Don't tell her I told you, but I doubt Elle even knows what the world record for 1,500 meters is.)

I'm not advocating you disregard your times. Racing hard doesn't mean blasting off the start line and hoping for the best. Split times give you valuable feedback early on that you haven't started too fast. Later in the race, they can motivate you to keep pushing. Just add to watching your watch the drive to beat as many of those around you as you can.

Courtesy of Justin Britton.

Compete hard and the times (and wins) will come.

Keep Racing in Perspective

Many runners train great but race poorly, especially at bigger events. This usually happens because they put too much stress on themselves about their performance. It's not so much their expectations of their performance that gets in the way as much as the pressure they perceive from the event. What if they don't run well? What will people think?

If that's you, take a step back. It's just a race. Before the Olympic Trials I told my team that even making the Olympic team didn't really change my life. Sure, I became a more popular runner, but making the Olympic team didn't change who I am. My parents and siblings were going to love me the same regardless of how I did. If someone wanted to suddenly be my friend because I made the team, or if someone wanted nothing to do with me because I didn't, I wouldn't want that person as a friend.

Treat big events like they're a low-key race. Take a step back and just run the best you can that day. Tell yourself, "I know I'm in good shape, I know I'm going to give it my best shot, and the world's not going to change no matter how I run. My family and friends are still going to be there for me."

7

Following the Programs

You're probably eager to pick a training program and get to work. That's good!

But sooner rather than later, I want you to read this chapter carefully. In it I'll describe the main types of runs in your training program, plus why and how fast to do them. I'll also help you decide which weekly mileage option and schedule length to choose. Finally, I'll give guidance on how to adjust the schedules and what to do if (or, more likely, when) you have a setback.

Types of Runs in the Training Programs

The training schedules in chapters 8 through 14 specify a type of run for each day of the week. (The occasional "day off" means, you guessed it, to not run that day.) Here are the types of runs you'll encounter in the schedules and what I mean by them.

Long Runs

This is your longest run of the week. It's usually at least a few miles longer than any other run I have you doing that week.

Long runs are a key part of all my training programs. Obviously, long runs are central to half-marathon and marathon training. But you need long runs to do your best at every distance from the mile on up. Look back at 1,500-meter Olympian Heather MacLean's training log excerpts in chapter 1. You'll see that Heather, whose longest race lasts just four minutes, does a long run almost every week, even as her goal races are approaching.

Long runs are one of the three main components of the aerobic monster principle I described in chapter 1. (Tempo runs and overall mileage are the other two.) You need long runs to build your endurance and enable you to hold a strong pace over the second half of your race. Long runs cause changes in your muscles, such as building a better network of the tiny blood vessels called capillaries that improve your ability to run aerobically. For races like the half-marathon and marathon, where running out of your body's fuel for high-end aerobic running can cause you to slow, long runs improve your ability to burn fat at a fast pace.

Besides helping you gain fitness, long runs callus you for racing. Being out on a long run can be very challenging mentally. You're almost certain to wish one or more long runs in your buildup would end around the halfway point. Sticking with it is great practice for handling the mental strain of racing.

The long runs in my programs are almost always at a conversational pace. They're basically extended regular runs (see page 94 for more on regular runs). It's the distance that's the challenging part of the run. You should be able to speak in complete sentences at any time during a long run. If you enjoy running with others, your weekly long run is a perfect opportunity to forge friendships and have a built-in way to know if you're sticking to a conversational pace.

There are a few long runs in the half-marathon and marathon schedules that incorporate some miles at half-marathon or marathon pace. You should still be able to say a short sentence during those parts of these long runs, but you'll probably prefer to concentrate rather than talk.

Tempo Runs

Tempo runs improve your ability to hold a strong pace while still running aerobically. They raise your lactate threshold—the point past which you can no longer clear lactate as quickly as you produce it. When you exceed your lactate threshold, you'll know it pretty quickly. All of a sudden your breathing increases dramatically, what had been discomfort becomes pain, and you know you won't be able to keep going for too many more minutes at that pace. If you raise your lactate threshold, then the pace when that unpleasant transition occurs becomes faster. You can then run farther at a given pace, or you can run for a set amount of time at a faster pace.

As with long runs, I have you doing tempo runs almost weekly, even if your target race is the mile. That's how important I think they are to being an aerobic monster.

I also like tempo runs because they deliver these benefits while not beating you up the way intense interval workouts can. You shouldn't feel exhausted after a tempo run. The day after, you shouldn't be sore or tight, like you might be after intervals. If you experience either of these, you did your tempo run too fast.

Many of the tempo runs in the schedules are to be done at 25 to 30 seconds per mile slower than your current 10K race pace. This is a more moderate effort level than some coaches prescribe for tempos. I have two reasons for that. First, I want to be sure you're not doing them too fast; tempo runs aren't supposed to be quasi time trials. Second, many of my tempos are longer than in other programs. Even in the 5K schedules, I have you doing up to six-mile tempos.

The half-marathon and marathon schedules often call for tempos at your half-marathon or marathon pace. I like the more race-specific tempos for half-marathon and marathon prep. In some cases, one of these paces might align with being 25 to 30 seconds slower per mile than your 10K pace.

If you train by heart rate, keep your tempos at 80 to 85 percent of your maximum heart rate. In terms of effort level, when I coached college runners who were unfamiliar with tempo runs, I would tell them to imagine I was riding a bike alongside. I would tell them that if I asked them a question, they should be able to give a short answer, like "I'm okay" or "this is hard," but they shouldn't be able to sing a song or recite a passage from their favorite book.

Do most of your tempo runs somewhere other than the track. Turning corners and going up and down hills adds variety to the workout and better mimics the demands of road racing. You'll probably also find something like a five-mile tempo run less psychologically draining if you're on the roads or a bike path. There are occasional workouts in the schedules that combine a short tempo run with faster

Courtesy of Justin Britton.

Working tempo runs into your training schedule will help you become an aerobic monster.

intervals. In those cases, you could do the tempo part on the track—a two- or three-mile tempo like that shouldn't be too mind numbing. But you could also do the tempo near the track.

Progression Runs

Think of these as a sibling of tempo runs. Both are sustained runs that improve your ability to hold a strong pace. Both also are great mental training for racing. A weekly tempo or progression run gets you used to concentrating and motivating yourself for a long time.

Progression runs differ from tempo runs in that they start out at a fairly easy pace and get faster throughout. Most of the progression runs in the schedules are three to six miles long, with your pace increasing five to ten seconds per mile each mile. By the final mile, you'll usually be around 10K race pace or even faster. You'll get to know what race pace feels like but not be exhausted at the end of the workout. Progressions also teach you how to run negative splits and ratchet up your effort despite growing fatigue.

You can do progression runs wherever you do tempo runs. It can be nice to do them on relatively flat courses, so that the main variable affecting your pace is you picking it up.

Intervals

These sessions are what most people mean when they think "hard workout." You do from a few to several repeats at a specified pace for a specified distance, with a recovery jog of a set distance between repeats. Intervals improve your aerobic capacity and get you used to exactly what your goal race pace feels like.

As I described in chapter 1, it's important to touch on all your energy systems in training, regardless of your target distance. So the interval workouts in the schedules aren't all at race pace for your target distance. Sometimes you'll run longer intervals at race pace for an event longer than your race, and sometimes you'll run shorter intervals at race pace for an event shorter than your race. For example, the 5K schedules have you sometimes running mile repeats at 10K pace and 400-meter repeats at mile pace. Sometimes you'll run race pace for two or more events in the same workout, usually ending with the shorter, faster repeats. Like progression runs, these workouts are great practice at bearing down when you get more tired.

I'll admit to a quirk in how I detail interval lengths. For repeats of less than a mile, the intervals are stated in meters, such as 400 meters (one lap of a standard track) or 800 meters. When the schedule says "1 mile" for an interval, I mean four laps of a standard track.

It's traditional to do interval workouts on the track, but I know having predictable access to a track is increasingly difficult when school boards tighten access restrictions. Also, not everyone lives near a track. When you're doing a hard workout soon before or after work, you might not have the time to travel to a track. So I'm all for doing interval workouts elsewhere if that's what's best for your situation. Use your GPS to mark off the appropriate distance, and get to work. (When the schedule says "400 meters," go with .25 mile on your watch, and on up for longer repeats stated in metric in the schedules.) Ideally, this will be on a flat stretch of road or bike path where you can run freely.

If you're that rare modern-day runner who doesn't use a GPS watch, and you can't get to a track, convert the intervals' distance and recovery jogs to time, and do the workout wherever is best for you. For example, if the schedule calls for six 800-meter repeats at 5K pace with a 400-meter jog, and you're aiming to run 20:00 for 5K, you could do six repeats of 3:12 and jog 2:15 between. (It's fine if you use a rounder figure like 3:10 to make the math easier.)

Even if you can usually get to a track, there might be times where the off-track, go-by-time option is the best. Weather or fatigue can make the unforgiving precision of a track undesirable. You'll probably have a more positive experience going by time and not worrying exactly how far you run. Also, it's important to learn what race effort feels like in different conditions without constant feedback. My team does workouts in this way during challenging winter weather in Boston.

Hill Workouts

Hill repeats combine the cardiorespiratory benefits of an interval session with the strength benefits of leg day at the gym. Hills make you faster, stronger, and more efficient. They also make you mentally tougher. There's really no such thing as cruising through a hill repeat, unlike the first few repeats of an interval session. Often the first hill repeat hurts as much as the last few.

What Pace Should I Run?

All of the workouts in the schedules specify a pace for the faster parts, such as 800-meter repeats at 5K pace or a tempo run at half-marathon pace. By "pace" I mean your goal pace for your upcoming race. I'm assuming you've picked a goal that's challenging but, on a great day, doable. For example, if in a recent 5K you ran 20:30, it's reasonable to set a goal of breaking 20:00 after following one of my 12-week 5K programs. (I like to think my training will prepare you better than the program you followed to run 20:30.) But if you trained pretty hard for that recent 20:30 and now set a goal of breaking 19:00, you're probably overshooting. If you haven't raced recently at your target distance, use an online calculator to find equivalent performances to distances you have raced in the past year.

Most of the schedules have you doing a workout at your goal race pace in the first week or two. Be honest about how difficult you find that pace. Although your race-specific fitness will increase a lot over the weeks of your training, you shouldn't strain to run, say, 400-meter repeats at your goal 5K pace or a few miles at your goal half-marathon pace. This is especially important if you're following one of the shorter schedules.

The schedules call for you to do workouts at race pace for events other than your target distance (or, in the case of many tempo runs, faster or slower than race pace for a standard distance). These sessions reflect my principle of working at a wide variety of effort levels. Use an online calculator to find the equivalent pace for these distances relative to your goal pace.

Don't freak out if your times are off on a given workout. Remember, you're doing the workout at your goal pace, not a pace you've recently held for a race at your target distances. It's a pace that's making you reach a bit, and you're not yet at the end of the program, when you'll (hopefully) have built the capacity to produce that pace on command. You'll learn pretty quickly what working at that pace should feel like. As always, concentrate on getting the work in at the right effort. If one week it turns out that effort results in running, say, 800-meter repeats five seconds slower than goal pace, you're fine. I'd much rather have you trust yourself and work at the right effort level than give up halfway through and conclude that meeting your goal is hopeless.

The hill repeats in the schedules usually call for eight ascents, with a jog back to your starting point for recovery. I call for distances between 300 meters and 800 meters, and either mile race effort or 5K effort, depending on which event you're training for.

Notice that I said mile or 5K *effort*, not pace. Don't get too caught up on time when doing hill repeats. Effort is what's most important here. Try to simulate the feeling you have when doing intervals at mile or 5K pace on the track. If you want reassurance you're being consistent, maybe time your first or second repeat, one toward the middle, and the second to last one.

My team often does hill repeats on the most famous hill in running, Heartbreak Hill, found in the 21st mile of the Boston Marathon. It's approximately half a mile long and has a grade of 3 to 4 percent. That's steep enough that you definitely know you're climbing, but still moderate enough to allow good running form. (It really only seems like a cliff that late in the marathon.) Try to find a similar hill. Steeper isn't necessarily better. If you do repeats on a hill that is challenging just to get up on a normal run, you'll struggle to maintain quick turnover and upright form.

You can simulate hill workouts on a treadmill. I wouldn't go steeper than a 5 percent incline. Play with the pacing until the effort feels appropriate. Put the incline at 0 percent for your recovery jog "down," and jog for about the same amount of time as your hard portions.

Easy Runs

These are gentle recovery runs that stimulate blood flow and otherwise help you to feel better the day after a hard effort. In a typical week in the schedules, you'll do an easy run on Monday (the day after a long run), Wednesday (the day after a hard workout), and Saturday (also the day after a hard workout).

Start these runs like you do your preworkout and prerace warm-up jog. As you loosen up, your pace might naturally increase at the same effort level. But don't force running faster. My team is really good at keeping easy runs easy. After a mile or two, they're purposefully holding back. They finish feeling refreshed, and often like they wish they had a few more miles to run.

That's the right way to do an easy run. You probably could run faster, but doing so is more likely to hurt than help your overall fitness. Consider the typical Wednesday easy day in the schedules. It follows a hard session the day before. Your next hard workout isn't until Friday. Why not run a little faster? Because if you don't take a true easy day on Wednesday, you won't be as recovered by Friday. Your times in that workout won't be as good. And you'll gain a lot more fitness by having a faster workout on Friday than a compromised workout because of

Courtesy of Justin Britton.

Keep your easy runs easy so you finish feeling refreshed and ready for your hard workouts.

running 10 seconds a mile faster on Wednesday. Pay special attention to running at a true recovery pace on the typical Mondays and Saturdays in the schedules, because those runs are either the day after a long run and the day before a workout or vice versa.

If there were ever a time to leave your watch at home, recovery runs are the day. There is no value in worrying about your pace. So why not remove the temptation to sneak a peek? Pick a course and stick to it. There are plenty of opportunities the rest of the week to focus on pace.

Regular Runs

These are what you probably mean when you think of just going out for a run. They're not too long or short, and they're not especially fast or slow. They're your everyday, getting-in-the-miles runs done at a conversational pace. They usually fall only on Thursdays in the schedules, but you could also count the Sunday long runs. Most of those are done at the same effort level as a regular run; they just last longer.

While regular runs are faster than easy runs, they're not meant to turn into borderline tempo runs. It's fine to speed up as you get going, as long as you're still at that conversational effort level of being able to speak in full sentences. Another sign that you're around the right effort level is that you don't have to concentrate to hold your pace and form like you do on tempo runs.

Avoid the common trap of basing your pace on regular runs on what your watch says. If you're someone who checks every mile split on regular runs, be sure you're just collecting the information rather than immediately acting on it. If you don't allow yourself to run slower than a given pace once you've run at that pace, stop reading this chapter right now and return to the final section of chapter 5. This is a bad habit that you need to break.

Easy to Regular Runs

These runs usually occur two days after a workout. Start at the gentle effort of an easy run. If, after a mile or two, you start feeling frisky, it's fine to go faster if it feels comfortable. If you're still tired once you've warmed up, it's fine to stay at an easy run effort the whole way. At no point should you be straining, and you should never feel like you're pushing the pace. Let your body dictate the proper effort on these runs, and let the pace be whatever it is.

▶ Strides

These are short segments of fast but relaxed running. The schedules call for strides that are 100 meters long. Generally, you'll do six to eight of these after a run on the day before a workout. You should also do at least a few as part of your warm-up before a workout or race.

Strides play a big part in my program. They have four main benefits.

1. Strides strengthen your muscles and tendons more than slower runs do.
2. Strides recruit fast-twitch muscle fibers, which you generally don't use on normal runs. If you never recruit these fibers in training, you won't be able to call on them when it's time to sprint at the end of a race. Fast interval sessions also recruit fast-twitch fibers, but those workouts tire you out and carry a higher injury risk than strides.

3. Strides move you through a fuller range of motion than regular running. Opening up with strides will energize you and loosen you up after a steady, slower pace. Strides are like postrun stretching in that way, in that they set you up to feel better at the beginning of the following day's run.

4. Strides also build confidence. It's great to feel like you can get to near top speed on demand. And they're fun! It feels good to run fast and relive being a kid sprinting around the playground.

To do a stride, find a flat, level surface. The straightaway of a track is ideal but usually not practical. A short stretch of road or bike path is fine. Build over the first 10 to 30 meters to around the pace you could hold for 800 meters. Hold that pace for the remainder. Don't strain. The goal isn't to go all out. It's to learn how to run fast while staying relaxed and efficient. Done this way, strides can improve your running form at all paces. On each stride, think about one element of good running form, such as a light, quick turnover, holding your shoulders low and level, or keeping your hands and arms relaxed.

Take a full recovery between strides. You're not trying to build cardiorespiratory capacity here like you do on intervals. You want to be able to run each stride fast but relaxed. Because strides are so short, it shouldn't take long until you feel ready for the next one.

The schedules call for 100-meter strides. Of course, there's no magic in that precise length. You can guesstimate by picturing the length of a track straightaway or a football field. Or you can mark off a stretch that takes you between 15 and 25 seconds to cover while running fast. Once you have your stride area set, don't time strides like you would intervals. Doing so could lead to treating them like intervals. You can also build strides into the last part of a run, such as by doing 20 seconds at the start of every minute. But this approach can mean encountering hills and turns. Again, the ideal setting is a flat, level, traffic-free setting where you can focus on fast, efficient turnover and good running form.

A set of eight strides shouldn't take more than 10 minutes. If you're pressed for time, I'd rather you run one less mile for the day and do your strides. (It would be even better if you accounted for the time strides take before starting your run.) No matter how tired you feel on the run, trust that you'll feel better after doing strides.

Warm-Ups and Cool-Downs

Finally, a word about your warm-up and cool-down on workout days. In chapter 1, I detailed all of the nonrunning things my team does as part of their preworkout and prerace warm-up. As I said there, the more of these elements you can incorporate into your warm-up, the better—you'll start your workout better prepared to hit the desired pace immediately. You should definitely at least do some strides between finishing your warm-up jog and starting your workout.

Actually, warm-up "jog" isn't entirely accurate. You should start at a gentle pace, like the beginning of a recovery run. Then gradually increase your pace so that you run most of the last mile at closer to your normal run pace. Don't force it, but run a little faster as feels natural. You want to finish your warm-up moving through a fuller range of motion and with your cardiorespiratory system working at a higher rate than when you started.

Cool-downs should definitely be jogs. Their purpose is to help your body gradually transition to its preworkout state. There is nothing to gain from thinking you have to hit a certain pace. Just aim for a nice gentle effort with relaxed form.

One or two easy miles will help you be less tight and sore the following day. Cool-downs are also a great time to think about the workout you just did. What went well? Where might you have done better? If you've worked out with others, it's a fun time to rehash what you just did. You'll probably finish your cool-down in a great mood and already be looking forward to your next workout.

I'm usually not a fan of really long cool-downs. Some runners head out for five or more miles after a workout. They often do this to pad their mileage for the week. Immediately after a workout isn't the time for this. You've just worked hard. It's time to start recovering from that work. If you do a longer cool-down, you might be running with compromised form by the end, exactly at the time when your body is most vulnerable. It's not worth risking injury or excess fatigue for the sake of a few more miles for the week.

Choosing a Weekly Mileage Schedule

All of the schedules have three weekly mileage ranges. For example, there are three 12-week 5K schedules: up to 50 miles per week, 35 to 60 miles per week, and 40 or more miles per week. For the three 16-week half-marathon schedules, the ranges are up to 65 miles per week, 40 to 75 miles per week, and 35 or more miles per week. I want to say a little about these mileage ranges to help you choose the most appropriate one.

You might notice from the examples above that there can be overlap in the weekly mileage among the three schedules. I didn't write the schedules to fall strictly within arbitrary mileage boundaries. I put together the mix of workouts, long runs, and everyday runs needed to best prepare you within a general framework of lower, middle, and higher mileage ranges. That's the approach I take with everyone I coach in person—I have a general goal for their mileage at various times of the year, but we do the training that's appropriate for their race plans and training and injury history. The exact weekly mileage falls where it does. We never work from the standpoint of "This week, your most important training goal is to hit X miles."

So don't just look at a given schedule's mileage range and decide that's the one for you. Compare at least two of the schedules for the race you're targeting. The far right column of the schedules shows the minimum and maximum possible mileage for each week (more on that in a bit). Get a feel for the general average of each schedule. Compare that with what's reasonable for both your recent training and your injury history. It's great if you're fired up to try higher mileage, but don't make a huge leap over what you've done in the past 6 to 12 months. And don't ignore if periods of higher mileage have led to more injuries.

You'll also want to consider what makes up the weekly mileage in the training schedules. It's one thing to feel okay running 50 miles a week of mostly medium-pace runs, with maybe occasional long runs or faster sessions. A 50-mile week that includes a long run and two hard workouts, which is typical in these training schedules, will likely be more demanding. You'll be doing that basic setup for several weeks in a row. You want to feel like you're absorbing your training, so that your fitness increases from week to week leading up to your goal race. Account for not just the quantity of miles but also the quality of miles when deciding which schedule to follow. You should be able to do the first week of your chosen program without being exhausted by the end.

What If I Want More Days Off?

My training schedules call for you to run almost every day. There are occasional optional days off, especially in the lower-mileage schedules. But like I said in chapter 1, consistency is key to peak performance. You've committed to following one of the schedules because you want to do well in an upcoming race. You owe it to yourself to be a little more devoted to regular running during the limited number of weeks of your buildup.

Still, some runners feel better if they take a day off each week. Other runners will regularly miss days for work or religious reasons. This is all fine and need not keep you from running your best. I have friends I ran with in the Olympics who took every Sunday off because of their religious beliefs, and they ran faster than I did. I also have Olympic friends who ran a whole year without missing a day, and they were also very successful.

If you want more days off in the schedule you're following, add a few miles into other days of the week. Maybe you can do a three-mile cool-down twice a week after your hard workouts instead of a one-mile cool-down. That gets you four extra miles that you could trade for one of the easy runs on Saturdays or Mondays.

Also, remember that all the weeks in the schedules have a fairly wide range of minimum and maximum mileages. You don't have to hit an exact number of miles each week; you just want to be in the mileage range that suits you best. It's okay to experiment with taking a day off each week and aiming for the higher end of the recommended mileage on long runs and the midweek runs between hard workouts.

Just make sure you don't become unhelpfully committed to getting your runs in. Training and racing are supposed to fun and exciting, not a chore you end up loathing.

At the same time, don't feel intimidated by a schedule's stated mileage range. Each week in each schedule has a fair amount of leeway. You can probably guess by now that I'm not someone who says, "Three Thursdays from now, you will run exactly eight miles come hell or high water." Most of the nonworkout days specify a range of miles for the day. Some workouts also have ranges of volume for the hard parts. You decide where to fall within that range, depending on factors such as fatigue, time constraints, weather, and whether you're aiming for the lower or higher end of that week's mileage range.

To illustrate, let's look at week 6 of the 35+ miles per week 15K–half-marathon 16-week schedule (table 7.1).

Look at the far-right column, which shows a minimum number of 52 miles for the week, and a maximum of 70. That's quite a range! Every day, including the two workouts, gives you the chance to go shorter or farther. So while you might conclude that a 70-mile week with two hard sessions is not in your best interest, you might be fine doing those workouts within the context of just more than 50 miles for the week.

Here's another example, this one from chapter 14, week 7, of the highest-mileage schedule for making a quick transition from the marathon to the 5K (8-Week 15K–Half-Marathon-to-Mile-or-5K Schedule 30+ Miles per Week, table 7.2).

TABLE 7.1 Week 6 of 35+ Miles per Week 15K-Half-Marathon 16-Week Schedule

Week 6							
Long run: 12-14 miles	Easy run: 6-8 miles, then 8 × 100-meter strides	Tempo run: 2- to 3-mile warm-up, 6-8 miles continuous at half-marathon pace; 1- to 2-mile cool-down	Easy run: 7-9 miles	Regular run: 6-9 miles, then 8 × 100-meter strides	Intervals: 2- to 3-mile warm-up; 6-8 × 800 meters at 10K pace with 400-meter jog between; 1- to 2-mile cool-down	Easy run: 4-6 miles	52-70

TABLE 7.2 Week 7 of 30+ Miles per Week 15K-Half-Marathon-to-Mile-or-5K 8-Week Schedule

Week 7							
Long run: 6-8 miles	Easy run: 4-6 miles	Intervals: 2- to 3-mile warm-up; 1,200 meters at 5K pace; 4 × 400 meters at mile pace; 400-meter jog between all intervals; 1- to 2-mile cool-down	Easy run: 4-6 miles	Regular run: 6-8 miles, then 6 × 100-meter strides	Tempo work: 2- to 3-mile warm-up; 2 miles continuous at 10K pace; 800-meter jog; 4 × 300 meters at mile pace with 100-meter walk between; 1- to 2-mile cool-down	Easy run: 4-6 miles OR Day off	32-50

Again, look at the weekly mileage range on the far right. The maximum is more than 50 percent greater than the minimum. Every day has a little leeway, but especially on Saturday, when one option is to take the day off from running. (These optional rest days appear more frequently in the lowest- and medium-mileage schedules.)

So, these aren't cookie-cutter schedules with nice, neat demarcations between mileage levels. They reflect both how I coach and how most runners in the real world go about their training. They merit a little investigation on your part to find the overall mileage range that's most appropriate at this point in your running life.

What About Running Twice a Day?

Doubles—that is, running twice in one day—are a great way to get extra mileage in if you can't reach your mileage goal running once a day. It might sound counterintuitive, but some runners feel better the day after doubling than they otherwise would. Doubles give you another chance to loosen up, especially if you're in the good habit of doing some flexibility exercises before and after every run. They can be a good recovery tool.

I like doing doubles on days that include an interval workout or other hard session. If you're working out in the afternoon, a short, easy morning run can make you feel better in the afternoon. If you work out in the morning, a gentle afternoon run can make you feel better the next day.

Don't do doubles after a long run or on a planned easy day. Let your body recover and have the 24 hours of rest. On my team, we do doubles on Monday, Tuesday, Thursday, and Friday. Wednesday and Saturday are our planned recovery days, and Sunday is long run day.

Aerobic cross-training, such as cycling, water running, or using an elliptical, is another option for adding work and promoting blood flow without the pounding of running.

Don't make doubles a stress. They're supposed to make your running better, not worse. Don't squeeze in doubles just to pad your weekly mileage. Do them only when you have enough time and the second run will boost your fitness and speed your recovery.

Choosing a Schedule Length

In addition to varying by mileage, the schedules in each chapter come in two lengths. For example, there are 6-week and 12-week schedules for the 5K, and 12-week and 16-week schedules for the marathon.

In general, I advise following the longer schedule for whatever distance you're targeting. The longer schedules build your fitness more comprehensively, allow your body more time to adapt to and absorb the training, and give you more practice at running your goal race pace. The longer schedules also have room for some easier weeks and tune-up races. They're long enough so that you won't feel rushed, but short enough that you'll still feel urgency in your training.

But sometimes the shorter schedules will be the better choice. Go with the shorter schedule if one or (ideally) more of these criteria apply to you:

- You've been injury-free for eight or more weeks and are feeling aerobically strong.
- Your harder runs over the past few months have been faster than average. For example, maybe you've been running with others once or twice a week and have run faster than you otherwise would to keep up with them. If so, you've been "training" a little bit despite not systematically following a program.
- You know your nonrunning life is going to be more stressful in a couple of months, so you'd like to shoot for a good race in the near future.
- You recently completed a different goal race, recovered well from it, and feel like you have good fitness from that cycle that you'd like to capitalize on. (Chapter 14 is for you!)
- Your training partners are focused on a race at your goal distance in the nearer future. It's nice to have others to do workouts with.
- You've had a difficult time sticking to longer programs in the past, whether because you lose focus or you start to break down. Twelve weeks can seem like a long time to train for a 5K. If the thought of the longer schedule deflates you while the shorter one excites, trust your gut.
- Weather and other elements make the shorter schedule the better option.
- You're new to the distance and want to see how your body handles training for it before committing too much time to it.
- There's a race that's really important to you for personal reasons, and it's coming up sooner rather than later.

Tweaking the Schedules

I created the schedules to follow the general pattern I used when competing and that my team now follows. That pattern is:

Sunday: long run

Monday: easy day

Tuesday: workout

Wednesday: easy day

Thursday: moderate day

Friday: workout

Saturday: easy day

You're not obligated to follow this pattern. The world will not end if you regularly do your long run on Saturday and hard sessions on Mondays and Thursdays. Or maybe your life is such that Wednesday is like most people's Sunday. Find the overall pattern that works best for you, including when potential training partners might most often be available.

It's also okay to occasionally move things around within a week to accommodate weather, travel, life, fatigue, and other aspects of real life. If you're generally on the basic Sunday-through-Saturday pattern seen in the schedules, but you know that next Friday you'll be traveling and won't be able to do a hard workout, it's fine to do the session that Thursday, on what would usually be a regular-run day.

Try not to make these adjustments a habit. The training schedules aren't a chess board for you to regularly move pieces around on. When planning adjustments, always try to follow the overall hard-easy pattern I've built into the schedules. Allow for adequate recovery after long runs and workouts. Never do a week's two hard sessions on consecutive days. If once or twice in your buildup you need to do a workout the day before a long run, plan for two truly easy days after the long run.

Some of the schedules include an optional tune-up race. It's okay to substitute a race for one of the hard workouts in a different week if that appeals to you. For example, if your local charity 5K falls on week 5 of your 12-week program and it's important to you to do that race, go with my blessing. Simply swap it for that week's tempo run (or whatever the workout with more sustained effort is that week).

Handling Setbacks in Training

It's rare to be able to precisely follow a multiweek training schedule. All sorts of things can interrupt your plans—injury, illness, weather, fatigue, and life itself, such as unforeseen family and work events. That's why, for the people I coach in person and see every day, our training plans are always written in pencil.

So don't freak out if you're unable to follow your chosen schedule to a T. Something is probably going to come up. I hope by now you've absorbed enough of my everything-isn't-always-going-to-be-perfect ethos that you can roll with the punches.

Here is some general guidance on what to do about some common setback scenarios.

• *You miss a few days of running because of life:* Life is more important than running. Don't beat yourself up if you need to have other priorities for a few days. You won't lose fitness, and missing one hard session never ruined a race. Get back on your schedule where you left off.

• *You miss a few days of running because of a slight injury or illness:* It's quite common to get little niggles—a newly tender Achilles, a little knee pain—when you've upped your training. Knowing how to handle them is usually a judgment call. If your slight injury keeps you from running with your normal form or gets worse as you run, you're better off not running on it. Similarly, if you're so sick that even a short, easy run leaves you more tired than you already were, time off is warranted.

It's much better to miss a few days of running than dig a hole you may not be able to get out of. If you make an injury more severe or get yourself really run down with an illness, successful training will be difficult. If you miss only a few days because of either situation, get back on your schedule where you left off. Don't worry about the one missed workout.

• *You miss a week of running because of life:* Once again, life is more important than running, so don't beat yourself up. Expect to feel a little awkward the first day or two back; start those runs a little slower than usual.

Try not to let missing a week ruin your long-term goals. Get back on your training schedule as quickly as possible. Early in a training program, I wouldn't worry too much about the time off. If you have to miss a week in the second half of your program, take a good look at when you want to race and see if maybe pushing your race out a week makes sense.

• *You miss a week of running because of injury or illness:* Make sure you're fully recovered before you jump back into serious training. I'd rather you miss a week of running and be healthy than resume running too soon and eventually have to miss more time. An off week won't kill your fitness, especially if your race is still weeks away, so just jump back into the schedule where you left off. If your race is a week or two away, you will want to move the race out another week or two. If that's not possible, you'll need to set a new goal for your original race that reflects your current fitness.

• *You miss two or more weeks of running because of life, injury, or illness:* You'll lose some fitness by not running for two weeks, but it will come back fairly quickly once you're running again. If you're on one of the shorter schedules, switch to the longer one in your mileage range, or resume where you left off in the shorter one. If you're following one of the longer schedules, resume where you left off. Picking up where you left off should be easier if your two-week break was because life got in the way than if you needed time off for injury or illness.

In any scenario, look into finding a substitute race later on the calendar. Focus first on being able to train well again. There will always be other races, even marathons, you can do.

• *You have a slight injury or illness that means you can still do an easy run, but you're not up for doing long runs and workouts:* If this is your situation for a week, don't sweat missing one or two hard workouts. Your body may have been asking for a few more easy days. Jump back into the training schedule where you left off.

If this is your situation for two or more weeks, there's good and bad news. The good news is that if you can keep running and your injury or illness doesn't get worse, you're not too bad off. You won't lose too much fitness, but you're certainly not advancing your fitness. The safest approach will likely be to pick another goal race so that you can resume your training schedule where you had to stop and still have a satisfying race. Make sure you're feeling injury-free and healthy before you start doing hard workouts again.

8

Training for and Racing the Mile

This chapter will prepare you for 1-mile races. Throughout this chapter, when you read "mile" you can substitute "1,600 meters" (four laps of a standard track, the standard distance in U.S. high school meets) or "1,500 meters" (three and three-quarter laps of a standard track, the Olympic event in this range). You can follow the schedules whether your mile race will be on the track or roads.

It's been great to see the renewed interest from non-elite runners in racing the mile. It's such a fun, challenging, and satisfying distance. Many of us who competed on a school team had as one of our first major running goals to run a certain time in the mile. Runners who took up the sport after school owe it to themselves to devote a season to the mile and its unique demands of endurance and speed. Even if you conclude the event isn't your favorite, training for the mile will help you be faster in longer races.

Following are six 1-mile schedules, three that are six weeks long and three that are 10 weeks long. The weekly mileage ranges for the 6-week schedules are up to 45, 30 to 45, and 40 or more. The weekly mileage ranges for the 10-week schedules are up to 50, 35 to 60, and 40 or more. As I said in chapter 7, there are many variables to consider when deciding which schedule to follow. Refer there for more details.

A Brief Guide to Following the Schedules

Most of the milers I've coached train a lot like a 5K runner. Many people training for the mile underestimate the need for overall volume and high-end aerobic work. That's why the schedules in this chapter call for regular long runs and tempo runs and don't have you doing four track workouts a week. You'll see a lot of similarities between the schedules in this chapter and the training log excerpts in chapter 1 from 1,500-meter Olympian Heather MacLean.

Each day's training in the schedules is described using the main types of runs I described at length in chapter 7. You'll want to refresh your memory occasionally by rereading those descriptions during your buildup. For quick reference, here are the types of runs you'll encounter in these schedules, and what I mean by each.

- *Easy run:* Done the day after your longest and hardest runs. Don't worry about pace. Just run at a comfortable, conversational effort level—no hard breathing, no bearing down. You should finish feeling energized for the next day's training.

- *Regular run:* A little faster and more effortful than an easy run, but still at a conversational pace. These are what you might think of as your getting-in-the-miles runs. It's okay to push things a little in the last few miles if you're feeling good.

- *Easy to regular run:* Start these runs as if they're a recovery run. If you're tired and want to stay at that gentle effort level for the whole run, that's fine. If you feel like going a little harder once you're warmed up, that's fine. But don't force yourself to go faster just because you think you "should" hit a certain pace.

- *Tempo run:* A sustained run, usually of two to six miles, at a "comfortably hard" effort level that requires concentration. For most runners, tempo runs should be around their 15K to half-marathon race pace. If I were riding a bike alongside and asked you a question, you should be able to answer in a complete sentence, but you shouldn't be able to carry on an in-depth conversation like you would on an easy or regular run.

- *Progression run:* A sustained run at an increasingly fast pace. Progression runs accomplish much of what conventional tempo runs do while also helping you practice increasing your effort as fatigue mounts. They tend to be a little longer than tempo runs because you start at a slower pace.

- *Intervals:* Repeats, usually between 200 meters and one mile long, usually run between mile and 5K race pace. You can do these on a track for precision and a uniform running surface, but you can also do them on roads or elsewhere with good footing. It's okay to roughly convert the distances stated in the training schedules to timed segments off the track, such as running at 5K effort for three minutes if the schedules prescribe 800-meter repeats at 5K pace.

There are a few workouts where I call for 200-meter repeats at your 800-meter race pace. If you're unsure what that is, aim to run two to three seconds faster per 200 meters than your mile race pace.

- *Hill workout:* Running at mile effort—not pace!—up a moderately steep hill, and jogging down for recovery. Ideally, the hill will be steep enough to make the climbing noticeable, but not so steep that it's difficult to maintain a good upright running form with quick turnover.

- *Long run:* Your longest run of the week, done at a conversational pace. Start at a gentle effort and gradually increase intensity to that of a regular run as your body warms up. Don't rush it—you've got plenty of time to get in a good rhythm for the second half of the run.

- *Strides:* Short (100 meters or so) bouts of fast running at around mile race pace, usually done either after an easy run or before a hard workout or race. Concentrate on maintaining good running form and staying relaxed while running fast. Strides should feel good and be fun; you'll usually feel better after doing them than you did before. Do strides on a flat, level surface with reliable footing.

This Schedule's A+ Workout

Remember from chapter 1 that I said I occasionally call for A+ workouts, the ones where you push yourself at least as hard as you do in a race? These schedules have a doozy of an A+ workout, on the Tuesday workout of week 5 in the 6-week schedules and week 9 in the 10-week schedules.

I like to have milers do an A+ workout about a week and a half before their race. Nailing it will give you great confidence for your race, and its intense mental demands will steel you for the unique pain of the mile.

If you add your time from the two 800-meter repeats in that workout, you'll have a good idea of your time in your mile race.

The Day Before Your Mile

The schedules all call for a short jog and some 100-meter strides the day before your mile race. Whenever possible, my runners do this light session at the facility where they'll be racing the next day. Wherever you do yours, visualize your race during this run. See yourself racing well. Imagine running strongly in the third quarter-mile to set yourself up for a strong finish and great time. Focus on running quickly and smoothly on your strides, and try to carry that feeling into the following day's race.

How to Race the Mile

Unlike Olympians, who often race for place instead of time in the mile, you're probably focused almost entirely on running as fast as you can. The best way to run a mile is to run as close to even splits as you can and have your last lap be the fastest. When I coached collegiate women who wanted to break 5:00 in the mile, I would tell them, "Let's try to run laps of 75, 75, 75, 74."

There's less room for making a mistake in the mile than in any other distance covered in this book. In a 5K or 10K, if you start to go anaerobic, you can usually back off a bit and recover quickly. In a half-marathon or marathon, if you lose concentration in the middle miles and unknowingly slow, you can get back on pace pretty easily. But the mile is over so quickly, and it demands riding such a fine line between aerobic and anaerobic running, that a brief mishap can derail your race.

The most common mistake is running the first lap (or on the roads, quarter-mile) too fast. As with the opening miles of a marathon, the first lap of a mile can feel deceptively easy. When I coached college runners, I regularly saw athletes (mostly on other teams!) who looked like they'd been shot out of a cannon. They were either not confident enough or familiar enough with the distance to hold back. They would tear through the first lap in 69 seconds, then maybe run 75 for the second lap, 77 for the third lap, and really tie up while running 82 seconds for the final lap. You'll never see an experienced, well-trained miler race like that.

Early on, you want to be as close as possible to the pace you really think you can maintain for the distance. You'll see that all of the schedules in this chapter call for doing a handful of 200-meter repeats at mile pace two days before your race. This is a great way to remind yourself what your goal pace should feel like from the start. Try to ingrain that feeling—your turnover, breathing, body carriage—so that you can hit it almost immediately in your race. If possible, do one or two 200s at mile pace as part of your race-day warm-up to again remind yourself what starting at the proper pace should feel like.

It's okay to give yourself a one- or two-second cushion in that first lap, in part to account for jostling and settling in during the first 200 meters. When I coached women who wanted to break 5:00, I would tell them not to be much faster than 73 seconds for the first lap. You can then carry that momentum into the second lap, during which your goal pace still shouldn't feel too demanding.

If you're going for a certain time, the third lap is crucial. You'll probably have to feel like you're picking it up just to maintain your pace. If your effort feels like you're maintaining the same pace on the third lap, you're probably slowing.

Don't start sprinting as soon as you hit the last lap. Instead, when going into the second-to-last turn, start building. Gradually increase your effort and (hopefully) pace as you come off that turn and into the final back straight. With half a lap to go, really try to get up to your top-end speed, and see if you can hold it to the finish.

Putting these track-based tips into practice in a road mile can be a little tricky. You won't necessarily know exactly where you are in the race like you do on the track. Many road miles have markers every quarter-mile. Use those as signposts for doling out your effort effectively.

Lessons From Coach Coogan's Miles

The best mile that I ever ran was in June 1989 on the Northeastern University track in Dedham, Massachusetts. It was my first track season after graduating from the University of Maryland the previous year.

There was a lot of hype about this mile because there were four or five guys who could possibly run under 4:00. At the time, no Massachusetts native had broken the magical 4:00 barrier. I figured I had a good shot at doing so.

I was running pretty well at the time. In March, I had run well at my first world cross-country championship, and earlier in the track season I had set personal bests at 3,000 meters and in the steeplechase.

The race was set up to help us run just under 4:00. There was a pacer who was supposed to take us through 800 meters in 1:58. When the gun went off, I immediately got myself into second place, right behind him. I felt my best shot at breaking 4:00 would be to run near the front, run the shortest possible distance, stay out of trouble, and not waste too much energy passing people. I needed to save all of my energy because I knew that if I did break 4:00, it wouldn't be by much.

Unfortunately, the pacer immediately slowed after the first lap, so I had to take the lead to keep the race honest. It was a little unnerving being in front with almost three laps to go. I told myself, "You're okay, Mark. Just keep it smooth and fast, Mark." I remember feeling the guys right on my butt as I became a pacer for the other racers. I didn't let this bother me because I knew I was strong from cross-country and all my training.

As I said earlier, you have to feel like you're picking it up on the third lap if you want to continue at the pace you're running. Otherwise, you're probably slowing a bit. As I tried to pick up the pace on the third lap, the rest of the field let me go, and I got a little bit of a lead. I saw the clock with one lap to go and knew I needed a 60-second last lap to break 4:00. I felt confident from my training that I could do this. I accelerated down the final backstretch and kicked as hard as I could over the last 200 meters, and I broke the line with a win and a time of 3:58.

It was one of the best races I ever ran, and it's also one of the races I'm most proud of. Being the first person from Massachusetts to break 4:00 is pretty cool! In the 1980s, breaking 4:00 was still a big deal, and I got to do so in front of my parents, siblings, and best friends. I will never forget when my friend Joey Keough said to me, "I knew you were fast, but that was just nuts how fast you were going to break 4:00." Needless to say, we headed to the Eliot Lounge, then a famous running bar, after the race to celebrate.

I wasn't as confident a miler in college. We often had dual meets, indoors and outdoors, with the Naval Academy. Their top runner, Ronnie Harris, was one of the best collegians in the country. I was sometimes intimidated by him when we raced early in my career. Ronnie had a bounce in his stride, and just watching him walk around you could see how confident he was. Also, Ronnie was from Southern California, and I was from Boston, so we had the Lakers-Celtics rivalry going. I used to pretend that Ronnie was "Showtime" and I was the blue-collar kid from Attleboro.

Ronnie and I always battled in our races, and they usually ended in photo finishes. Ours were some of the most competitive races I ever ran. Ronnie brought the best out of me in these dual meets, but I could never beat him. He always just nipped me at the line. Why did he always come out on top?

I now realize I didn't have the best strategies when I raced him. I would usually try to make the race fast in the hope of tiring him. Ronnie would try to pass me on the third lap, and I would use everything I had to not let him by. I was wasting precious energy. Then he would regroup and pass me right at the line. If I hadn't tried to hold him off, and instead had saved energy for a big move in the final straight, maybe I could have won one or two of those races. In a competitive mile, it's often the last person to make a move who wins. Ronnie was always that person when we raced in college.

A great thing about running is that you can be fierce competitors in a race and good friends before and after. Ronnie and I have stayed close since college, and he's one of the first people who congratulates me with a text when one of the athletes I coach runs well.

6-Week 1-Mile Schedule: Up to 45 Miles per Week

	Sunday	Monday	Tuesday	Wednesday	Thursday	Friday	Saturday	Week's mileage
Week 1	Long run: 6-8 miles	Easy run: 4-6 miles, then 8 × 100-meter strides	Intervals: 2-mile warm-up; 6 × 400 meters at 5K pace with 200-meter jog between; 1-mile cool-down	Easy run: 4-6 miles	Regular run: 4-6 miles, then 8 × 100-meter strides	Tempo run: 2-mile warm-up; 3 miles continuous at 25-30 seconds per mile slower than 10K pace; 6 × 150-meter strides; 1-mile cool-down	Easy to regular run: 3-4 miles OR Day off	30-40
Week 2	Long run: 6-8 miles	Easy run: 4-6 miles, then 8 × 100-meter strides	Hills: 2-mile warm-up; 6 × 200-meter hill at mile effort; jog down for recovery; 1-mile cool-down	Easy run: 4-6 miles	Regular run: 4-6 miles, then 8 × 100-meter strides	Tempo run: 2-mile warm-up; 3 miles continuous at 25-30 seconds per mile slower than 10K pace; 800-meter jog; 4 × 300 meters at mile pace with 100-meter walk/jog between; 1 mile cool-down	Easy to regular run: 3-4 miles OR Day off	32-44
Week 3	Long run: 6-8 miles	Easy run: 4-6 miles, then 8 × 100-meter strides	Intervals: 2-mile warm-up; 4 × 1,000 meters at 5K pace with 400-meter jog between; 4 × 200 meters at 800-meter pace with 200-meter jog between; 1-mile cool-down	Easy run: 4-6 miles	Regular run: 4-6 miles, then 8 × 100-meter strides	Tempo work: 2-mile warm-up; 2-3 × 1 mile at 10K pace with 400-meter jog between; 1-mile cool-down	Easy to regular run: 3-4 miles OR Day off	31-43

	Sunday	Monday	Tuesday	Wednesday	Thursday	Friday	Saturday	Week's mileage
Week 4	Long run: 6-8 miles	Easy run: 4-6 miles, then 6 × 100-meter strides	Intervals: 2-mile warm-up; 4 × 800 meters at 3K pace; 2 × 400 meters at mile pace; 400-meter jog between all intervals; 1-mile cool-down	Easy run: 4-6 miles	Regular run: 4-6 miles, then 6 × 100-meter strides	Tempo run: 2-mile warm-up; 3-4 miles continuous at 25-30 seconds per mile slower than 10K pace; 1-mile cool-down	Easy to regular run: 3-4 miles OR Day off	31-44
Week 5	Long run: 5-7 miles	Easy run: 4-6 miles, then 8 × 100-meter strides	Intervals: 2-mile warm-up; 400 meters, 800 meters, 800 meters, 400 meters, all at mile pace; 400-meter jog between intervals; 1-mile cool-down	Easy run: 4-6 miles	Regular run: 4-6 miles, then 8 × 100-meter strides	Tempo/Intervals: 2-mile warm-up; 2 miles continuous at 20 seconds per mile slower than 10K pace; 800-meter jog; 4 × 300 meters at mile pace with 100-meter walk/jog between; 1-mile cool-down	Easy to regular run: 3-4 miles OR Day off	28-40
Week 6	Long run: 5-7 miles	Easy run: 4-6 miles, then 8 × 100-meter strides	Intervals: 2-mile warm-up; 6 × 400 meters at mile pace with 200-meter jog between; 1-mile cool-down	Easy run: 3-4 miles	Intervals: 2-mile warm-up; 4 × 200 meters at mile pace with 200-meter jog between; 1-mile cool-down	Easy run: 2-3 miles, then 6 to 8 100-meter strides	Race mile	23-29 (not including race)

6-Week 1-Mile Schedule: 30-45 Miles per Week

	Sunday	Monday	Tuesday	Wednesday	Thursday	Friday	Saturday	Week's mileage
Week 1	Long run: 7-10 miles	Easy run: 4-6 miles, then 8 × 100-meter strides	Intervals: 2-mile warm-up; 6 × 400 meters at 5K pace with 200-meter jog between; 1-mile cool-down	Easy run: 6-8 miles	Regular run: 4-6 miles, then 8 × 100-meter strides	Tempo run: 2-mile warm-up; 3 miles continuous at 25-30 seconds per mile slower than 10K pace; 6 × 150-meter strides; 1-mile cool-down	Easy to regular run: 3-4 miles OR Day off	32-45
Week 2	Long run: 7-10 miles	Easy run: 4-6 miles, then 8 × 100-meter strides	Hills: 2-mile warm-up; 6 × 200-meter hill at mile effort; jog down for recovery; 1-mile cool-down	Easy run: 6-8 miles	Regular run: 4-6 miles, then 8 × 100-meter strides	Tempo run: 2-mile warm-up; 3 miles continuous at 25-30 seconds per mile slower than 10K pace; 800-meter jog; 4 × 300 meters at mile pace with 100-meter walk/jog between; 1-mile cool-down	Easy to regular run: 3-4 miles OR Day off	33-46
Week 3	Long run: 6-8 miles	Easy run: 4-6 miles, then 8 × 100-meter strides	Intervals: 2-mile warm-up; 4 × 1,000 meters at 5K pace with 400-meter jog between; 4 × 200 meters at 800-meter pace with 200-meter jog between; 1-mile cool-down	Easy run: 5-7 miles	Regular run: 4-6 miles, then 8 × 100-meter strides	Tempo work: 2-mile warm-up; 3 × 1 mile at 10K pace with 400-meter jog between; 1-mile cool-down	Easy to regular run: 3-4 miles OR Day off	33-45

	Sunday	Monday	Tuesday	Wednesday	Thursday	Friday	Saturday	Week's mileage
Week 4	Long run: 6-8 miles	Easy run: 4-6 miles, then 6 × 100-meter strides	Intervals: 2-mile warm-up; 4 × 800 meters at 3K pace; 2 × 400 meters at mile pace; 400-meter jog between all intervals; 1-mile cool-down	Easy run: 5-7 miles	Regular run: 4-6 miles, then 6 × 100-meter strides	Tempo run: 2-mile warm-up; 4 miles continuous at 25-30 seconds slower than 10K pace; 1-mile cool-down	Easy to regular run: 3-4 miles OR Day off	33-45
Week 5	Long run: 6-8 miles	Easy run: 4-6 miles, then 8 × 100-meter strides	Intervals: 2-mile warm-up; 400 meters, 800 meters, 800 meters, 400 meters, all at mile pace; 400-meter jog between intervals; 1-mile cool-down	Easy run: 4-7 miles	Regular run: 4-6 miles, then 8 × 100-meter strides	Tempo/Intervals: 2-mile warm-up; 2 miles continuous at 20 seconds per mile slower than 10K pace; 800-meter jog; 4 × 300 meters at mile pace with 100-meter walk/jog between intervals; 1-mile cool-down	Easy to regular run: 3-4 miles OR Day off	29-42
Week 6	Long run: 5-7 miles	Easy run: 4-6 miles, then 8 × 100-meter strides	Intervals: 2-mile warm-up; 6 × 400 meters at mile pace with 200-meter jog between; 1-mile cool-down	Easy run: 3-4 miles	Intervals: 2-mile warm-up; 4 × 200 meters at mile pace with 200-meter jog between; 1-mile cool-down	Easy run: 2-3 miles, then 6-8 100-meter strides	Race mile	22-28 (not including race)

6-Week 1-Mile Schedule: 40+ Miles per Week

	Sunday	Monday	Tuesday	Wednesday	Thursday	Friday	Saturday	Week's mileage
Week 1	Long run: 10-14 miles	Easy run: 6-8 miles, then 8 × 100-meter strides	Intervals: 2- to 3-mile warm-up; 8 × 400 meters at 5K pace with 200-meter jog between; 1- to 2-mile cool-down	Easy run: 8-10 miles	Regular run: 6-8 miles, then 8 × 100-meter strides	Tempo run: 2- to 3-mile warm-up; 3-4 miles continuous at 25-30 seconds per mile slower than 10K pace; 6 × 150-meter strides; 1- to 2-mile cool-down	Easy to regular run: 3-4 miles OR Day off	42-61
Week 2	Long run: 10-14 miles	Easy run: 6-8 miles, then 8 × 100-meter strides	Hills: 2- to 3-mile warm-up; 8-10 × 200-meter hill at mile effort; jog down for recovery; 1- to 2-mile cool-down	Easy run: 8-10 miles	Regular run: 6-8 miles, then 8 × 100-meter strides	Tempo run: 2- to 3-mile warm-up; 4-6 miles continuous at 25-30 seconds per mile slower than 10K pace; 4 × 300 meters at mile pace; 800-meter jog; 4 × 300 meters at mile pace with 100-meter walk/jog between; 1- to 2-mile cool-down	Easy to regular run: 3-4 miles	44-64
Week 3	Long run: 10-14 miles	Easy run: 6-8 miles, then 8 × 100-meter strides	Intervals: 2- to 3-mile warm-up; 6 × 1,000 meters at 5K pace with 400-meter jog between; 4 × 200 meters at mile pace with 200-meter jog between; 1- to 2-mile cool-down	Easy run: 8-10 miles	Regular run: 6-8 miles, then 8 × 100-meter strides	Tempo work: 2-mile warm-up; 2 × 1 mile at 5K pace with 400-meter jog after each; 4 × 400 meters at mile pace with 400-meter jog between; 1- to 2-mile cool-down	Easy to regular run: 3-4 miles OR Day off	46-63

	Sunday	Monday	Tuesday	Wednesday	Thursday	Friday	Saturday	Week's mileage
Week 4	Long run: 10-14 miles	Easy run: 6-8 miles, then 6 × 100-meter strides	Intervals: 2-3 mile warm-up; 4 × 800, 2 × 400 meters, with the 800s at 3K pace and 400s at mile pace; 400-meter jog between all intervals; 1- to 2-mile cool-down	Easy run: 8-10 miles	Regular run: 6-8 miles, then 6 × 100-meter strides	Tempo run: 2- to 3-mile warm-up; 4-5 miles continuous at 25-30 seconds per mile slower than 10K pace; 1- to 2-mile cool-down	Easy to regular run: 3-4 miles	44-63
Week 5	Long run: 8-10 miles	Easy run: 6-8 miles, then 8 × 100-meter strides	Intervals: 2- to 3-mile warm-up; 400 meters, 800 meters, 800 meters, 400 meters, all at mile pace; 400-meter jog between all intervals; 1- to 2-mile cool-down	Easy run: 6-8 miles	Regular run: 6-8 miles, then 8 × 100-meter strides	Tempo/Intervals: 2- to 3-mile warm-up; 3 miles continuous at 20 seconds per mile slower than 10K pace; 800-meter jog; 4 × 300 meters at mile pace with 100-meter walk/jog between; 1- to 2-mile cool-down	Easy to regular run: 3-4 miles OR Day off	28-41
Week 6	Long run: 5-7 miles	Easy run: 4-6 miles, then 8 × 100-meter strides	Intervals: 2- to 3-mile warm-up; 8 × 400 meters at mile pace with 200-meter jog between; 1-mile cool-down	Easy run: 5-7 miles	Intervals: 2- to 3-mile warm-up; 4-6 × 200 meters at mile pace with 200-meter jog between; 1-mile cool-down	Easy run: 2-3 miles, then 6-8 100-meter strides	Race mile	26-36 (not including race)

40+ Miles per Week
6-Week 1-Mile Schedule

10-Week 1-Mile Schedule: Up to 50 Miles per Week

	Sunday	Monday	Tuesday	Wednesday	Thursday	Friday	Saturday	Week's mileage
Week 1	Regular run: 6-8 miles	Easy run: 4-6 miles, then 8 × 100-meter strides	Intervals: 2-mile warm-up; 4-6 × 1,000 meters at 5K pace with 400-meter jog between; 1-mile cool-down	Easy run: 6-8 miles	Regular run: 4-6 miles, then 8 × 100-meter strides	Tempo run: 2-mile warm-up; 3 miles continuous at 25-30 seconds per mile slower than 10K pace; 1-mile cool-down	Easy to regular run: 3-5 miles OR Day off	33-46
Week 2	Regular run: 6-8 miles	Easy run: 6-8 miles, then 8 × 100-meter strides	Hills: 2-mile warm-up; 6-8 × 200-meter hill at mile effort, jog down for recovery; 1-mile cool-down	Easy run: 6-8 miles	Regular run: 4-6 miles, then 8 × 100-meter strides	Tempo work: 2-mile warm-up; 2 miles continuous at 15-20 seconds per mile slower than 10K pace; 800-meter jog; 4 × 300 meters at mile pace with 100-meter walk/jog between; 1-mile cool-down	Easy to regular run: 3-5 miles	36-46
Week 3	Regular run: 6-8 miles	Easy run: 6-8 miles, then 8 × 100-meter strides	Intervals: 2-mile warm-up; 3-4 × set of 800 meters at 5K pace, 200-meter jog, 200 meters at mile pace, 400-meter jog; 1-mile cool-down	Easy run: 6-8 miles	Regular run: 4-6 miles, then 8 × 100-meter strides	Progression run: 2-mile warm-up; 3 miles continuous, starting at 30 seconds per mile slower than 10K pace and increasing pace 5-10 seconds per mile after each mile; 1-mile cool-down	Easy to regular run: 3-5 miles OR Day off	34-48

	Sunday	Monday	Tuesday	Wednesday	Thursday	Friday	Saturday	Week's mileage
Week 4	Regular run: 6-8 miles	Easy run: 6-8 miles, then 8 × 100-meter strides	Intervals: 2-mile warm-up; 4 × 200 meters, 4 × 400 meters, 4 × 200 meters, all at mile pace; 200-meter jog after 200s and 400-meter jog after 400s; 1-mile cool-down	Easy run: 4-6 miles	Regular run: 4-6 miles, then 8 × 100-meter strides	Tempo run: 2-mile warm-up; 3-4 miles continuous at 25-30 seconds per mile slower than 10K pace; 1-mile cool-down	Easy to regular run: 2-4 miles	35-46
Week 5	Regular run: 6-8 miles	Easy run: 6-8 miles, then 8 × 100-meter strides	Intervals: 2-mile warm-up; 8 × 400 meters at 5K pace with 200-meter jog between; 1-mile cool-down	Easy run: 6-8 miles	Regular run: 4-6 miles, then 8 × 100-meter strides	Tempo/Intervals: 2-mile warm-up; 3-5 miles continuous at 25-30 seconds per mile slower than 10K pace; 800-meter jog; 6 × 200 meters at mile pace with 200-meter jog between; 1-mile cool-down	Easy to regular run: 3-5 miles OR Day off	36-51
Week 6	Regular run: 6-8 miles	Easy run: 6-8 miles, then 8 × 100-meter strides	Hills: 2-mile warm-up; 8-10 × 200-meter hill at hard effort; jog down for recovery; 1-mile cool-down	Easy run: 6-8 miles	Regular run: 4-6 miles, then 8 × 100-meter strides	Tempo run: 2-mile warm-up; 3-4 miles continuous at 25-30 seconds per mile slower than 10K pace; 800-meter jog; 4 × 300 meters at mile pace with 100-meter walk/jog between; 1-mile cool-down	Easy to regular run: 3-5 miles	36-49

(continued)

115

10-Week 1-Mile Schedule: Up to 50 Miles per Week (continued)

	Sunday	Monday	Tuesday	Wednesday	Thursday	Friday	Saturday	Week's mileage
Week 7	Regular run: 6-8 miles	Easy run: 6-8 miles, then 8 × 100-meter strides	Intervals: 2-mile warm-up; 4-6 × 1,000 meters at 5K pace with 400-meter jog between; 4 × 200 meters at 800-meter pace with 200-meter jog between; 1-mile cool-down	Easy run: 6-8 miles	Regular run: 4-6 miles, then 8 × 100-meter strides	Tempo work: 2-mile warm-up; 2 × 1 mile at 5K pace with 800-meter jog after each; 4 × 400 meters at mile pace with 400-meter jog between; 1-mile cool-down	Easy to regular run: 3-5 miles OR Day off	36-51
Week 8	Regular run: 6-8 miles	Easy run: 6-8 miles, then 6 × 100-meter strides	Intervals: 2-mile warm-up; 3-4 × 800 meters at 3K pace; 4 × 400 meters at mile pace; 400-meter jog between intervals; 1-mile cool-down	Easy run: 6-8 miles	Regular run: 4-6 miles, then 6 × 100-meter strides	Tempo run: 2-mile warm-up; 3-4 miles continuous at 25-30 seconds per mile slower than 10K pace; 1-mile cool-down	Easy to regular run: 3-5 miles	38-50
Week 9	Regular run: 6 miles	Easy run: 4-6 miles, then 8 × 100-meter strides	Intervals: 2-mile warm-up; 400 meters, 800 meters, 800 meters, 400 meters, all at mile pace; 400-meter jog between intervals; 1-mile cool-down	Easy run: 4-6 miles	Regular run: 4-6 miles, then 8 × 100-meter strides	Tempo/Intervals: 2-mile warm-up; 2-3 miles at 20 seconds per mile slower than 10K pace; 800-meter jog; 4 × 300 meters at mile pace with 100-meter walk/jog between; 1-mile cool-down	Easy to regular run: 3-4 miles OR Day off	29-41
Week 10	Regular run: 5 miles	Easy run: 3-4 miles, then 8 × 100-meter strides	Intervals: 2-mile warm-up; 6-8 × 400 meters at mile pace with 200-meter jog between; 1-mile cool-down	Easy run: 3-4 miles	Intervals: 2-mile warm-up; 4-6 × 200 meters at mile pace with 200-meter jog between; 1-mile cool-down	Easy run: 2-3 miles, then 6-8 100-meter strides	Race mile	22-26 (not including race)

10-Week 1-Mile Schedule: 35-60 Miles per Week

	Sunday	Monday	Tuesday	Wednesday	Thursday	Friday	Saturday	Week's mileage
Week 1	Long run at a slightly faster pace than Wednesday's easy run: 8-10 miles	Easy run: 6-8 miles, then 8 × 100-meter strides	Intervals: 2-mile warm-up; 6 × 1,000 meters at 5K pace with 400-meter jog between; 1- to 2-mile cool-down	Easy run: 8-10 miles	Regular run: 6-8 miles, then 8 × 100-meter strides	Tempo run: 2-mile warm-up; 3-4 miles continuous at 25-30 seconds per mile slower than 10K pace; 1- to 2-mile cool-down	Easy to regular run: 3-5 miles OR Day off	43-59
Week 2	Long run at a slightly faster pace than Wednesday's easy run: 8-10 miles	Easy run: 6-8 miles, then 8 × 100-meter strides	Hills: 2-mile warm-up; 8 × 200-meter hill at mile effort, jog down for recovery; 1- to 2-mile cool-down	Easy run: 8-10 miles	Regular run: 6-8 miles, then 8 × 100-meter strides	Tempo work: 2-mile warm-up; 2-3 miles continuous at 15-20 seconds per mile slower than 10K pace; 800-meter jog; 4 × 300 meters at mile pace with 100-meter walk/jog between; 1- to 2-mile cool-down	Easy to regular run: 3-5 miles	42-54
Week 3	Long run at a slightly faster pace than Wednesday's easy run: 8-12 miles	Easy run: 6-8 miles, then 8 × 100-meter strides	Intervals: 2-mile warm-up; 4 × set of 800 meters at 5K pace, 200-meter jog, 200 meters at mile pace; 400-meter jog; 1- to 2-mile cool-down	Easy run: 8-10 miles	Regular run: 6-8 miles, then 8 × 100-meter strides	Progression run: 2-mile warm-up; 3 miles continuous, starting at 30 seconds per mile slower than 10K pace and increasing pace 5-10 seconds per mile after each mile; 1- to 2-mile cool-down	Easy to regular run: 3-5 miles OR Day off	41-58

(continued)

10-Week 1-Mile Schedule: 35-60 Miles per Week (continued)

	Sunday	Monday	Tuesday	Wednesday	Thursday	Friday	Saturday	Week's mileage
Week 4	Long run at a slightly faster pace than Wednesday's easy run: 8-12 miles	Easy run: 6-8 miles, then 8 × 100-meter strides	Intervals: 2-mile warm-up; 4 × 200 meters, 5 × 400 meters, 4 × 200 meters, all at mile pace; 200-meter jog after 200s and 400-meter jog after 400s; 1- to 2-mile cool-down	Easy run: 6-8 miles	Regular run: 4-6 miles, then 8 × 100-meter strides	Tempo run: 2-mile warm-up; 3-4 miles continuous at 25-30 seconds per mile slower than 10K pace; 1- to 2-mile cool-down	Easy to regular run: 2-4 miles	39-54
Week 5	Long run at a slightly faster pace than Wednesday's easy run: 8-12 miles	Easy run: 6-8 miles, then 8 × 100-meter strides	Intervals: 2-mile warm-up; 8 × 400 meters at 5K pace with 200-meter jog between; 1- to 2-mile cool-down	Easy run: 8-10 miles	Regular run: 6-8 miles, then 8 × 100-meter strides	Tempo run: 2-mile warm-up; 3-5 miles continuous at 25-30 seconds per mile slower than 10K pace; 6 × 200 meters at mile pace with 200-meter jog between; 1- to 2-mile cool-down	Easy to regular run: 3-5 miles OR Day off	41-60
Week 6	Long run at a slightly faster pace than Wednesday's easy run: 8-12 miles	Easy run: 6-8 miles, then 8 × 100-meter strides	Hills: 2-mile warm-up; 8-10 × 200-meter hill at mile effort; jog down for recovery; 1- to 2-mile cool-down	Easy run: 8-10 miles	Regular run: 6-8 miles, then 8 × 100-meter strides	Tempo run: 2-mile warm-up; 4-5 miles continuous at 25-30 seconds per mile slower than 10K pace; 4 × 300 meters at mile pace with 100-meter walk/jog between; 1- to 2-mile cool-down	Easy to regular run: 3-5 miles	44-60

	Sunday	Monday	Tuesday	Wednesday	Thursday	Friday	Saturday	Week's mileage
Week 7	Long run at a slightly faster pace than Wednesday's easy run: 8-12 miles	Easy run: 6-8 miles, then 8 × 100-meter strides	Intervals: 2-mile warm-up; 6 × 1,000 meters at 5K pace with 400-meter jog between; 4 × 200 meters at 800-meter pace with 200-meter jog between; 1- to 2-mile cool-down	Easy run: 8-10 miles	Regular run: 6-8 miles, then 8 × 100-meter strides	Tempo work: 2-mile warm-up; 2 × 1 mile at 5K pace with 800-meter jog after each; 4 × 400 meters at mile pace with 400-meter jog between; 1- to 2-mile cool-down	Easy to regular run: 3-5 miles OR Day off	48-60
Week 8	Long run at a slightly faster pace than Wednesday's easy run: 8-12 miles	Easy run: 6-8 miles, then 6 × 100-meter strides	Intervals: 2-mile warm-up; 4 × 800 meters at 3K pace; 4 × 400 meters at mile pace; 400-meter jog between intervals; 1- to 2-mile cool-down	Easy run: 8-10 miles	Regular run: 6-8 miles, then 6 × 100-meter strides	Tempo run: 2-mile warm-up; 4-5 miles continuous at 25-30 seconds per mile slower than 10K pace; 1- to 2-mile cool-down	Easy to regular run: 3-5 miles	46-60
Week 9	Long run at a slightly faster pace than Wednesday's easy run: 6-8 miles	Easy run: 6-8 miles, then 8 × 100-meter strides	Intervals: 2-mile warm-up; 400 meters, 800 meters, 800 meters, 400 meters, all at mile pace; 400-meter jog between intervals; 1- to 2-mile cool-down	Easy run: 6-8 miles	Regular run: 6-8 miles, then 8 × 100-meter strides	Tempo/Intervals: 2-mile warm-up; 3 miles continuous at 20 seconds per mile slower than 10K pace; 800-meter jog; 4 × 300 meters at mile pace with 100-meter walk/jog between; 1- to 2-mile cool-down	Easy to regular run: 3-4 miles OR Day off	37-51
Week 10	Long run at a slightly faster pace than Wednesday's easy run: 5-7 miles	Easy run: 4-6 miles, then 8 × 100-meter strides	Intervals: 2-mile warm-up; 6-8 × 400 meters at mile pace with 200-meter jog between; 1- to 2-mile cool-down	Easy run: 5-7 miles	Intervals: 2-mile warm-up; 4-6 × 200 meters at mile pace with 200-meter jog between; 1-mile cool-down	Easy run: 2-3 miles, then 6-8 100-meter strides	Race mile	25-34 (not including race)

10-Week 1-Mile Schedule: 40+ Miles per Week

	Sunday	Monday	Tuesday	Wednesday	Thursday	Friday	Saturday	Week's mileage
Week 1	Long run: 10-12 miles	Easy run: 6-8 miles, then 8 × 100-meter strides	Intervals: 2- to 3-mile warm-up; 6 × 1,000 meters at 5K pace with 400-meter jog between; 1- to 2-mile cool-down	Easy run: 8-10 miles	Regular run: 6-8 miles, then 8 × 100-meter strides	Tempo run: 2- to 3-mile warm-up; 3-4 miles continuous at 25-30 seconds per mile slower than 10K pace; 1- to 2-mile cool-down	Easy to regular run: 3-7 miles OR Day off	44-64
Week 2	Long run: 10-12 miles	Easy run: 6-8 miles, then 8 × 100-meter strides	Hills: 2- to 3-mile warm-up; 8 × 200-meter hill at mile effort; jog down for recovery; 1- to 2-mile cool-down	Easy run: 8-10 miles	Regular run: 6-8 miles, then 8 × 100-meter strides	Tempo work: 2- to 3-mile warm-up; 2-3 miles continuous at 15-20 seconds per mile slower than 10K pace; 800-meter jog; 4 × 300 meters at mile pace with 100-meter walk/jog between; 1- to 2-mile cool-down	Easy to regular run: 3-7 miles	44-62
Week 3	Long run: 10-14 miles	Easy run: 6-8 miles, then 8 × 100-meter strides	Intervals: 2- to 3-mile warm-up; 4 × set of 800 meters at 5K pace, 200-meter jog, 200 meters at mile pace, 400-meter jog; 1- to 2-mile cool-down	Easy run: 8-10 miles	Regular run: 6-8 miles, then 8 × 100-meter strides	Progression run: 2- to 3-mile warm-up; 3 miles continuous, starting at 30 seconds per mile slower than 10K pace and increasing pace 5-10 seconds per mile after each mile; 1- to 2-mile cool-down	Easy to regular run: 3-7 miles OR Day off	47-68

	Sunday	Monday	Tuesday	Wednesday	Thursday	Friday	Saturday	Week's mileage
Week 4	Long run: 10-14 miles	Easy run: 6-8 miles, then 8 × 100-meter strides	Intervals: 2- to 3-mile warm-up; 4 × 200 meters, 5 × 400 meters, 4 × 200 meters, all at mile pace; 200-meter jog after 200s and 400-meter jog after 400s; 1- to 2-mile cool-down	Easy run: 6-8 miles	Regular run: 4-6 miles, then 8 × 100-meter strides	Tempo run: 2- to 3-mile warm-up; 3-4 miles continuous at 25-30 seconds per mile slower than 10K pace; 1- to 2-mile cool-down	Easy to regular run: 2-5 miles	41-59
Week 5	Long run: 10-14 miles	Easy run: 6-8 miles, then 8 × 100-meter strides	Intervals: 2- to 3-mile warm-up; 8 × 400 meters at 5K pace with 200-meter jog between; 1- to 2-mile cool-down	Easy run: 8-10 miles	Regular run: 6-8 miles, then 8 × 100-meter strides	Tempo run: 2- to 3-mile warm-up; 3-5 miles continuous at 25-30 seconds per mile slower than 10K pace; 6 × 200 meters at mile pace with 200-meter jog between; 1- to 2-mile cool-down	Easy to regular run: 4-8 miles OR Day off	44-68
Week 6	Long run: 10-14 miles	Easy run: 6-8 miles, then 8 × 100-meter strides	Hills: 2- to 3-mile warm-up; 8-10 × 200-meter hill at mile effort; jog down for recovery; 1- to 2-mile cool-down	Easy run: 8-10 miles	Regular run: 6-8 miles, then 8 × 100-meter strides	Tempo run: 2- to 3-mile warm-up; 4-5 miles continuous at 25-30 seconds per mile slower than 10K pace; 800-meter jog; 4 × 300 meters at mile pace with 100-meter walk/jog between; 1- to 2-mile cool-down	Easy to regular run: 3-7 miles	46-66

(continued)

10-Week 1-Mile Schedule: 40+ Miles per Week (continued)

	Sunday	Monday	Tuesday	Wednesday	Thursday	Friday	Saturday	Week's mileage
Week 7	Long run: 10-14 miles	Easy run: 6-8 miles, then 8 × 100-meter strides	Intervals: 2- to 3-mile warm-up; 6 × 1,000 meters at 5K pace with 400-meter jog between; 4 × 200 meters at 800-meter pace with 200-meter jog between; 1- to 2-mile cool-down	Easy run: 8-10 miles	Regular run: 6-8 miles, then 8 × 100-meter strides	Tempo work: 2- to 3-mile warm-up; 2 × 1 mile at 5K pace with 800-meter jog after each; 4 × 400 meters at mile pace with 400-meter jog between; 1- to 2-mile cool-down	Easy to regular run: 3-7 miles OR Day off	47-68
Week 8	Long run: 10-14 miles	Easy run: 6-8 miles, then 6 × 100-meter strides	Intervals: 2- to 3-mile warm-up; 4 × 800 meters at 3K pace; 4 × 400 meters at mile pace; 400-meter jog between intervals; 1- to 2-mile cool-down	Easy run: 8-10 miles	Regular run: 6-8 miles, then 6 × 100-meter strides	Tempo run: 2- to 3-mile warm-up; 4-5 miles continuous at 25-30 seconds per mile slower than 10K pace; 1- to 2-mile cool-down	Easy to regular run: 3-7 miles	48-67
Week 9	Long run: 10-12 miles	Easy run: 6-8 miles, then 8 × 100-meter strides	Intervals: 2- to 3-mile warm-up: 400 meters, 800 meters, 800 meters, 400 meters, all at mile pace; 400-meter jog between intervals; 1- to 2-mile cool-down	Easy run: 6-8 miles	Regular run: 6-8 miles, then 8 × 100-meter strides	Tempo/Intervals: 2- to 3-mile warm-up; 3 miles continuous at 20 seconds per mile slower than 10K pace; 800-meter jog; 4 × 300 meters at mile pace with 100-meter walk/jog between; 1- to 2-mile cool-down	Easy to regular run: 3-4 miles OR Day off	40-56
Week 10	Long run: 5-7 miles	Easy run: 4-6 miles, then 8 × 100-meter strides	Intervals: 2- to 3-mile warm-up; 6-8 × 400 meters at mile pace with 200-meter jog between; 1-mile cool-down	Easy run: 5-7 miles	Intervals: 2- to 3-mile warm-up; 4-6 × 200 meters at mile pace with 200-meter jog between; 1-mile cool-down	Easy run: 2-3 miles, then 6-8 100-meter strides	Race mile	25-35 (not including race)

Training for and Racing the 5K

This chapter will prepare you for 5-kilometer (3.1-mile) races. Better known as the 5K, this distance remains among the most popular because of its satisfying challenge. You're running a little slower than in the mile, but noticeably faster than in a 10K. You need to have all your bases covered in training and all your wits about you on race day to run your best 5K.

Following are six 5K schedules, three that are six weeks long and three that are 12 weeks long. The weekly mileage ranges for the 6-week schedules are up to 45, 35 to 55, and 40 or more. The weekly mileage ranges for the 12-week schedules are up to 50, 35 to 60, and 40 or more. As I said in chapter 7, there are many variables to consider when deciding which schedule to follow. Refer there for more details.

A Brief Guide to Following the Schedules

Each day's training in the schedules is described using the main types of runs I described at length in chapter 7. You'll want to refresh your memory occasionally by rereading those descriptions during your buildup. For quick reference, here are the types of runs you'll encounter in these schedules, and what I mean by each.

- *Easy run:* Done the day after your longest and hardest runs. Don't worry about pace. Just run at a comfortable, conversational effort level—no hard breathing, no bearing down. You should finish feeling energized for the next day's training.

- *Regular run:* A little faster and more effortful than an easy run, but still at a conversational pace. These are what you might think of as your getting-in-the-miles runs. It's okay to push things a little in the last few miles if you're feeling good.

- *Easy to regular run:* Start these runs as if they're a recovery run. If you're tired and want to stay at that gentle effort level for the whole run, that's fine. If you feel like going a little harder once you're warmed up, that's fine. But don't force yourself to go faster just because you think you "should" hit a certain pace.

- *Tempo run:* A sustained run, usually of two to six miles, at a "comfortably hard" effort level that requires concentration. For most runners, tempo runs should be around their 15K to half-marathon race pace. If I were riding a bike alongside and asked you a question, you should be able to answer in a complete sentence, but you shouldn't be able to carry on an in-depth conversation as on an easy or regular run.

- *Progression run:* A sustained run at an increasingly fast pace. Progression runs accomplish much of what conventional tempo runs do while also helping you practice increasing your effort as fatigue mounts. They tend to be a little longer than tempo runs because you start at a slower pace.

- *Intervals:* Repeats, usually between 400 meters and one mile long, usually run between mile and 10K race pace. You can do these on a track for precision and a uniform running surface, but you can also do them on roads or elsewhere with good footing. It's okay to roughly convert the distances stated in the training schedules to timed segments off the track, such as running at 5K effort for three minutes if the schedules prescribe 800-meter repeats at 5K pace.

- *Hill workout:* Running at mile effort—not pace!—up a moderately steep hill, and jogging down for recovery. Ideally, the hill will be steep enough to make the climbing noticeable, but not so steep that it's difficult to maintain a good upright running form with quick turnover.

- *Long run:* Your longest run of the week, done at a conversational pace. Start at a gentle effort and gradually increase intensity to that of a regular run as your body warms up. Don't rush it—you've got plenty of time to get in a good rhythm for the second half of the run.

- *Strides:* Short (100 meters or so) bouts of fast running at around mile race pace, usually done either after an easy run or before a hard workout or race. Concentrate on maintaining good running form and staying relaxed while running fast. Strides should feel good and be fun; you'll usually feel better after doing them than you did before. Do strides on a flat, level surface with reliable footing.

How to Race a 5K

I think the 5K is the toughest event to run, because you're close to your aerobic max the whole way if you're trying to get a PR or running to the best of your current ability. Even in a properly paced mile you have a short stretch early on where you don't feel like you're pressing.

Adding to the challenge of the 5K is that you immediately have to gauge where that red line is. If you start too slow, it can be difficult to make that time back. Although elites increasingly run negative splits when going for a record or personal best, doing so requires extraordinary aerobic fitness and the ability to run close to your mile race pace for the final kilometer. That's a tall order for most recreational runners, whose best bet is almost always to run close to even pace.

Much more common, and disastrous, is starting too fast. You might run a few seconds shy of what you're capable of with a too-slow start. But you could lose dozens of seconds with a too-quick start. It's not uncommon to slow by 30 seconds per mile in the final mile if you've run the first mile too fast. And you might not even know you're starting too fast. Say you want to break 20:00 for 5K, which is an average of roughly 6:25 per mile. You might reach the first mile marker between 6:20 and 6:25 and tell yourself you're right on pace. But if you ran the first few hundred yards ridiculously fast and then settled into a more sustainable rhythm, you didn't get to the mile mark at an even pace. You'll almost certainly be off pace by the two-mile mark because you've been slowing ever since that initial burst off the start line.

One way to contain yourself early on is by including one to three longer strides, up to 200 meters, in your warm-up. From your training you should know what 5K pace feels like. Re-create that feeling in these prerace strides, and then commit to not running the first minute of the race faster than that. Don't worry about how many people are in front of you at this point. You'll pass many of them by the time you reach the mile marker.

Even if you start at perfectly even pace, you need to stay intensely focused, because the middle section can be really tough. You can get constant feedback from lap splits in a track 5K. That's trickier on the roads, where it's easy to let your guard down in the second mile and not realize you're slowing. I think a few glances at your GPS during this stretch are okay. But don't constantly stare at your watch at the expense of being engaged in the race and focusing on your body's signals.

A better use of your watch, whether or not it has GPS, is to look at the time in the closing stages and tell yourself there's not much running left. Use positive self-talk to tell yourself something like, "You're doing fine. You can keep this up for a little bit more, and then you can push for the final two minutes."

If possible, warm up over the final half-mile of the course prior to the race. Those last few minutes of a 5K can feel like an eternity. Knowing if they contain turns or hills helps you cover them with confidence. You can also pick a spot from which you'll launch your finishing sprint and picture yourself hitting that spot running strong and then closing the best you can.

Lessons From Coach Coogan's 5Ks

One of the best 5,000-meter races I ever ran was at the U.S. championships in June 1995 in Sacramento, California. I ran a lifetime best 13:23 and qualified for the world championships later that summer.

Why did this race go so well for me? The top reason was that I had prepared well for it and was strong, fit, and healthy. I had trained hard for the Pan American Games marathon that March in Argentina and finished second there. I then almost immediately channeled the fitness I acquired getting ready for the marathon into my track season. I ran a few track races before the U.S. championships, including the 2-mile at the Prefontaine Classic. I came in third in the 2-mile behind Olympians Bob Kennedy and Todd Williams and ran 8:21, which was a big PR for me. The 5K was 12 days later. I took the confidence I gained at the Prefontaine meet with me to Sacramento.

Bob was the clear favorite in the 5,000. He had already been an Olympian in the event and was among a handful of people in the world with the potential to break 13:00 for the distance. I was a big fan of Bob's racing skills and toughness, and I knew he would make the race tough.

Bob took the race out really hard, running just over 4:00 mile pace for the first 400 meters. Only Olympian Matt Guisto and I went with him. We immediately had about 25 meters' lead in front of fourth place. This was good, because the top three finishers would make the team for the world championships in Sweden in August.

Then on the third lap Bob slowed to a crawl. I thought, "Oh God, now we are jogging and we are going to let the rest of the field back into the race. I just ran really hard and now here the rest of the field comes, and they won't be as tired as me." I had to think quickly on my feet. Matt was on my shoulder, and I was right behind Bob. I said, "Bob, get out of the way and I'll take it." Bob moved over, and I took the lead and injected a bit of pace back into the race. Bob got right behind me and Matt went right behind Bob.

I was pretty sure I could handle the new pace I took up because I was controlling the race and I could back off if I had to. None of the other competitors could catch up to the three of us and we kept clicking off 64-second laps. With one lap to go Bob quickly moved to the lead, but I kept him close the rest of the way and finished second, just behind Bob. Matt finished third and also set a personal best. My time of 13:23 was a fast one in the mid-1990s; at the time, our race was one of the fastest 5Ks in U.S. championship history.

I ran well because I knew my fitness level and I put myself in position to succeed without going too hard and dying or too slow and letting the miler types use their kicks. I really took advantage of the situation that I was given that evening. I'm proud of myself for taking the lead when I needed to and having the confidence in my training and fitness to lead for most of the U.S. championship. I did a great job of trusting but not overestimating my fitness and running just what I thought I was capable of that day.

The bad 5Ks I ran were usually races in which I ran recklessly (wasting energy for no reason) or overestimated my fitness. This happened at the Penn Relays when I was a sophomore at the University of Maryland.

When I was a young runner, it was easy for me to go out too hard and run beyond my abilities and then fall apart. I suspect that I had a little too much confidence and needed to learn some running lessons the hard way. At Penn I was racing a lot of the top college guys from around the country. Almost all of them had run faster than me. But for some idiotic reason, I went to the lead after the mile. I was probably in the lead for three or four laps before reality set in, the pack went by me, and I slowed and struggled to the finish.

I had no business leading and forcing the issue. I wasted so much energy surging through the field to the lead. I would have been so much better off running a pace that was suited to my fitness. If I had sat back, run in lane 1, and not surged much, my time would have been much better. When I coach now, I let young runners know about the mistakes I made, and I ask them to not go out as hard or recklessly as I did. I stress trying to run within themselves.

A happy coda: I returned to the Penn Relays 5,000 in 1995, didn't repeat my collegiate mistakes, and ended up winning.

6-Week 5K Schedule: Up to 45 Miles per Week

	Sunday	Monday	Tuesday	Wednesday	Thursday	Friday	Saturday	Week's mileage
Week 1	Long run: 6-8 miles	Easy run: 3-5 miles, then 6 × 100-meter strides	Intervals: 2-mile warm-up; 6 × 1,000 meters at 5K pace; 400-meter jog between intervals; 1- to 2-mile cool-down	Easy run: 6 miles	Regular run: 3-5 miles, then 6 × 100-meter strides	Tempo run: 2-mile warm-up; 3 miles continuous at 25-30 seconds per mile slower than 10K pace; 1- to 2-mile cool-down	Day off	32-40
Week 2	Long run: 7-8 miles	Easy run: 3-5 miles, then 6 × 100-meter strides	Intervals: 2-mile warm-up; 3 × set of 800 meters, 400 meters, 400 meters, with 800 at 5K pace and 400s at mile pace; 400-meter jog between all repeats; 1- to 2-mile cool-down	Easy run: 6 miles	Regular run: 4-5 miles, then 6 × 100-meter strides	Progression run: 2-mile warm-up; 3 miles continuous, starting at 30 seconds per mile slower than 10K pace and increasing pace 5-10 seconds per mile after each mile; 1- to 2-mile cool-down	Easy to regular run: 3-4 miles	36-46
Week 3	Long run: 7-8 miles	Easy run: 3-5 miles, then 6 × 100-meter strides	Intervals: 2-mile warm-up; 4 × 400 meters at mile pace with 200-meter jog after each; 2 × 800 meters at 5K pace with 400-meter jog after each; 4 × 400 meters at mile pace with 200-meter jog after each; 1- to 2-mile cool-down	Easy run: 6 miles	Regular run: 3-5 miles, then 6 × 100-meter strides	Intervals and tempo run: 2-mile warm-up; 3 × 600 meters at 5K pace with 400-meter jog after each; 2 miles continuous at 25 seconds per mile slower than 10K pace; 400-meter jog; 2 × 400 meters at mile pace with 200-meter jog between; 1- to 2-mile cool-down	Easy run: 1-3 miles OR Day off	33-43

(continued)

6-Week 5K Schedule: Up to 45 Miles per Week (continued)

	Sunday	Monday	Tuesday	Wednesday	Thursday	Friday	Saturday	Week's mileage
Week 4	Long run: 7-8 miles	Easy run: 3-5 miles, then 6 × 100-meter strides	Intervals: 2-mile warm-up; 8 × 400 meters at 5K pace with 200-meter jog between; 1- to 2-mile cool-down	Easy run: 4-6 miles	Regular run: 3-5 miles, then 6 × 100-meter strides	Tempo run: 2-mile warm-up; 3 miles continuous at 25-30 seconds per mile slower than 10K pace; 1- to 2-mile cool-down	Easy run: 3-4 miles	32-43
Week 5	Long run: 6-8 miles	Easy run: 1-3 miles OR Day off	Intervals: 2-mile warm-up; 1 mile at 5K pace or a few seconds slower; 4 × 400 meters at mile pace; 1 mile at 5K pace or a few seconds slower; 400-meter jog between all intervals; 1- to 2-mile cool-down	Easy run: 4-6 miles	Regular run: 3-5 miles, then 6 × 100-meter strides	Tempo work: 2-mile warm-up; 2-3 miles continuous at 15-20 seconds per mile slower than 10K pace; 800-meter jog; 4 × 300 meters at mile pace with 100-meter walk between; 1- to 2-mile cool-down	Easy run: 2-4 miles	29-40
Week 6	Long run: 6 miles	Easy run: 3 miles	Intervals: 2-mile warm-up; 8 × 300 meters at 5K pace with 200-meter jog between; 1- to 2-mile cool-down	Day off	Easy run: 3 miles, then 6 × 100-meter strides	Easy run: 3 miles, then 4-6 × 100-meter strides	Race 5K	18-22 (not including race)

6-Week 5K Schedule: 35-55 Miles per Week

	Sunday	Monday	Tuesday	Wednesday	Thursday	Friday	Saturday	Week's mileage
Week 1	Long run: 8-10 miles	Easy run: 4-6 miles, then 6 × 100-meter strides	Intervals: 2-mile warm-up; 6 × 1,000 meters at 5K pace; 400-meter jog between intervals; 1- to 2-mile cool-down	Easy run: 6-8 miles	Regular run: 5-8 miles, then 8 × 100-meter strides	Tempo run: 2-mile warm-up; 3 miles continuous at 25-30 seconds per mile slower than 10K pace; 1- to 2-mile cool-down	Easy run: 1-4 miles OR Day off	36-53
Week 2	Long run: 8-12 miles	Easy run: 4-6 miles, then 6 × 100-meter strides	Intervals: 2-mile warm-up; 3 × set of 800 meters, 400 meters, 400 meters, with 800 at 5K pace and 400s at mile pace; 400-meter jog between all repeats; 1- to 2-mile cool-down	Easy run: 6-8 miles	Regular run: 6-8 miles, then 8 × 100-meter strides	Progression run: 2-mile warm-up; 3 miles continuous, starting at 30 seconds per mile slower than 10K pace and increasing pace 5-10 seconds per mile after each mile; 1- to 2-mile cool-down	Easy run: 3-4 miles	41-52
Week 3	Long run: 8-12 miles	Easy run: 4-6 miles, then 6 × 100-meter strides	Intervals: 2-mile warm-up; 4 × 400 meters at mile pace with 200-meter jog after each; 2 × 800 meters at 5K pace with 400-meter jog after each; 4 × 400 meters at mile pace with 200-meter jog after each; 1- to 2-mile cool-down	Easy run: 6-8 miles	Regular run: 5-8 miles, then 8 × 100-meter strides	Intervals and tempo run: 2-mile warm-up; 3 × 600 meters at 5K pace with 400-meter jog after each; 2 miles continuous at 25 seconds per mile slower than 10K pace; 400-meter jog; 2 × 400 meters at mile pace with 200-meter jog between; 1- to 2-mile cool-down	Easy run: 3-5 miles	41-55

(continued)

6-Week 5K Schedule: 35-55 Miles per Week (continued)

	Sunday	Monday	Tuesday	Wednesday	Thursday	Friday	Saturday	Week's mileage
Week 4	Long run: 8-10 miles	Easy run: 4-6 miles, then 6 × 100-meter strides	Intervals: 2-mile warm-up; 8 × 400 meters at 5K pace with 200-meter jog between; 1- to 2-mile cool-down	Easy run: 6-8 miles	Regular run: 5-8 miles, then 6 × 100-meter strides	Tempo run: 2-mile warm-up; 3 miles continuous at 25-30 seconds per mile slower than 10K pace; 1- to 2-mile cool-down	Easy run: 1-4 miles OR Day off	36-53
Week 5	Long run: 8-9 miles	Easy run: 3-4 miles, then 6 × 100-meter strides	Intervals: 2-mile warm-up; 1 mile at 5K pace or a few seconds slower; 4 × 400 meters at mile pace; 1 mile at 5K pace or a few seconds slower; 400-meter jog between all intervals; 1- to 2-mile cool-down	Easy run: 4-6 miles	Regular run: 4-6 miles, then 6 × 100-meter strides	Tempo work: 2-mile warm-up; 2-3 miles continuous at 15-20 seconds slower than 10K pace; 800-meter jog; 4 × 300 meters at mile pace with 100-meter walk between; 1- to 2-mile cool-down	Easy run: 3-4 miles	36-45
Week 6	Long run: 6-8 miles	Easy run: 4 miles, then 6 × 100-meter strides	Intervals: 2-mile warm-up; 8 × 300 meters at 5K pace with 200-meter jog between; 1- to 2-mile cool-down	Day off	Easy run: 3-4 miles, then 6 × 100-meter strides OR Day off	Easy run: 3 miles, then 4-6 × 100-meter strides	Race 5K	19-28 (not including race)

6-Week 5K Schedule: 40+ Miles per Week

	Sunday	Monday	Tuesday	Wednesday	Thursday	Friday	Saturday	Week's mileage
Week 1	Long run: 10-14 miles	Easy run: 7-9 miles, then 8 × 100-meter strides	Intervals: 2-mile warm-up; 6 × 1,000 meters at 5K pace; 400-meter jog between intervals; 1- to 2-mile cool-down	Easy run: 7-10 miles	Regular run: 7-9 miles, then 8 × 100-meter strides	Tempo run: 2-mile warm-up; 3 miles continuous at 25-30 seconds per mile slower than 10K pace; 1- to 2-mile cool-down	Easy run: 4-6 miles	50-69
Week 2	Long run: 10-14 miles	Easy run: 7-9 miles, then 8 × 100-meter strides	Intervals: 2-mile warm-up; 3 × set of 800 meters, 400 meters, 400 meters, with 800 at 5K pace and 400s at mile pace; 400-meter jog between all repeats; 1- to 2-mile cool-down	Easy run: 7-10 miles	Regular run: 7-9 miles, then 8 × 100-meter strides	Progression run: 2-mile warm-up; 3 miles continuous, starting at 30 seconds per mile slower than 10K pace and increasing pace 5-10 seconds per mile after each mile; 1- to 2-mile cool-down	Easy to regular run: 4-6 miles	49-66
Week 3	Long run: 12-15 miles	Easy run: 1-4 miles OR Day off	Intervals: 2-mile warm-up; 4 × 400 meters at mile pace with 200-meter jog after each; 2 × 800 meters at 5K pace with 400-meter jog after each; 4 × 400 meters at mile pace with 200-meter jog after each; 1- to 2-mile cool-down	Easy run: 6-8 miles	Regular run: 7-9 miles, then 8 × 100-meter strides	Intervals and tempo run: 2-mile warm-up; 3 × 600 meters at 5K pace with 400-meter jog after each; 2-mile tempo run at 25 seconds per mile slower than 10K pace; 400-meter jog; 2 × 400 meters at mile pace with 200-meter jog between; 1- to 2-mile cool-down	Easy run: 4-6 miles	44-63

(continued)

6-Week 5K Schedule: 40+ Miles per Week (continued)

	Sunday	Monday	Tuesday	Wednesday	Thursday	Friday	Saturday	Week's mileage
Week 4	Long run: 10-14 miles	Easy run: 6-8 miles, then 8 × 100-meter strides	Intervals: 2-mile warm-up; 8 × 400 meters at 5K pace with 200-meter jog between all repeats; 1- to 2-mile cool-down	Easy run: 8 miles	Regular run: 7-9 miles, then 8 × 100-meter strides	Tempo run: 2-mile warm-up; 3 miles continuous at 25-30 seconds per mile slower than 10K pace; 1- to 2-mile cool-down	Easy run: 4-6 miles	45-63
Week 5	Long run: 10-12 miles	Day off (preferred) OR Easy run: 3 miles, then 8 × 100-meter strides	Intervals: 2-mile warm-up; 1 mile at 5K pace or a few seconds slower; 4 × 400 meters at mile pace; 1 mile at 5K pace or a few seconds slower; 400-meter jog between all intervals; 1- to 2-mile cool-down	Easy run: 6-8 miles	Regular run: 6-8 miles, then 6 × 100-meter strides	Tempo work: 2-mile warm-up; 2-3 miles continuous at 15-20 seconds slower than 10K pace; 800-meter jog; 4 × 300 meters at mile pace with 100-meter walk between; 1- to 2-mile cool-down	Easy run: 4 miles	40-51
Week 6	Long run: 8 miles	Easy run: 4 miles	Intervals: 2-mile warm-up; 8 × 300 meters at 5K pace with 200-meter jog between repeats; 1- to 2-mile cool-down	Easy run: 4-6 miles	Easy run: 3-4 miles, then 8 × 100-meter strides OR Day off	Easy run: 3 miles, then 4-6 × 100-meter strides	Race 5K	25-34 (not including race)

12-Week 5K Schedule: Up to 50 Miles per Week

	Sunday	Monday	Tuesday	Wednesday	Thursday	Friday	Saturday	Week's mileage
Week 1	Long run: 6-8 miles	Easy run: 3-5 miles, then 6 × 100-meter strides	Intervals: 2-mile warm-up; 6-8 × 400 meters at 5K pace with 200-meter jog between; 1- to 2-mile cool-down	Easy run: 6 miles	Regular run: 3-5 miles, then 6 × 100-meter strides	Tempo run: 2-mile warm-up; 3-4 miles continuous at 25-30 seconds per mile slower than 10K pace; 1- to 2-mile cool-down	Day off	31-40
Week 2	Long run: 6-8 miles	Easy run: 3-5 miles, then 6 × 100-meter strides	Hill workout: 2-mile warm-up; 6-8 × 200-meter hill at mile effort; jog down for recovery; 1- to 2-mile cool-down	Easy run: 6 miles	Regular run: 4-5 miles, then 6 × 100-meter strides	Tempo run: 2-mile warm-up; 3 miles continuous at 25-30 seconds per mile slower than 10K pace; 800-meter jog; 4 × 300 meters at mile pace with 200-meter jog between; 1- to 2-mile cool-down	Easy to regular run: 3-4 miles OR Day off	33-44
Week 3	Long run: 7-8 miles	Easy run: 3-5 miles, then 6 × 100-meter strides	Intervals: 2-mile warm-up; 4-5 × 800 meters at 5K pace with 400-meter jog between; 1- to 2-mile cool-down	Easy run: 6 miles	Regular run: 4-5 miles, then 6 × 100-meter strides	Pace work: 2-mile warm-up; 1.5 miles at 10K pace; 800-meter jog; 1 mile at 5K pace; 400-meter jog; 1 mile at 10K pace; 1- to 2-mile cool-down	Easy to regular run: 2-4 miles OR Day off	36-44
Week 4	Long run: 7-8 miles	Easy run: 3-5 miles, then 6 × 100-meter strides	Hill workout: 2-mile warm-up; 6-8 × 400-meter hill at mile effort; jog down for recovery; 1- to 2-mile cool-down	Easy run: 6 miles	Regular run: 3-5 miles, then 6 × 100-meter strides	Tempo run: 2-mile warm-up; 4-5 miles continuous at 25-30 seconds per mile slower than 10K pace; 1- to 2-mile cool-down	Easy to regular run: 1-4 miles OR Day off	33-48

(continued)

Up to 50 Miles per Week
12-Week 5K Schedule

133

12-Week 5K Schedule: Up to 50 Miles per Week (continued)

	Sunday	Monday	Tuesday	Wednesday	Thursday	Friday	Saturday	Week's mileage
Week 5	Long run: 8-10 miles	Easy run: 3-5 miles, then 6 × 100-meter strides	Intervals: 2-mile warm-up; 8 × 400 meters at 5K pace; 200-meter jog between; 1- to 2-mile cool-down	Easy run: 6 miles	Regular run: 4-5 miles, then 6 × 100-meter strides	Progression run: 2-mile warm-up; 3 miles continuous starting at 25-30 seconds slower than 10K pace, increasing pace 5-8 seconds per mile after each mile; 1- to 2-mile cool-down	Easy to regular run: 2-3 miles OR Day off	36-44
Week 6	Long run: 8-10 miles	Easy run: 3-5 miles, then 8 × 100-meter strides	Intervals: 2-mile warm-up; 6 × 800 meters at 5K pace with 400-meter jog between; 1- to 2-mile cool-down	Easy run: 4-6 miles	Regular run: 4-6 miles, then 6 × 100-meter strides	Tempo work: 2-mile warm-up; 2 miles continuous at 25-30 seconds per mile slower than 10K pace; 800-meter jog; 1 mile at 10 seconds slower than 5K pace; 800-meter jog; 4 × 400 meters at 5K pace with 400-meter jog between; 1- to 2-mile cool-down	Easy to regular run: 2-4 miles OR Day off	35-48
Week 7	Long run: 8-10 miles	Easy run: 3-5 miles, then 6 × 100-meter strides	Intervals: 2-mile warm-up; 3 × 1 mile at 5K pace with 800-meter jog between; 1- to 2-mile cool-down	Easy run: 4-6 miles	Regular run: 4-6 miles, then 6 × 100-meter strides	Tempo run: 2-mile warm-up; 3-4 miles continuous at 25-30 seconds per mile slower than 10K pace; 1- to 2-mile cool-down	Easy to regular run: 2-4 miles	34-49

	Sunday	Monday	Tuesday	Wednesday	Thursday	Friday	Saturday	Week's mileage
Week 8	Long run: 6-8 miles	Easy run: 3-5 miles, then 6 × 100-meter strides	Hill workout: 2-mile warm-up; 8 × 300-meter hill at mile effort; jog down for recovery; 1- to 2-mile cool-down	Easy run: 3-5 miles	Regular run: 3-5 miles, then 6 × 100-meter strides	Tempo work: 2-mile warm-up; 1 mile at 10K pace; 800-meter jog; 2 × 800 meters at 5K pace with 400-meter jog after each; 2 × 400 meters at mile pace with 200-meter jog between; 1- to 2-mile cool-down	Easy to regular run: 1-4 miles OR Day off	29-43
Week 9	Long run: 8-10 miles	Easy run: 3-5 miles, then 6 × 100-meter strides	Intervals: 2-mile warm-up; 8 × 400 meters at 5K pace with 200-meter jog between; 1- to 2-mile cool-down	Easy run: 4-6 miles	Regular run: 4-6 miles, then 6 × 100-meter strides	If racing tomorrow: Easy run: 2-4 miles If not racing tomorrow: Pace work: 2-mile warm-up; 2-3 miles continuous at 10K pace; 1- to 2-mile cool-down	5K-8K race OR Easy to regular run: 3-4 miles	30-46
Week 10	Long run: 8-10 miles	Easy run: 3-5 miles, then 6 × 100-meter strides	Intervals: 2-mile warm-up; 400 meters at mile pace; 800 meters at 5K pace; 1,200 meters at 10K pace; 800 meters at 5K pace; and 400 meters at mile pace; 400-meter jog between all intervals; 1- to 2-mile cool-down	Easy run: 4-6 miles	Regular run: 4-6 miles, then 6 × 100-meter strides	Tempo run: 2-mile warm-up; 3-4 miles continuous at 25-30 seconds per mile slower than 10K pace; 800-meter jog; 2 × 400 meters at mile pace with 200-meter jog between; 1- to 2-mile cool-down	Easy to regular run: 2-4 miles	33-45

(continued)

135

12-Week 5K Schedule: Up to 50 Miles per Week (continued)

	Sunday	Monday	Tuesday	Wednesday	Thursday	Friday	Saturday	Week's mileage
Week 11	Long run: 4-7 miles	Easy run: 3-5 miles, then 6 × 100-meter strides	Intervals: 2-mile warm-up; 5-6 × 1,000 meters at 5K pace with 400-meter jog between; 1- to 2-mile cool-down	Easy run: 4-6 miles	Regular run: 4-6 miles, then 6 × 100-meter strides	Tempo work: 2-mile warm-up; 2 × 400 meters at 5K pace with 200-meter jog between; 1.5 miles at 10K pace; 800-meter jog; 4 × 200 meters at mile pace with 200-meter jog between; 1- to 2-mile cool-down	Easy to regular run: 1-4 miles OR Day off	28-48
Week 12	Long run: 4-6 miles	Easy run: 3-4 miles, then 6 × 100-meter strides	Intervals: 2-mile warm-up; 6-8 × 400 meters at 5K pace with 200-meter jog between; 1- to 2-mile cool-down	Easy run: 3-4 miles	Easy run: 2-3 miles, then 6 × 100-meter strides	Easy run: 2-3 miles, then 6 × 100-meter strides	Race 5K	20-30 (not including race)

12-Week 5K Schedule: 35-60 Miles per Week

	Sunday	Monday	Tuesday	Wednesday	Thursday	Friday	Saturday	Week's mileage
Week 1	Long run: 7-10 miles	Easy run: 4-6 miles, then 6 × 100-meter strides	Intervals: 2-mile warm-up; 6-8 × 400 meters at 5K pace with 200-meter jog between; 1- to 2-mile cool-down	Easy run: 6-8 miles	Regular run: 5-8 miles, then 6 × 100-meter strides	Tempo run: 2-mile warm-up; 3-4 miles continuous at 25-30 seconds per mile slower than 10K pace; 1- to 2-mile cool-down	Easy run: 2-4 miles	38-52
Week 2	Long run: 7-10 miles	Easy run: 4-6 miles, then 6 × 100-meter strides	Hill workout: 2-mile warm-up; 6-8 × 300-meter hill at mile effort; jog down for recovery; 1- to 2-mile cool-down	Easy run: 6-8 miles	Regular run: 5-8 miles, then 6 × 100-meter strides	Progression run: 2-mile warm-up; 3-5 miles continuous starting at 35 seconds slower than 10K pace, increasing pace 5-10 seconds per mile after each mile; 1- to 2-mile cool-down	Easy to regular run: 3-4 miles	40-53
Week 3	Long run: 8-10 miles	Easy run: 4-6 miles, then 6 × 100-meter strides	Intervals: 2-mile warm-up; 5-6 × 800 meters at 5K pace with 400-meter jog between; 1- to 2-mile cool-down	Easy run: 6-8 miles	Regular run: 6-8 miles, then 6 × 100-meter strides	Tempo work: 2-mile warm-up; 2 × 1.5 miles at 20-25 seconds slower per 1.5-mile segment than 5K pace; 800-meter jog between the two intervals; 1- to 2-mile cool-down	Easy to regular run: 3-4 miles	39-53
Week 4	Long run: 8-10 miles	Easy run: 4-6 miles, then 6 × 100-meter strides	Hill workout: 2-mile warm-up; 8 × 400-meter hill at mile effort; jog down for recovery; 1- to 2-mile cool-down	Easy run: 5-6 miles	Regular run: 5-7 miles, then 6 × 100-meter strides	Tempo run: 2-mile warm-up; 4-5 miles continuous at 25-30 seconds per mile slower than 10K pace; 1- to 2-mile cool-down	Easy to regular run: 1-6 miles OR Day off	37-53

(continued)

12-Week 5K Schedule: 35-60 Miles per Week (continued)

	Sunday	Monday	Tuesday	Wednesday	Thursday	Friday	Saturday	Week's mileage
Week 5	Long run: 8-12 miles	Easy run: 4-6 miles, then 6 × 100-meter strides	Intervals: 2-mile warm-up; 2 sets of 4 × 400 meters, with 5K pace for first set and mile pace for second set; 200-meter jog between repeats in a set and 400-meter jog between sets; 1- to 2-mile cool-down	Easy run: 6-8 miles	Regular run: 5-8 miles, then 6 × 100-meter strides	Progression run: 2-mile warm-up; 4-5 miles continuous starting at 30-35 seconds slower than 10K pace, increasing pace 5-10 seconds per mile after each mile; 1- to 2-mile cool-down	Easy to regular run: 3-4 miles	43-57
Week 6	Long run: 8-12 miles	Easy run: 4-6 miles, then 8 × 100-meter strides	Intervals: 2-mile warm-up; 6 × 800 meters at 5K pace with 400-meter jog between; 1- to 2-mile cool-down	Easy run: 6-8 miles	Regular run: 5-7 miles, then 6 × 100-meter strides	Tempo work: 2-mile warm-up; 2 miles continuous at 25-30 seconds per mile slower than 10K pace; 800-meter jog; 1 mile at 10 seconds slower than 5K pace; 800-meter jog; 4 × 400 meters at mile to 5K pace with 400-meter jog between; 1- to 2-mile cool-down	Easy to regular run: 3-4 miles	44-56
Week 7	Long run: 10-12 miles	Easy run: 4-6 miles, then 6 × 100-meter strides	Intervals: 2-mile warm-up; 3 × 1 mile at 5K pace with 800-meter jog between; 1- to 2-mile cool-down	Easy run: 6-8 miles	Regular run: 6-8 miles, then 6 × 100-meter strides	Tempo run: 2-mile warm-up; 4-5 miles continuous at 25-30 seconds per mile slower than 10K pace; 1- to 2-mile cool-down	Easy to regular run: 3-4 miles	46-56
Week 8	Long run: 8-10 miles	Easy run: 4-6 miles, then 6 × 100-meter strides	Hill workout: 2-mile warm-up; 8 × 300-meter hill at mile effort; jog down for recovery; 1- to 2-mile cool-down	Easy run: 4-6 miles	Regular run: 3-5 miles, then 6 × 100-meter strides	Tempo work: 2-mile warm-up; 1 mile at 10K pace; 800-meter jog; 2 × 800 meters at 5K pace with 400-meter jog after each; 2 × 400 meters at mile pace with 200-meter jog between; 1- to 2-mile cool-down	Easy to regular run: 1-4 miles OR Day off	32-47

138

	Sunday	Monday	Tuesday	Wednesday	Thursday	Friday	Saturday	Week's mileage
Week 9	Long run: 10-12 miles	Easy run: 4-6 miles, then 6 × 100-meter strides	Intervals: 2-mile warm-up; 8 × 400 meters at 5K pace with 200-meter jog between; 1- to 2-mile cool-down	Easy run: 6-8 miles	Regular run: 6-8 miles, then 6 × 100-meter strides	If racing tomorrow: Easy run: 2-4 miles. If not racing tomorrow: Pace work: 2-mile warm-up; 3 miles continuous at 10K pace; 1- to 2-mile cool-down	5K-8K race OR Easy to regular run: 3-5 miles	43-52
Week 10	Long run: 8-12 miles	Easy run: 4-6 miles, then 6 × 100-meter strides	Interval ladder: 2-mile warm-up; 400 meters at mile pace; 800 meters at 5K pace; 2 × 1,200 meters at 10K pace; 800 meters at 5K pace; 400 meters at mile pace; 400-meter jog between all repeats; 1- to 2-mile cool-down	Easy run: 5-7 miles	Regular run: 5-7 miles, then 6 × 100-meter strides	Tempo run: 2-mile warm-up; 3-4 miles continuous at 25-30 seconds per mile slower than 10K pace; 800-meter jog; 4 × 400 meters at 5K pace with 200-meter jog between; 1- to 2-mile cool-down	Easy to regular run: 3-4 miles	42-56
Week 11	Long run: 7-10 miles	Easy run: 4-6 miles, then 6 × 100-meter strides	Intervals: 2-mile warm-up; 5-6 × 1,000 meters at 5K pace with 400-meter jog between; 1- to 2-mile cool-down	Easy run: 4-6 miles	Regular run: 4-6 miles, then 6 × 100-meter strides	Pace work: 2-mile warm-up; 2 × 800 meters at 5K pace; 400-meter jog after both; 4 × 400 meters at 5K pace with 200-meter jog between; 1- to 2-mile cool-down	Easy to regular run: 1-4 miles OR Day off	33-44
Week 12	Long run: 6-8 miles	Easy run: 4-5 miles, then 6 × 100-meter strides	Intervals: 2-mile warm-up; 6-8 × 400 meters at 5K pace with 200-meter jog between; 1- to 2-mile cool-down	Easy run: 3-5 miles	Easy run: 3-4 miles, then 6 × 100-meter strides	Easy run: 2-4 miles, then 6 × 100-meter strides	Race 5K	22-30 (not including race)

12-Week 5K Schedule: 40+ Miles per Week

	Sunday	Monday	Tuesday	Wednesday	Thursday	Friday	Saturday	Week's mileage
Week 1	Long run: 8-12 miles	Easy run: 6-8 miles, then 8 × 100-meter strides	Intervals: 2- to 3-mile warm-up; 8 × 400 meters at 5K pace with 200-meter jog between; 1- to 2-mile cool-down	Easy run: 7-9 miles	Regular run: 6-9 miles, then 8 × 100-meter strides	Tempo run: 2- to 3-mile warm-up; 3-4 miles continuous at 25-30 seconds per mile slower than 10K pace; 1- to 2-mile cool-down	Easy run: 4-6 miles	44-62
Week 2	Long run: 8-12 miles	Easy run: 6-8 miles, then 8 × 100-meter strides	Hill workout: 2- to 3-mile warm-up; 8 × 300-meter hill at mile effort; jog down for recovery; 1- to 2-mile cool-down	Easy run: 7-9 miles	Regular run: 6-9 miles, then 8 × 100-meter strides	Progression run: 2- to 3-mile warm-up; 4-5 miles continuous starting at 35 seconds slower than 10K pace, increasing pace 5-10 seconds per mile after each mile; 1- to 2-mile cool-down	Easy to regular run: 4-6 miles	45-64
Week 3	Long run: 8-12 miles	Easy run: 6-8 miles, then 8 × 100-meter strides	Intervals: 2- to 3-mile warm-up; 6 × 800 meters at 5K pace with 400-meter jog between; 1- to 2-mile cool-down	Easy run: 7-10 miles	Regular run: 6-9 miles, then 8 × 100-meter strides	Tempo work: 2- to 3-mile warm-up; 3 × 1.5 miles at 20-25 seconds slower per 1.5-mile segment than 10K pace; 800-meter jog between; 1- to 2-mile cool-down	Easy to regular run: 4-6 miles	46-65
Week 4	Long run: 8-12 miles	Easy run: 6-8 miles, then 6 × 100-meter strides	Hill workout: 2- to 3-mile warm-up; 8 × 400-meter hill at mile effort; jog down for recovery; 1- to 2-mile cool-down	Easy run: 7-10 miles	Regular run: 6-9 miles, then 6 × 100-meter strides	Tempo run: 2- to 3-mile warm-up; 5-6 miles continuous at 25-30 seconds per mile slower than 10K pace; 1- to 2-mile cool-down	Easy to regular run: 1-6 miles OR Day off	43-66

	Sunday	Monday	Tuesday	Wednesday	Thursday	Friday	Saturday	Week's mileage
Week 5	Long run: 10-14 miles	Easy run: 6-8 miles, then 8 × 100-meter strides	Intervals: 2- to 3-mile warm-up; 2 × sets of 4 × 400 meters with 5K pace for first set and mile pace for second set; 200-meter jog between repeats in a set and 400-meter jog between sets; 1- to 2-mile cool-down	Easy run: 7-10 miles	Regular run: 6-9 miles, then 8 × 100-meter strides	Progression run: 2-3 mile warm-up; 4-6 miles continuous starting at 35 seconds slower than 10K pace, increasing pace 5-10 seconds per mile after each mile; 1- to 2-mile cool-down	Easy to regular run: 4-6 miles	45-65
Week 6	Long run: 10-14 miles	Easy run: 6-8 miles, then 8 × 100-meter strides	Intervals: 2- to 3-mile warm-up; 6-8 × 800 meters at 5K pace with 400-meter jog between; 1- to 2-mile cool-down	Easy run: 7-10 miles	Regular run: 6-9 miles, then 8 × 100-meter strides	Tempo work: 2-mile warm-up; 2-3 miles continuous at 25-30 seconds per mile slower than 10K pace; 800-meter jog; 1 mile at 10 seconds slower than 5K pace; 800-meter jog; 4 × 400 meters at mile pace with 400-meter jog between; 1- to 2-mile cool-down	Easy to regular run: 4-6 miles	52-68
Week 7	Long run: 10-14 miles	Easy run: 6-8 miles, then 8 × 100-meter strides	Intervals: 2- to 3-mile warm-up; 3 × 1 mile at 5K pace with 800-meter jog between; 1- to 2-mile cool-down	Easy run: 7-10 miles	Regular run: 6-9 miles, then 8 × 100-meter strides	Tempo run: 2- to 3-mile warm-up; 4-6 miles continuous at 25-30 seconds per mile slower than 10K pace; 1- to 2-mile cool-down	Easy to regular run: 4-6 miles	49-67

(continued)

40+ Miles per Week
6-Week 5K Schedule

12-Week 5K Schedule: 40+ Miles per Week (continued)

	Sunday	Monday	Tuesday	Wednesday	Thursday	Friday	Saturday	Week's mileage
Week 8	Long run: 8-12 miles	Easy run: 5-7 miles, then 8 × 100-meter strides	Hill workout: 2- to 3-mile warm-up; 8 × 300-meter hill at mile effort; jog down for recovery; 1- to 2-mile cool-down	Easy run: 6-8 miles	Regular run: 5-7 miles, then 8 × 100-meter strides	Tempo work: 2- to 3-mile warm-up; 1 mile at 10K pace; 800-meter jog; 4 × 800 meters at 5K pace with 400-meter jog between; 2 × 400 meters at mile pace with 200-meter jog between; 1- to 2-mile cool-down	Easy to regular run: 1-6 miles OR Day off	39-58
Week 9	Long run: 12-14 miles	Easy run: 6-8 miles, then 8 × 100-meter strides	Intervals: 2- to 3-mile warm-up; 2 sets of 4 × 400 meters, with 5K pace for first set and mile pace for second set; 200-meter jog between repeats in a set and 400-meter jog between sets; 1- to 2-mile cool-down	Easy run: 7-10 miles	Regular run: 6-9 miles, then 8 × 100-meter strides	If racing tomorrow: Easy run: 3-4 miles. If not racing tomorrow: Pace work: 2- to 3-mile warm-up; 3 miles continuous at 10K pace; 1- to 2-mile cool-down	5K-8K race OR Easy to regular run: 4-6 miles	48-64

	Sunday	Monday	Tuesday	Wednesday	Thursday	Friday	Saturday	Week's mileage
Week 10	Long run: 12-14 miles	Easy run: 6-8 miles, then 8 × 100-meter strides	Interval ladder: 2- to 3-mile warm-up; 400 meters at mile pace; 800 meters at 5K pace; 2 × 1,200 meters at 10K pace; 800 meters at 5K pace; 400 meters at mile pace; 400-meter jog between all repeats; 1- to 2-mile cool-down	Easy run: 7-10 miles	Regular run: 6-9 miles, then 8 × 100-meter strides	Tempo run: 2- to 3-mile warm-up; 3-4 miles continuous at 20-30 seconds per mile slower than 10K pace; 800-meter jog; 4 × 400 meters at 5K pace with 200-meter jog between; 1- to 2-mile cool-down	Easy to regular run: 4-6 miles	54-70
Week 11	Long run: 8-12 miles	Easy run: 5-7 miles, then 8 × 100-meter strides	Intervals: 2- to 3-mile warm-up; 6 × 1,000 meters at 5K pace with 400-meter jog between; 1- to 2-mile cool-down	Easy run: 6-8 miles	Regular run: 5-7 miles, then 8 × 100-meter strides	Pace work: 2- to 3-mile warm-up; 2 × 800 meters at 5K pace; 400-meter jog after both; 4 × 400 meters at 5K pace with 200-meter jog between; 1- to 2-mile cool-down	Easy to regular run: 1-6 miles OR Day off	40-60
Week 12	Long run: 8 miles	Easy run: 4-6 miles, then 8 × 100-meter strides	Intervals: 2- to 3-mile warm-up; 6-8 × 400 meters at 5K pace with 200-meter jog between; 1- to 2-mile cool-down	Easy run: 4-6 miles	Easy run: 3-4 miles, then 6 × 100-meter strides	Easy run: 3-4 miles, then 6 × 100-meter strides	Race 5K	28-36 (not including race)

10

Training for and Racing the 10K

This chapter will prepare you for 10-kilometer (6.21-mile) races. Better known as the 10K, this distance remains among the most popular because of its satisfying challenge. You're running a little slower than in a 5K, but noticeably faster than in a half-marathon. You need to have all your bases covered in training and all your wits about you on race day to run your best 10K.

Following are six 10K schedules, three that are six weeks long and three that are 12 weeks long. The weekly mileage ranges for the 6-week schedules are up to 45, 35 to 55, and 40 or more. The weekly mileage ranges for the 12-week schedules are up to 50, 35 to 60, and 40 or more. As I said in chapter 7, there are many variables to consider when deciding which schedule to follow. Refer there for more details.

A Brief Guide to Following the Schedules

Each day's training in the schedules is described using the main types of runs I described at length in chapter 7. You'll want to refresh your memory occasionally by rereading those descriptions during your buildup. For quick reference, here are the types of runs you'll encounter in these schedules, and what I mean by each.

- *Easy run:* Done the day after your longest and hardest runs. Don't worry about pace. Just run at a comfortable, conversational effort level—no hard breathing, no bearing down. You should finish feeling energized for the next day's training.

- *Regular run:* A little faster and more effortful than an easy run, but still at a conversational pace. These are what you might think of as your getting-in-the-miles runs. It's okay to push things a little in the last few miles if you're feeling good.

- *Easy to regular run:* Start these runs as if they're a recovery run. If you're tired and want to stay at that gentle effort level for the whole run, that's fine. If you feel like going a little harder once you're warmed up, that's fine. But don't force yourself to go faster just because you think you "should" hit a certain pace.

- *Tempo run:* A sustained run, usually of two to six miles, at a "comfortably hard" effort level that requires concentration. For most runners, tempo runs should be around their 15K to half-marathon race pace. If I were riding a bike alongside and asked you a question, you should be able to answer in a complete sentence, but you shouldn't be able to carry on an in-depth conversation as on an easy or regular run.

- *Progression run:* A sustained run at an increasingly fast pace. Progression runs accomplish much of what conventional tempo runs do while also helping you practice increasing your effort as fatigue mounts. They tend to be a little longer than tempo runs because you start at a slower pace.

- *Intervals:* Repeats, usually between 400 meters and one mile long, usually run between mile and 10K race pace. You can do these on a track for precision and a uniform running surface, but you can also do them on roads or elsewhere with good footing. It's okay to roughly convert the distances stated in the training schedules to timed segments off the track, such as running at 5K effort for three minutes if the schedules prescribe 800-meter repeats at 5K pace.

- *Hill workout:* Running at mile effort—not pace!—up a moderately steep hill, and jogging down for recovery. Ideally, the hill will be steep enough to make the climbing noticeable, but not so steep that it's difficult to maintain a good upright running form with quick turnover.

- *Long run:* Your longest run of the week, done at a conversational pace. Start at a gentle effort and gradually increase intensity to that of a regular run as your body warms up. Don't rush it—you've got plenty of time to get in a good rhythm for the second half of the run.

- *Strides:* Short (100 meters or so) bouts of fast running at around mile race pace, usually done either after an easy run or before a hard workout or race. Concentrate on maintaining good running form and staying relaxed while running fast. Strides should feel good and be fun; you'll usually feel better after doing them than you did before. Do strides on a flat, level surface with reliable footing.

Don't Forget the 8K!

You can use the schedules in this chapter to prepare for an 8-kilometer or 5-mile race. (The two are essentially the same race, with five miles being a little more than 50 yards longer than eight kilometers). You don't even have to worry about tweaking the schedules to get ready for an 8K or 5-miler. The range of paces on the harder days will have you just as ready to race these slightly shorter distances.

On race day, the same pacing advice I have for 10Ks works for 8Ks and 5-milers. You could either try to run even pace from the start, or you could go out a little slower than your goal pace and pick it up past the halfway point. An 8K or 5-miler is still long enough that you'll suffer for quite a while in the second half if you start too aggressively.

Most well-trained runners—which will include you if you follow one of this chapter's schedules—can run a few seconds per mile faster for 8K or 5-mile races than they can for 10K. Again, don't get carried away early on. Starting at 10 seconds per mile faster than your 10K pace puts you in 5K pace territory. It's unlikely you can hold that pace for another two miles past the 5K mark.

How to Race a 10K

As with most distances, one good way to race a 10K is to run as even a pace as possible. This is a good approach if your race will be on a uniform course like a track or a flat road race.

Another option I often recommend is to run the first four or so miles at three to five seconds slower than your goal pace, then gradually pick up the pace all the way to the finish, culminating with a sprint.

Notice I said "gradually." Don't suddenly start running 10 seconds per mile faster. The increase in pace should be noticeable, but each incremental increase should feel like something you can hold to the finish.

This approach has a lot going for it. As I often say, you can't win a distance race in the first 400 meters, but you can certainly lose one then. Starting even just a little too fast will detract from your ability to hold goal pace in the second half of the race and will probably keep you from being able to kick in hard from the six-mile mark. Planning to start slower than goal pace keeps you from sabotaging your race in its opening minutes.

Another plus of this strategy is that you'll be passing people over the final two miles. You'll get a confidence boost every time you do so. After you pass one person, pick another a little ahead of you and concentrate on chasing that runner down. This will keep you mentally engaged in the act of racing instead of thinking about how tired you're getting.

I definitely recommend this approach if you're running the first 10K of your life, or even the first of a racing season. You want a good experience that you can build from and that makes you excited to train for the next one. I'm not saying to run overly conservatively in those circumstances. But you don't want to be too aggressive early on, because doing so will almost certainly mean not running what you're capable of that day.

Coogan's Crew: Katrina Coogan

Personal Bests: 15:14 5,000 meters; 31:56 10,000 meters

Career Highlights: Olympic Trials qualifier; 11-time All-American

Years With Coach Coogan: 2016-

Yes, you read that last name correctly.

Katrina is the oldest of my three children, runners all. I now have the privilege of coaching her as part of New Balance Boston. If you've ever coached one of your kids in any sport, you know it can be difficult to balance your roles as parent and coach. I think I get it right most of the time!

One of the great things about having Katrina on our team is how it

Courtesy of Justin Britton.

helps me to be a better coach to everyone else. Like I said in chapter 4, a good training group should feel like a family. We always want to care for each other a lot more as people than as runners. Having a literal member of my family on our team reminds me of this important idea on a daily basis.

In May 2021, Katrina ran her first 10K on the track. Running 31:56 and qualifying for the Olympic Trials in her debut was an awesome accomplishment. There are lessons for all 10K runners in Katrina's race.

Katrina's training leading up to the 10K didn't go well. New Balance Boston was training in Flagstaff, Arizona, that spring to get ready for the late-June Olympic Trials. In the six weeks leading into the meet, she rarely had a good workout because of her allergies and a chronically sore foot. Whenever we did a track workout, Katrina would have a hard time breathing. She was rarely able to finish strongly, and sometimes she even had to cut the workout short. This was not the normal Katrina; she's usually one of the toughest and most consistent people on our team.

So why did Katrina have a good race? Katrina knew that she had started training well in the fall of 2020 and had been working toward this May race for a long time. Instead of dwelling on a few not-great weeks of training, she drew confidence from the work she'd done the previous six months, and even over the prior few years. Not having the perfect preparation going into the 10K allowed her to come to the race relaxed and without added pressure to run super fast. Her attitude was "I can only do my best. Let's see what I can do."

Her training coming into the race also forced her to race slightly conservatively and not run aggressively early on. She stayed patient and stuck to her game plan of running around 32:00 pace. She found the early pace comfortable, and this let her stay composed as fatigue set in and runners ahead of her fell apart.

Katrina worked through her tough patches by staying positive mentally. She told herself that she might feel bad for a lap or two (out of 25), but she would then feel better. She did a good job of running the race one lap at a time, not getting overwhelmed by the distance. Passing runners over the last mile kept her positive and engaged in the race. Her last lap was her fastest of the race.

Katrina's positive attitude, the accumulation of training, and staying engaged throughout the race led her to an excellent first 10K. Sometimes your training will not go as planned, but you can certainly still have a successful race.

Regardless of your pacing strategy, the 10K is a beast mentally. Concentrating for that long when you're running not that much slower than 5K pace is hard! Do what you can in the week before an important 10K to lessen stress in your life so that you start the race mentally fresh.

I often tell my runners "go to sleep" early in a 10K. I don't mean they should daydream or not be fully engaged in the race. I mean that, after the initial scramble off the start line, they should get in a good rhythm. I also mean that, if there are other runners near them, they should settle into a comfortable position rather than fight to be near the front of their group. "Go to sleep" reminds my runners not to be aggressive early on and to save the racing for the second half.

The 10K is the first distance where you might want to take fluids. A small sip or pouring water over your head might not make a ton of difference for dehydration, but it can make you feel better. It's a chance to take a little mental break before bearing back down for the remaining distance.

Consider Cross-Country

I love cross-country races. Some of my favorite and most satisfying experiences as an elite runner were in the U.S. and world cross-country championships. It's such a pure form of racing—times don't really matter, so you're focused on simply getting the best out of yourself on the day. There's also often a team element to cross-country that's lacking in road and track racing.

So as a coach, I'm a big fan of runners committing themselves to cross-country for a season. The training and racing will make you physically and mentally stronger. There are so many examples from running history of world-class runners excelling on the track or roads, from the mile to the marathon, in the same year that they ran a cross-country season.

You can use the schedules in this chapter to prepare for an 8K or 10K cross-country race. The only real adjustment to make is to do some of the interval workouts on grass, ideally on a course with similar ups and downs to what you'll be racing on. I liked to get on grass for workouts in the last few weeks before a big cross-country race. If you're following one of the 6-week schedules, at the least you should do the Tuesday workout in week 3 on grass. If you're following one of the 12-week schedules, try to do the Tuesday workout in weeks 7, 10, and 11 on grass.

Cross-country races often feature a wide start that winnows to a more narrow path in the first half-mile. You could slightly tweak these workouts to better simulate a cross-country race by running the first interval a little faster than you

Courtesy of Justin Britton.

Cross-country training can make you physically and mentally stronger.

would on the track or road. Then do the middle intervals at race-pace effort, and finish with the final interval a little harder. That pattern will get you accustomed to going out hard to get good position, then settling into a good rhythm, and then finishing hard.

Don't get too hung up on precisely measuring these workouts on grass. As we say often during New Balance Boston practices, get the work in. One good way to convert the hard workouts in the schedules for cross-country is to go by time rather than distance. For example, instead of mile repeats at 10K pace, run hard for what you roughly estimate your per-mile pace will be on grass, such as 5:30 or 6:30. Doing workouts like this on grass will have you running fast (and doing recovery jogs) over all sorts of terrain, just like you'll be doing in your cross-country race.

Lessons From Coach Coogan's 10Ks

One of my best races as a pro was a track 10,000 meters. So was one of my worst. Here's how they went, and what you can learn from them.

My first 10,000-meter track race took place on April 23, 1992, at the famous Penn Relays. It was a hot and humid day in Philadelphia, and the race was in the evening. I remember being nervous and confident at the same time, which I see as being in a good place going into a race. I remember going to a movie during the day to stay cool and relaxed, but I don't recall what the movie was.

Among the runners in the race were past or future Olympians Sydney Maree, Rod DeHaven, and Are Nakkim, along with most of the top 10K guys on the East Coast. In the days leading up to the race, I kept telling myself to just relax, stay in lane 1, and cover any gaps that formed. My plan was to get in the front group and not worry if I was third or eighth whatever, as long as I was connected to the lead pack.

The early pace was honest but not too difficult. I knew I had to bide my time. My more-experienced training partners had told me a bad 10K on the track is worse than a bad marathon. If you get the pacing wrong, the 10K can hurt more mentally and physically than most races. (More on that on page 146!) Plus, on the track, there's no hiding if you're having a bad race.

A key thing I knew about Penn Relays was that the finish line comes up extremely quickly when you come off the final turn. You rarely see someone get passed off the last turn of that track. I had mentally prepared myself to go as hard as I could before I hit the last turn. I knew how fast some of the other guys in the race were—Sydney had held the world record for 1,500 meters—and didn't want to have to try to outsprint them in the final lap.

As the race played out, what had been a big lead pack dwindled, as guys let go as they had to slow. I moved past each of them as easily and smoothly as possible. Coming up to one lap to go, Nakkim was in first and I was in second. He was starting to get a step on me, but I was able to stay close, and as we hit the final lap I told myself to hold on and get ready to kick.

As we ran down the back straight, I started to pick up the pace. When I was just about to pass Nakkim, I went into an all-out sprint and jumped him. I went into the turn flying. He had no chance to regroup and catch up to me, especially because of the short straight to the finish line. I ended up winning the race by one second in 28:23, which was a good time in the early '90s for my first 10K.

This debut is a good example of how to run a 10K. I knew I could handle the early pace. I can't remember if people discussed what they were trying to do pace-wise, but most of the runners knew each other and I was comfortable with my decision to just get into the lead group. I was able to catch a groove and not push myself to the limits too early in the race. I was able to stay positive and engaged mentally, telling myself "you're good, Mark," and other simple phrases. I didn't race out in lane 2; I ran the shortest distance possible. When I kicked for the finish line, I did so decisively, aided by my prerace plan of picking a spot to start my final sprint. All in all, a good 10K.

Now, for the not so good.

In the spring of 1998, my agent, Ray Flynn, told me there would probably be a world-record attempt at 10,000 meters at the Hengelo meet in the Netherlands in June, and that I could probably get in the race. At the time, there were few top-level 10Ks on the track in the U.S. I was really excited about the opportunity to be in a fast 10K and lower my personal best, which was still the 28:23 I'd run at Penn six years earlier.

The problem with the Hengelo race was the pace was going to be too fast for me to handle. The great Haile Gebrselassie of Ethiopia wanted to reclaim the world record and was targeting a time of 26:20. I now realize it was good for me to be excited about the opportunity, but that maybe I shouldn't have run the race—all of the focus was on Haile chasing the world record, so if I wanted to meet my goal of breaking 28:00, I'd be mostly on my own. In 1998, however, I jumped at the chance to race it.

I remember sitting in the warm-up area behind the stadium just relaxing before warming up. It was a little hot that day. The meet director told us that, if the track was being watered down soon before our race, the record attempt was on. (Haile liked to have tracks watered down before he raced. I'm not sure whether he thought doing so made the track bouncier or cooled it off.) When we were called to the track and walked into the stadium, I saw a fire truck spraying down the track. I took a deep breath because I knew the record attempt was on.

As for my race, I thought if I was 14:05 at 5K, I'd have a shot at breaking 28:00. There were a few other athletes in the field with the same goal.

The race almost immediately broke into three distinct packs. Haile tucked in behind three pacemakers who were running 62 to 63 seconds per lap—way over my head! I was in the third pack, which was smart, but unfortunately, we let ourselves be affected by Haile's record attempt. Instead of starting out at 67 seconds per lap (roughly 4:30 mile), we ran 64s or 65s for the first 8 to 10 laps. This was too fast—I was basically running my 5K race pace. By 3,000 meters, I was already tired and knew my race was in the tank.

Soon after he passed halfway, Haile lapped me. My early stupidity really started to crush me. I lost all mental fight I had left and dropped out of the race soon after. I sat down in the outside lane and watched Haile run 26:22 to break the world record by five seconds.

Why did I have such a crappy race? A few reasons come to mind.

First, I was overzealous coming into the race. I think my goals were out of reach in those conditions. I should have reevaluated what I could have run as the race approached. Maybe I should have tried to run 28:15 pace and hoped to have a good kick and get close to breaking 28:00. Having a realistic game plan is very important.

Second, I should have found a race where I would be closer to the front (like my debut at the Penn Relays) so that I would stay mentally engaged. It's so easy to go negative in your head when you're getting smoked in a race. The year after Hengelo, I lowered my personal best to 28:19 in a much more tightly grouped race.

Finally, don't drop out of races just because you're not doing well. Doing so sets a bad precedent for the inevitable other tough days.

6-Week 10K Schedule: Up to 45 Miles per Week

	Sunday	Monday	Tuesday	Wednesday	Thursday	Friday	Saturday	Week's mileage
Week 1	Long run: 6-8 miles	Easy run: 3-5 miles, then 6 × 100-meter strides	Intervals: 2-mile warm-up; 3 × 1 mile at 5-10 seconds per mile faster than 10K pace; 400-meter jog between intervals; 1- to 2-mile cool-down	Easy run: 6 miles	Regular run: 3-5 miles, then 6 × 100-meter strides	Tempo run: 2-mile warm-up; 3-4 miles continuous at 25-30 seconds per mile slower than 10K pace; 1- to 2-mile cool-down	Day off	31-38
Week 2	Long run: 7-8 miles	Easy run: 3-5 miles, then 6 × 100-meter strides	Intervals: 2-mile warm-up; 6 × 800 meters at 10-20 seconds per mile faster than 10K pace; 400-meter jog between intervals; 1- to 2-mile cool-down	Easy run: 6 miles	Regular run: 4-5 miles, then 6 × 100-meter strides	Progression run: 2-mile warm-up; 3 miles continuous, starting at 30 seconds per mile slower than 10K pace and increasing pace 5-10 seconds per mile after each mile; 1- to 2-mile cool-down	Easy to regular run: 3-4 miles	36-46
Week 3	Long run: 7-8 miles	Easy run: 3-5 miles, then 6 × 100-meter strides	Intervals: 2-mile warm-up; 2 × 1,200 meters at 10K pace; 2 × 800 meters at 5K pace; 2 × 400 meters at mile pace; 400-meter jog after all intervals; 1- to 2-mile cool-down	Easy run: 6 miles	Regular run: 3-5 miles, then 6 × 100-meter strides	Intervals and tempo run: 2-mile warm-up; 2 × 800 meters at 10K pace with 400-meter jog after each; 2-mile tempo run at 25 seconds per mile slower than 10K pace; 400-meter jog; 2 × 400 meters with 200-meter jog between; 1- to 2-mile cool-down	Easy run: 1-3 miles OR Day off	33-43

	Sunday	Monday	Tuesday	Wednesday	Thursday	Friday	Saturday	Week's mileage
Week 4	Long run: 7-8 miles	Easy run: 3-5 miles, then 6 × 100-meter strides	Intervals: 2-mile warm-up; 8 × 400 meters at 5K pace with 200-meter jog between; 1- to 2-mile cool-down	Easy run: 4-6 miles	Regular run: 3-5 miles, then 6 × 100-meter strides	Tempo run: 2-mile warm-up; 3-4 miles continuous at 25-30 seconds per mile slower than 10K pace (see if you can go a bit faster than 3 weeks ago at the same effort); 1- to 2-mile cool-down	Easy run: 3-4 miles	32-43
Week 5	Long run: 6-8 miles	Easy run: 1-3 miles OR Day off	Intervals: 2-mile warm-up; 6 × 800 meters at 20 seconds per mile faster than 10K pace with 400-meter jog between; 1- to 2-mile cool-down	Easy run: 4-6 miles	Regular run: 3-5 miles, then 6 × 100-meter strides	Race pace work: 2-mile warm-up; 3 × 1 mile at 10K pace with 400-meter jog between; 1- to 2-mile cool-down	Easy run: 2-4 miles	29-40
Week 6	Long run: 6 miles	Easy run: 3 miles	Intervals: 2-mile warm-up; 8 × 400 meters at 5K pace with 200-meter jog between; 1- to 2-mile cool-down	Day off	Easy run: 3 miles, then 6 × 100-meter strides OR Day off	Easy run: 3 miles, then a few 100-meter strides	Race 10K	18-22 (not including race)

6-Week 10K Schedule: 35-55 Miles per Week

	Sunday	Monday	Tuesday	Wednesday	Thursday	Friday	Saturday	Week's mileage
Week 1	Long run: 8-10 miles	Easy run: 4-6 miles, then 6 × 100-meter strides	Intervals: 2-mile warm-up; 3 or 4 × 1 mile at 5-10 seconds per mile faster than 10K pace; 400-meter jog between intervals; 1- to 2-mile cool-down	Easy run: 6-8 miles	Regular run: 5-8 miles, then 8 × 100-meter strides	Tempo run: 2-mile warm-up; 4 miles continuous at 25-30 seconds per mile slower than 10K pace; 1- to 2-mile cool-down	Easy run: 1-4 miles OR Day off	36-53
Week 2	Long run: 8-12 miles	Easy run: 4-6 miles, then 6 × 100-meter strides	Intervals: 2-mile warm-up; 6 × 800 meters at 20 seconds per mile faster than 10K pace; 400-meter jog between intervals; 1- to 2-mile cool-down	Easy run: 6-8 miles	Regular run: 6-8 miles, then 8 × 100-meter strides	Progression run: 2-mile warm-up; 4 miles continuous, starting at 30 seconds per mile slower than 10K pace and increasing pace 5-10 seconds per mile after each mile; 1- to 2-mile cool-down	Easy run: 3-4 miles	41-52
Week 3	Long run: 8-12 miles	Easy run: 4-6 miles, then 6 × 100-meter strides	Intervals: 2-mile warm-up; 1 mile at 10K pace; 800-meter jog; 1,200 meters at 10K pace; 800-meter jog; 800 meters at 5K pace; 400-meter jog; 400 meters at mile pace; 1- to 2-mile cool-down	Easy run: 6-8 miles	Regular run: 5-8 miles, then 8 × 100-meter strides	Intervals and tempo run: 2-mile warm-up; 2 × 800 meters at 10K pace with 400-meter jog after each; 3 miles continuous at 30 seconds per mile slower than 10K pace; 800-meter jog; 2 × 400 meters at 5K pace with 200-meter jog between; 1- to 2-mile cool-down	Easy run: 3-5 miles	41-55

	Sunday	Monday	Tuesday	Wednesday	Thursday	Friday	Saturday	Week's mileage
Week 4	Long run: 8-10 miles	Easy run: 4-6 miles, then 6 × 100-meter strides	Intervals: 2-mile warm-up; 8-10 × 400 meters at 5K race pace with 200-meter jog between; 1- to 2-mile cool-down	Easy run: 6-8 miles	Regular run: 5-8 miles, then 6 × 100-meter strides	Tempo run: 2-mile warm-up; 4-5 miles continuous at 25-30 seconds per mile slower than 10K pace (see if you can go a bit faster than 3 weeks ago at the same effort); 1- to 2-mile cool-down	Easy run: 1-4 miles OR Day off	36-53
Week 5	Long run: 8-9 miles	Easy run: 3-4 miles, then 6 × 100-meter strides	Intervals: 2-mile warm-up; 6 × 800 meters at 5K pace with 400-meter jog between; 1- to 2-mile cool-down	Easy run: 4-6 miles	Regular run: 4-6 miles, then 6 × 100-meter strides	Race pace work: 2-mile warm-up; 3 × 1 mile at 10K pace with 400-meter jog between; 1- to 2-mile cool-down	Easy run: 3-4 miles	36-45
Week 6	Long run: 6-8 miles	Easy run: 4 miles, then 6 × 100-meter strides	Intervals: 2-mile warm-up; 8 × 400 meters at 5K pace with 200-meter jog between; 1- to 2-mile cool-down	Day off	Easy run: 3-4 miles, then 6 × 100-meter strides OR Day off	Easy run: 3 miles, then 6 × 100-meter strides	Race 10K	19-28 (not including race)

6-Week 10K Schedule: 40+ Miles per Week

	Sunday	Monday	Tuesday	Wednesday	Thursday	Friday	Saturday	Week's mileage
Week 1	Long run: 10-14 miles	Easy run: 7-9 miles, then 8 × 100-meter strides	Intervals: 2- to 3-mile warm-up; 4 × 1 mile at 5-10 seconds per mile faster than 10K pace; 400-meter jog between; 1- to 2-mile cool-down	Easy run: 7-10 miles	Regular run: 7-9 miles, then 8 × 100-meter strides	Tempo run: 2- to 3-mile warm-up; 4-6 miles continuous at 25-30 seconds per mile slower than 10K pace; 1- to 2-mile cool-down	Easy run: 4-6 miles	50-69
Week 2	Long run: 10-14 miles	Easy run: 7-9 miles, then 8 × 100-meter strides	Intervals: 2- to 3-mile warm-up; 6 × 800 meters at 20 seconds per mile faster than 10K pace; 400-meter jog between; 1- to 2-mile cool-down	Easy run: 7-10 miles	Regular run: 7-9 miles, then 8 × 100-meter strides	Progression run: 2- to 3-mile warm-up; 4 miles continuous, starting at 30 seconds per mile slower than 10K pace and increasing pace 5-10 seconds per mile after each mile; 1- to 2-mile cool-down	Easy to regular run: 4-6 miles	49-66
Week 3	Long run: 12-15 miles	Easy run: 1-4 miles OR Day off	Intervals: 2- to 3-mile warm-up; mile at 10K pace; 800-meter jog; 1,200 meters at 10K pace; 800-meter jog; 800 meters at 5K pace; 400-meter jog; 400 meters at mile pace; 1- to 2-mile cool-down	Easy run: 6-8 miles	Regular run: 7-9 miles, then 8 × 100-meter strides	Intervals and tempo run: 2- to 3-mile warm-up; 1 mile at 10K pace; 400-meter jog; 3 miles continuous at 25-30 seconds per mile slower than 10K pace; 800-meter jog; 4-6 × 400 meters at 5K pace with 200-meter jog between; 1- to 2-mile cool-down	Easy run: 4-6 miles	44-63

	Sunday	Monday	Tuesday	Wednesday	Thursday	Friday	Saturday	Week's mileage
Week 4	Long run: 10-12 miles	Easy run: 6-8 miles, then 8 × 100-meter strides	Intervals: 2- to 3-mile warm-up; 12 × 400 meters at 5K pace with 200-meter jog between; 1- to 2-mile cool-down	Easy run: 8 miles	Regular run: 7-9 miles, then 8 × 100-meter strides	Tempo run: 2- to 3-mile warm-up; 4-6 miles continuous at 25-30 seconds per mile slower than 10K pace (see if you can go a bit faster than 3 weeks ago at the same effort); 1- to 2-mile cool-down	Easy run: 4-6 miles	45-63
Week 5	Long run: 10-12 miles	Day off (preferred) OR Easy run: 3 miles, then 8 × 100-meter strides	Intervals: 2- to 3-mile warm-up; 6 × 800 meters at 5K pace with 400-meter jog between; 1- to 2-mile cool-down	Easy run: 6-8 miles	Regular run: 6-8 miles, then 6 × 100-meter strides	Race pace work: 2- to 3-mile warm-up; 3 × 1 mile at 10K pace with 400-meter jog between; 1- to 2-mile cool-down	Easy run: 4 miles	40-51
Week 6	Long run: 8 miles	Easy run: 4 miles	Intervals: 2- to 3-mile warm-up; 8 × 400 meters at 5K pace with 200-meter jog between; 1- to 2-mile cool-down	Easy run: 4-6 miles	Easy run: 3-4 miles, then 8 × 100-meter strides OR Day off	Easy run: 3-4 miles, then 4 × 100-meter strides	Race 10K	25-34 (not including race)

**40+ Miles per Week
6-Week 5K Schedule**

12-Week 10K Schedule: Up to 50 Miles per Week

	Sunday	Monday	Tuesday	Wednesday	Thursday	Friday	Saturday	Week's mileage
Week 1	Long run: 6-8 miles	Easy run: 3-5 miles, then 6 × 100-meter strides	Intervals: 2-mile warm-up; 6-8 × 400 meters at 5K pace with a 200-meter jog between; 1- to 2-mile cool-down	Easy run: 6 miles	Regular run: 3-5 miles, then 6 × 100-meter strides	Tempo run: 2-mile warm-up; 3-4 miles continuous at 25-30 seconds per mile slower than 10K pace; 1- to 2-mile cool-down	Day off	29-36
Week 2	Long run: 6-8 miles	Easy run: 3-5 miles, then 6 × 100-meter strides	Hill workout: 2-mile warm-up; 6-8 × 300-meter hill at mile effort; jog down for recovery; 1- to 2-mile cool-down	Easy run: 6 miles	Regular run: 4-5 miles, then 6 × 100-meter strides	Progression run: 2-mile warm-up; 3 miles continuous starting at 35 seconds slower than 10K pace, then increasing pace 5-10 seconds per mile after each mile; 1- to 2-mile cool-down	Easy to regular run: 3-4 miles	34-40
Week 3	Long run: 7-8 miles	Easy run: 3-5 miles, then 6 × 100-meter strides	Intervals: 2-mile warm-up; 4-6 × 800 meters at 5K pace with a 400-meter jog between; 1- to 2-mile cool-down	Easy run: 6 miles	Regular run: 4-5 miles, then 6 × 100-meter strides	Tempo work: 2-mile warm-up; 3 × 1.5 miles at 20-30 seconds slower per 1.5-mile segment than 10K pace; 800-meter jog after each; 1- to 2-mile cool-down	Easy to regular run: 2-4 miles OR Day off	35-46
Week 4	Long run: 7-8 miles	Easy run: 3-5 miles, then 6 × 100-meter strides	Hill workout: 2-mile warm-up; 6-8 × 400-meter hill at mile effort; jog down for recovery; 1- to 2-mile cool-down	Easy run: 6 miles	Regular run: 3-5 miles, then 6 × 100-meter strides	Tempo run: 2-mile warm-up; 3-5 miles continuous at 25-30 seconds per mile slower than 10K pace; 1- to 2-mile cool-down	Easy to regular run: 1-4 miles OR Day off	32-48

	Sunday	Monday	Tuesday	Wednesday	Thursday	Friday	Saturday	Week's mileage
Week 5	Long run: 8-10 miles	Easy run: 3-5 miles, then 6 × 100-meter strides	Intervals: 2-mile warm-up; 2 sets of 4 × 400 meters at 5K pace; 200-meter jog between intervals and 400-meter jog between sets; 1- to 2-mile cool-down	Easy run: 6 miles	Regular run: 4-5 miles, then 6 × 100-meter strides	Progression run: 2-mile warm-up; 3 miles continuous starting at 30 seconds slower than 10K pace, then increasing pace 5-10 seconds per mile after each mile; 1- to 2-mile cool-down	Easy to regular run: 2-3 miles OR Day off	33-43
Week 6	Long run: 8-10 miles	Easy run: 3-5 miles, then 8 × 100-meter strides	Intervals: 2-mile warm-up; 6 × 800 meters at 5K pace with a 400-meter jog between; 1- to 2-mile cool-down	Easy run: 4-6 miles	Regular run: 4-6 miles, then 6 × 100-meter strides	Tempo work: 2-mile warm-up; 2 miles continuous at 25-30 second per mile slower than 10K pace; 800-meter jog; 2 miles continuous at 25-30 seconds per mile slower than 10K pace; 800-meter jog; 800 meters at 10K pace; 1- to 2-mile cool-down	Easy to regular run: 2-4 miles OR Day off	35-49
Week 7	Long run: 8-10 miles	Easy run: 3-5 miles, then 6 × 100-meter strides	Intervals: 2-mile warm-up; 4 × 1 mile at 10K pace with 400-meter jog between; 1- to 2-mile cool-down	Easy run: 4-6 miles	Regular run: 4-6 miles, then 6 × 100-meter strides	Tempo run: 2-mile warm-up; 3-5 miles continuous at 25-30 seconds per mile slower than 10K pace; 1- to 2-mile cool-down	Easy to regular run: 2-4 miles	35-49

(continued)

12-Week 10K Schedule: Up to 50 Miles per Week (continued)

	Sunday	Monday	Tuesday	Wednesday	Thursday	Friday	Saturday	Week's mileage
Week 8	Long run: 6-8 miles	Easy run: 3-5 miles, then 6 × 100-meter strides	Hill workout: 2-mile warm-up; 8 × 300-meter hill; jog down for recovery; 1- to 2-mile cool-down	Easy run: 3-5 miles	Regular run: 3-5 miles, then 6 × 100-meter strides	Tempo work: 2-mile warm-up; 1 mile at 10K pace; 800-meter jog; 2 miles continuous at 25-30 seconds slower than 10K pace; 800-meter jog; 2 × 400 meters at 5K pace; 200-meter jog between 400s; 1- to 2-mile cool-down	Easy to regular run: 1-4 miles OR Day off	28-42
Week 9	Long run: 8-10 miles	Easy run: 3-5 miles, then 6 × 100-meter strides	Intervals: 2-mile warm-up; 2 sets of 4 × 400 meters at 5K pace with a 200-meter jog between intervals and 400-meter jog between sets; 1- to 2-mile cool-down	Easy run: 4-6 miles	Regular run: 4-6 miles, then 6 × 100-meter strides	If racing tomorrow: Easy run: 2-4 miles OR If not racing tomorrow: Pace work: 2-mile warm-up; 3 miles continuous at 10K pace; 1- to 2-mile cool-down	5K-8K race OR Easy to regular run: 3-4 miles	31-47
Week 10	Long run: 8-10 miles	Easy run: 3-5 miles, then 6 × 100-meter strides	Intervals: 2-mile warm-up; 400 meters at mile pace; 800 meters at 5K pace; 2 × 1,200 meters at 10K pace; 800 meters at 5K pace; 400 meters at mile pace; 400-meter jog between all repeats; 1- to 2-mile cool-down	Easy run: 4-6 miles	Regular run: 4-6 miles, then 6 × 100-meter strides	Tempo run: 2-mile warm-up; 3-4 miles continuous at 20-30 seconds per mile slower than 10K pace; 800-meter jog; 2 × 400 meters at 5K pace with a 200-meter jog between; 1- to 2-mile cool-down	Easy to regular run: 2-4 miles	37-51

	Sunday	Monday	Tuesday	Wednesday	Thursday	Friday	Saturday	Week's mileage
Week 11	Long run: 4-7 miles	Easy run: 3-5 miles, then 6 × 100-meter strides	Intervals: 2-mile warm-up; 3 × 1 mile at 5-10 seconds faster than 10K pace with 400-meter jog between; 1- to 2-mile cool-down	Easy run: 4-6 miles	Regular run: 4-6 miles, then 6 × 100-meter strides	Tempo work: 2-mile warm-up; 2 × 400 meters at 5K pace; 200-meter jog between; 2 miles continuous at 10K pace; 800-meter jog; 4 × 400 meters at 5K pace; 200-meter jog between; 1- to 2-mile cool-down	Easy to regular run: 1-4 miles OR Day off	29-44
Week 12	Long run: 4-6 miles	Easy run: 3-4 miles, then 6 × 100-meter strides	Intervals: 2-mile warm-up; 4-6 × 400 meters at 5K pace with a 200-meter jog between; 1- to 2-mile cool-down	Easy run: 3-4 miles	Easy run: 2-3 miles, then 6 × 100-meter strides	Easy run: 2-3 miles, then 6 × 100-meter strides	Race 10K	16-24 (not including race)

12-Week 10K Schedule: 35 to 60 Miles per Week

	Sunday	Monday	Tuesday	Wednesday	Thursday	Friday	Saturday	Week's mileage
Week 1	Long run: 7-10 miles	Easy run: 4-6 miles, then 6 × 100-meter strides	Intervals: 2-mile warm-up; 6-8 × 400 meters at 5K pace with a 200-meter jog between; 1- to 2-mile cool-down	Easy run: 6-8 miles	Regular run: 5-8 miles, then 6 × 100-meter strides	Tempo run: 2-mile warm-up; 3-4 miles continuous at 25-30 seconds per mile slower than 10K pace; 1- to 2-mile cool-down	Easy run: 2-4 miles	35-52
Week 2	Long run: 7-10 miles	Easy run: 4-6 miles, then 6 × 100-meter strides	Hill workout: 2-mile warm-up; 6-8 × 300-meter hill at mile effort; jog down for recovery; 1- to 2-mile cool-down	Easy run: 6-8 miles	Regular run: 5-8 miles, then 6 × 100-meter strides	Progression run: 2-mile warm-up; 3-5 miles continuous starting at 35 seconds slower than 10K pace, increasing pace 5-10 seconds per mile after each mile; 1- to 2-mile cool-down	Easy to regular run: 3-4 miles	36-53
Week 3	Long run: 8-10 miles	Easy run: 4-6 miles, then 6 × 100-meter strides	Intervals: 2-mile warm-up; 5-6 × 800 meters at 5K pace with a 400-meter jog between; 1- to 2-mile cool-down	Easy run: 6-8 miles	Regular run: 6-8 miles, then 6 × 100-meter strides	Tempo work: 2-mile warm-up; 3 × 1.5 miles at 20-30 seconds slower per 1.5-mile segment than 10K pace; 800-meter jog after each; 1- to 2-mile cool-down	Easy to regular run: 3-4 miles	42-55
Week 4	Long run: 8-10 miles	Easy run: 4-6 miles, then 6 × 100-meter strides	Hill workout: 2-mile warm-up; 8 × 400-meter hill at mile effort; jog down for recovery; 1- to 2-mile cool-down	Easy run: 5-6 miles	Regular run: 5-7 miles, then 6 × 100-meter strides	Tempo run: 2-mile warm-up; 4-5 miles continuous at 25-30 seconds per mile slower than 10K pace; 1- to 2-mile cool-down	Easy to regular run: 1-6 miles OR Day off	38-53

	Sunday	Monday	Tuesday	Wednesday	Thursday	Friday	Saturday	Week's mileage
Week 5	Long run: 8-12 miles	Easy run: 4-6 miles, then 6 × 100-meter strides	Intervals: 2-mile warm-up; 2-3 sets of 4 × 400 meters at 5K pace; 200-meter jog between intervals and 400-meter jog between sets; 1- to 2-mile cool-down	Easy run: 6-8 miles	Regular run: 5-8 miles, then 6 × 100-meter strides	Progression run: 2-mile warm-up; 4-5 miles continuous starting at 35 seconds slower than 10K pace, increasing pace 5-10 seconds per mile after each mile; 1- to 2-mile cool-down	Easy to regular run: 3-4 miles	39-55
Week 6	Long run: 8-12 miles	Easy run: 4-6 miles, then 8 × 100-meter strides	Intervals: 2-mile warm-up; 6 × 800 meters at 5K pace with a 400-meter jog between; 1- to 2-mile cool-down	Easy run: 6-8 miles	Regular run: 5-7 miles, then 6 × 100-meter strides	Tempo work: 2-mile warm-up; 2 miles continuous at 25-30 seconds per mile slower than 10K pace; 800-meter jog; 2 miles continuous at 25-30 second per mile slower than 10K pace; 800-meter jog; 800 meters at 10K pace; 1- to 2-mile cool-down	Easy to regular run: 3-4 miles	43-59
Week 7	Long run: 10-12 miles	Easy run: 4-6 miles, then 6 × 100-meter strides	Intervals: 2-mile warm-up; 4-5 × 1 mile at 10K pace with 400-meter jog between; 1- to 2-mile cool-down	Easy run: 6-8 miles	Regular run: 6-8 miles, then 6 × 100-meter strides	Tempo run: 2-mile warm-up; 4-6 miles continuous at 25-30 seconds per mile slower than 10K pace; 1- to 2-mile cool-down	Easy to regular run: 3-4 miles	44-57

(continued)

12-Week 10K Schedule: 35 to 60 Miles per Week (continued)

	Sunday	Monday	Tuesday	Wednesday	Thursday	Friday	Saturday	Week's mileage
Week 8	Long run: 8-10 miles	Easy run: 4-6 miles, then 6 × 100-meter strides	Hill workout: 2-mile warm-up; 8 × 300-meter hill at mile effort; jog down for recovery; 1- to 2-mile cool-down	Easy run: 4-6 miles	Regular run: 3-5 miles, then 6 × 100-meter strides	Tempo work: 2-mile warm-up; 1 mile at 10K pace; 800-meter jog; 2 miles continuous at 25-30 seconds slower than 10K pace; 800-meter jog; 4 × 400 meters at 5K pace; 200-meter jog between 400s; 1- to 2-mile cool-down	Easy to regular run: 1-4 miles OR Day off	36-50
Week 9	Long run: 10-12 miles	Easy run: 4-6 miles, then 6 × 100-meter strides	Intervals: 2-mile warm-up; 3 sets of 4 × 400 meters at 5K pace; 200-meter jog between intervals and 400-meter jog between sets; 1- to 2-mile cool-down	Easy run: 6-8 miles	Regular run: 6-8 miles, then 6 × 100-meter strides	If racing tomorrow: Easy run: 2-4 miles OR If not racing tomorrow: Pace work: 2-mile warm-up; 3 miles continuous at 10K pace; 1- to 2-mile cool-down	5K-8K race OR Easy to regular run: 3-5 miles	40-57
Week 10	Long run: 10-12 miles	Easy run: 4-6 miles, then 6 × 100-meter strides	Interval ladder: 2-mile warm-up; 400 meters at mile pace; 800 meters at 5K pace; 1,200 meters at 5K pace; 1,600 meters at 10K pace; 1,200 meters at 10K pace; 800 meters at 10K pace; 400 meters at 5K pace; mile pace; 400-meter jog between all intervals; 1- to 2-mile cool-down	Easy run: 5-7 miles	Regular run: 5-7 miles, then 6 × 100-meter strides	Tempo run: 2-mile warm-up; 3-4 miles continuous at 20-30 seconds per mile slower than 10K pace; 800-meter jog; 4 × 400 meters at 5K pace with 200-meter jog between; 1- to 2-mile cool-down	Easy to regular run: 3-4 miles	42-53

	Sunday	Monday	Tuesday	Wednesday	Thursday	Friday	Saturday	Week's mileage
Week 11	Long run: 7-10 miles	Easy run: 4-6 miles, then 6 × 100-meter strides	Intervals: 2-mile warm-up; 3-4 × 1 mile at 5-10 seconds faster than 10K pace with 400-meter jog between; 1- to 2-mile cool-down	Easy run: 4-6 miles	Regular run: 4-6 miles, then 6 × 100-meter strides	Pace work: 2-mile warm-up; 2 × 800 meters at 5K pace; 400-meter jog after both; 2 miles continuous at 10K pace; 4 × 400 meters at 5K pace; 200-meter jog between; 1- to 2-mile cool-down	Easy to regular run: 1-4 miles OR Day off	34-50
Week 12	Long run: 6-8 miles	Easy run: 4-5 miles, then 6 × 100-meter strides	Intervals: 2-mile warm-up; 6-8 × 400 meters at 5K pace with a 200-meter jog between; 1- to 2-mile cool-down	Easy run: 3-5 miles	Easy run: 3-4 miles, then 6 × 100-meter strides	Easy run: 2-4 miles, then 6 × 100-meter strides	Race 10K	22-30 (not including race)

12-Week 10K Schedule: 40+ Miles per Week

	Sunday	Monday	Tuesday	Wednesday	Thursday	Friday	Saturday	Week's mileage
Week 1	Long run: 8-12 miles	Easy run: 6-8 miles, then 8 × 100-meter strides	Intervals: 2- to 3-mile warm-up; 8 × 400 meters at 5K pace with a 200-meter jog between; 1- to 2-mile cool-down	Easy run: 7-9 miles	Regular run: 6-9 miles, then 8 × 100-meter strides	Tempo run: 2- to 3-mile warm-up; 3-4 miles continuous at 25-30 seconds per mile slower than 10K pace; 1- to 2-mile cool-down	Easy run: 4-6 miles	43-61
Week 2	Long run: 8-12 miles	Easy run: 6-8 miles, then 8 × 100-meter strides	Hill workout: 2- to 3-mile warm-up; 8 × 300-meter hill at mile effort; jog down for recovery; 1- to 2-mile cool-down	Easy run: 7-9 miles	Regular run: 6-9 miles, then 8 × 100-meter strides	Progression run: 2- to 3-mile warm-up; 4-5 miles continuous starting at 35 seconds slower than 10K pace, increasing pace 5-10 seconds per mile after each mile; 1- to 2-mile cool-down	Easy to regular run: 4-6 miles	44-61
Week 3	Long run: 8-12 miles	Easy run: 6-8 miles, then 8 × 100-meter strides	Intervals: 2- to 3-mile warm-up; 6 × 800 meters at 5K pace with a 400-meter jog between; 1- to 2-mile cool-down	Easy run: 7-10 miles	Regular run: 6-9 miles, then 8 × 100-meter strides	Tempo work: 2- to 3-mile warm-up; 3 × 2 miles at 20-30 seconds slower per 2-mile segment than 10K pace; 800-meter jog between; 1- to 2-mile cool-down	Easy to regular run: 4-6 miles	49-67
Week 4	Long run: 8-12 miles	Easy run: 6-8 miles, then 6 × 100-meter strides	Hill workout: 2- to 3-mile warm-up; 8 × 400-meter hill at mile effort; jog down for recovery; 1- to 2-mile cool-down	Easy run: 7-10 miles	Regular run: 6-9 miles, then 6 × 100-meter strides	Tempo run: 2- to 3-mile warm-up; 5-6 miles continuous at 25-30 seconds per mile slower than 10K pace; 1- to 2-mile cool-down	Easy to regular run: 1-6 miles OR Day off	42-65

	Sunday	Monday	Tuesday	Wednesday	Thursday	Friday	Saturday	Week's mileage
Week 5	Long run: 10-14 miles	Easy run: 6-8 miles, then 8 × 100-meter strides	Intervals: 2- to 3-mile warm-up; 3 sets of 4 × 400 meters at 5K pace; 200-meter jog between intervals and 400-meter jog between sets; 1- to 2-mile cool-down	Easy run: 7-10 miles	Regular run: 6-9 miles, then 8 × 100-meter strides	Progression run: 2- to 3-mile warm-up; 4-6 miles continuous starting at 35 seconds slower than 10K pace, increasing pace 5-10 seconds per mile after each mile; 1- to 2-mile cool-down	Easy to regular run: 4-6 miles	47-67
Week 6	Long run: 10-14 miles	Easy run: 6-8 miles, then 8 × 100-meter strides	Intervals: 2- to 3-mile warm-up; 6-8 × 800 meters at 5K pace with a 400-meter jog between; 1- to 2-mile cool-down Note: If doing 8 repeats, break into two sets of 4, with an 800-meter jog between sets.	Easy run: 7-10 miles	Regular run: 6-9 miles, then 8 × 100-meter strides	Tempo work: 2- to 3-mile warm-up; 3 miles continuous at 25-30 seconds per mile slower than 10K pace; 800-meter jog; 2 miles continuous at 25-30 seconds slower than 10K pace; 800-meter jog; 1 mile at 10K pace; 1- to 2-mile cool-down	Easy to regular run: 4-6 miles	50-69
Week 7	Long run: 10-14 miles	Easy run: 6-8 miles, then 8 × 100-meter strides	Intervals: 2- to 3-mile warm-up; 5 × 1 mile at 10K pace with a 400-meter jog between; 1- to 2-mile cool-down	Easy run: 7-10 miles	Regular run: 6-9 miles, then 8 × 100-meter strides	Tempo run: 2- to 3-mile warm-up; 5-6 miles continuous at 25-30 seconds per mile slower than 10K pace; 1- to 2-mile cool-down	Easy to regular run: 4-6 miles	50-69

(continued)

12-Week 10K Schedule: 40+ Miles per Week (continued)

	Sunday	Monday	Tuesday	Wednesday	Thursday	Friday	Saturday	Week's mileage
Week 8	Long run: 8-12 miles	Easy run: 5-7 miles, then 8 × 100-meter strides	Hill workout: 2- to 3-mile warm-up; 8 × 300-meter hill at mile effort; jog down for recovery; 1- to 2-mile cool-down	Easy run: 6-8 miles	Regular run: 5-7 miles, then 8 × 100-meter strides	Tempo work: 2- to 3-mile warm-up; 1 mile at 10K pace; 800-meter jog; 3 miles continuous at 25-30 seconds slower than 10K pace; 800-meter jog; 4 × 400 meters at 5K pace; 200-meter jog between 400s; 1- to 2-mile cool-down	Easy to regular run: 1-6 miles OR Day off	42-62
Week 9	Long run: 12-14 miles	Easy run: 6-8 miles, then 8 × 100-meter strides	Intervals: 2- to 3-mile warm-up; 3 sets of 4 × 400 meters at 5K pace; 200-meter jog between intervals and 400-meter jog between sets; 1- to 2-mile cool-down	Easy run: 7-10 miles	Regular run: 6-9 miles, then 8 × 100-meter strides	If racing tomorrow: Easy run: 3-4 miles OR If not racing tomorrow: Pace work: 2- to 3-mile warm-up; 3 miles continuous at 10K pace; 1- to 2-mile cool-down	5K-8K race OR Easy to regular run: 4-6 miles	43-65
Week 10	Long run: 12-14 miles	Easy run: 6-8 miles, then 8 × 100-meter strides	Interval ladder: 2- to 3-mile warm-up; 400 meters at mile pace; 800 meters at 5K pace; 1,200 meters at 10K pace; 1,600 meters, at 10K pace; 1,200 meters at 10K pace; 800 meters at 5K pace; 400 meters at mile pace; 400-meter jog between all repeats; 1- to 2-mile cool-down	Easy run: 7-10 miles	Regular run: 6-9 miles, then 8 × 100-meter strides	Tempo run: 2- to 3-mile warm-up; 3-4 miles continuous at 20-30 seconds slower than 10K pace; 800-meter jog; 4 × 400 meters at 5K pace with 200-meter jog between; 1- to 2-mile cool-down	Easy to regular run: 4-6 miles	51-67

	Sunday	Monday	Tuesday	Wednesday	Thursday	Friday	Saturday	Week's mileage
Week 11	Long run: 8-12 miles	Easy run: 5-7 miles, then 8 × 100-meter strides	Intervals: 2- to 3-mile warm-up; 4 × 1 mile at 5-10 seconds faster than 10K pace with a 400-meter jog between; 1- to 2-mile cool-down	Easy run: 6-8 miles	Regular run: 5-7 miles, then 8 × 100-meter strides	Tempo work: 2- to 3-mile warm-up; 2 × 800 meters at 5K pace; 400-meter jog after each; 2 miles continuous at 10K pace; 800-meter jog; 4 × 400 meters at 5K pace; 200-meter jog between 400s; 1- to 2-mile cool-down	Easy to regular run: 1-6 miles OR Day off	41-59
Week 12	Long run: 8 miles	Easy run: 4-6 miles, then 8 × 100-meter strides	Intervals: 2- to 3-mile warm-up; 8 × 400 meters at 5K pace with a 200-meter jog between; 1- to 2-mile cool-down	Easy run: 4-6 miles	Easy run: 3-4 miles, then 6 × 100-meter strides	Easy run: 3-4 miles, then 6 × 100-meter strides	Race 10K	28-36 (not including race)

11

Training for and Racing the 15K to Half-Marathon

This chapter will prepare you to race events between 15 kilometers (9.3 miles) and the half-marathon (13.1 miles, 21.1 kilometers). Ten-milers and 20Ks are the other popular distances in this range.

Focusing on one of these races can be extremely satisfying. If you've mostly been a 5K or 10K runner but want to do a marathon, they're a great stepping-stone to racing 26.2 miles. You'll learn how you handle higher mileage and longer races without jumping immediately to the marathon. A lot of runners will benefit from targeting a 15K to half-marathon in one season before moving up to the marathon the following season.

Of course, you're not obligated to run marathons. Many pros find their sweet spot in the 15K to half-marathon range. These are great distances if you enjoy tempo runs and long runs more than shorter, faster workouts. The races are long enough to merit significant dedication, but not so long that they'll take over your life, which is how it may feel when you're training for a marathon.

This chapter has six schedules, three that are 12 weeks long and three that are 16 weeks long. The weekly mileage ranges for the 12-week schedules are up to 60, 35 to 70, and 45 or more. The weekly mileage ranges for the 16-week schedules are up to 60, 35 to 70, and 35 or more. As I said in chapter 7, there are many variables to consider when deciding which schedule to follow. Refer there for more details.

A Brief Guide to Following the Schedules

Each day's training in the schedules is described using the main types of runs I described at length in chapter 7. You'll want to refresh your memory occasionally by rereading those descriptions during your buildup. For quick reference, here are the types of runs you'll encounter in these schedules, and what I mean by each.

- *Easy run:* Done the day after your longest and hardest runs. Don't worry about pace. Just run at a comfortable, conversational effort level—no hard breathing, no bearing down. You should finish feeling energized for the next day's training.

- *Regular run:* A little faster and more effortful than an easy run, but still at a conversational pace. These are what you might think of as your getting-in-the-miles runs. It's okay to push things a little in the last few miles if you're feeling good.

- *Easy to regular run:* Start these runs as if they're a recovery run. If you're tired and want to stay at that gentle effort level for the whole run, that's fine. If you feel like going a little harder once you're warmed up, that's fine. But don't force yourself to go faster just because you think you "should" hit a certain pace.

- *Tempo run:* A sustained run at a "comfortably hard" effort level that requires concentration. In these schedules, you'll do some tempo runs at half-marathon pace and some at marathon pace. The shorter tempos tend to be at half-marathon pace. To gauge the right effort for those tempo runs, imagine I were riding a bike alongside and asked you a question. You should be able to answer in a complete sentence, but you shouldn't be able to carry on an in-depth conversation as on an easy or regular run. For marathon-pace runs, you should be even more able to speak in complete sentences, but it's likely that toward the end of them you'll need to concentrate a bit to do so.

- *Progression run:* A sustained run at an increasingly fast pace. Progression runs accomplish much of what conventional tempo runs do while also helping you practice increasing your effort as fatigue mounts. They tend to be a little longer than tempo runs because you start at a slower pace.

- *Intervals:* Repeats, usually between 400 meters and one mile long, usually run between mile and 10K race pace. You can do these on a track for precision and a uniform running surface, but you can also do them on roads or elsewhere with good footing. It's okay to roughly convert the distances stated in the training schedules to timed segments off the track, such as running at 5K effort for three minutes if the schedules prescribe 800-meter repeats at 5K pace.

- *Hill workout:* Running at 5K effort—not pace!—up a moderately steep hill, and jogging down for recovery. Ideally, the hill will be steep enough to make the climbing noticeable, but not so steep that it's difficult to maintain a good upright running form with quick turnover.

- *Long run:* Your longest run of the week, done at a conversational pace. Start at a gentle effort and gradually increase intensity to that of a regular run as your body warms up. Don't rush it—you've got plenty of time to get in a good rhythm for the second half of the run.

- *Strides:* Short (100 meters or so) bouts of fast running at around mile race pace, usually done either after an easy run or before a hard workout or race. Concentrate on maintaining good running form and staying relaxed while running fast. Strides should feel good and be fun; you'll usually feel better after doing them than you did before. Do strides on a flat, level surface with reliable footing.

How to Race the 15K to Half-Marathon

These races call for just the right combination of patience and aggression. Your pace probably won't be vastly different between a 15K and a half-marathon, but those few to several seconds per mile are key. A half-marathon is about 40 percent longer than a 15K. If you start a 20K or half-marathon at your 15K or 10-mile race pace, you'll pay that time back and then some as you slow in the second half. If you run the first half of a 15K or 10-miler at something like your 20K or half-marathon pace, you might find it difficult to make up the time in the final miles. That's a more enjoyable experience than going out too fast in a half-marathon and then having to slow, but still. You trained for these longer races to do your best at them, and they're not like a 5K where you can try again the following week if you're unsatisfied.

I usually tried to run 15Ks like a controlled 10K. I would start five to seven seconds slower per mile than 10K pace and work hard to hold that to the end. I would never take that approach in a half-marathon. From the many tempo runs you'll do at half-marathon pace in your buildup, you should have a good feel for what's possible at 20K or the half-marathon.

If you get your early pacing right, one of the biggest challenges in these races is mental. In the middle portion you really need to concentrate to keep from slowing. It's not so much that your breathing will suddenly get more rapid, signaling that you need to bear down. You can kind of fall asleep mentally around, say, mile eight of a half-marathon or mile six of a 10-miler. Even though your effort feels the same, your mile splits can fall off by 10 seconds or more. In these stretches, try to recall how you concentrated toward the end of your tempo runs in training. Once you get past this middle stage and you have only two or three miles to go, the distance will get physically difficult enough that it will focus your attention.

Depletion starts to be a factor in these races. Depending on the weather, you might need to take in a small amount of fluids at every opportunity. Don't be stubborn and think, "It's just 10 miles; I can do this without any help." Especially in a 20K or half-marathon, have a plan for getting in some carbohydrates, either in a drink or via a gel, before halfway. The carbs help preserve the stores you'll need to call on in the last few miles to maintain a strong pace. Consuming carbs between five kilometers and five miles is early enough in the race that your stomach shouldn't get upset.

These races are also long enough that you'll want to do all the little things right. Much more so than in a 5K, make sure your socks are on correctly, your shoes are secured but not tied too tightly, and that your racing outfit isn't going to chafe you. If it's a cooler day, base what to race in on what's appropriate after a few miles, when you're fully warmed up and generating a lot of heat.

Lessons From Coach Coogan's 15Ks and Half-Marathons

On Labor Day in 1997, I finished 11th in the New Haven 20K. I was hoping to do better—the race was the U.S. championship—but I didn't listen to my own advice leading into this fairly big race. My mistake was planning too many other activities leading into the race. This is the opposite of what I preach to my team—to reduce their outside activities in the week before a big race.

When I lived in Boulder, I became good friends with Bobby Beathard, who at the time was the general manager of the San Diego Chargers. Bobby is a big fan of running and was an avid road racer back then. For opening day of the NFL season that year, the Chargers were in Foxboro, Massachusetts, where the New England Patriots would be raising the AFC Championship flag. I wanted to go to the game with my best friends from high school. I surprised them with sideline passes that Bobby got for me. I was in the locker room before the game and sat on the end of the Chargers' bench during the game.

The only problem was that it was extremely hot and humid, and early the next morning I was running the 20K. If you're running a big race, you should try to take it easy the day before, not use all your energy up by tailgating and baking in the sun for four hours. I didn't even drive to New Haven for the race until the next morning, whereas my smarter competitors spent the night before the race close to the start.

When the race started, my legs were heavy and stiff. I just never felt good or comfortable the entire race. I was dehydrated from the Patriots game and lacked sleep. I finished more than a minute behind the top American, Brian Clas, and was beaten soundly by guys I usually beat.

The main lesson to take from this story is that you should try to prioritize your running in the few days going into a race. Try not to add any new stressors to your life, even if they're fun and enjoyable. These extracurricular activities will affect your performance.

On the other hand, the New Haven 20K wasn't a goal race for me that year. I was running it as part of my buildup for the New York City Marathon, but that race was still two months away. Plus, I knew I had the Philadelphia Distance Run three weeks later. I wound up setting my half-marathon PR in that race.

I made the choice to be with my best friends, and I'm extremely happy I put them first on this day. These many years later, I barely remember the race, but I do remember all the laughs and good times I had at the Patriots game. You're always going to have to balance being a runner with having fun in the rest of your life.

One of my best races in this range of distances was in March 1995. My main goal that spring was the Pan American Games Marathon, to be held on March 25. The Gate River Run 15K in Jacksonville, Florida, was always one of my favorite races as a pro. That year, with it falling on March 11, it served as my final really hard effort before the marathon. I was coming off my last big week of training and wasn't completely sure how I was going to feel once the race started.

The race was the U.S. championship and had a large prize money purse, so all the top Americans were there. Olympian Todd Williams told me before the race that he was going to go out hard and chase the American record. I knew it was best to let Todd go immediately. (Good decision! He won in 42:22, which is still the American record.) My strategy was to hide in the chase pack until it was time to try to outkick everyone for second place and the $5,000 runner-up check.

Sure enough, as soon as the race started, Todd just took off. I settled into the pace I thought I could handle. I still remember how easy the pace felt that day. My preparation for the marathon had been going really well. I was mostly unsure how my legs would feel when it was time to dash for the cash.

During the race, I used a lot of positive self-talk. I kept telling myself, "You're good; just sit here." I was able to get some water, take a few sips, cool myself off, and maintain my groove. It's always a good feeling to get some fluids in without it bugging you. I just kept hanging in there until in the last mile, when I moved closer to the front of the chase pack.

On my prerace warm-up, I picked a spot on the road near the finish and told myself from there I'd kick as hard as I could. We came around a corner and I saw the spot. I did as planned, and it worked! I outsprinted everyone around me and finished second in a personal best of 43:47.

I was extremely happy how the race turned out, and it gave me great confidence leading into the marathon two weeks later, where I won the silver medal. Use tune-up races to gain confidence for your big races later in the season or during a buildup for a longer race.

12-Week 15K–Half-Marathon Schedule: Up to 60 Miles per Week

	Sunday	Monday	Tuesday	Wednesday	Thursday	Friday	Saturday	Week's mileage
Week 1	Long run: 7-9 miles	Easy run: 4-8 miles, then 8 × 100-meter strides	Tempo run: 2-mile warm-up; 4 miles continuous at half-marathon pace; 1-mile cool-down	Easy run: 7-8 miles	Regular run: 5-7 miles, then 8 × 100-meter strides	Intervals: 2-mile warm-up; 8 × 400 meters at 10K pace with 200-meter jog between; 1-mile cool-down	Easy run: 1-4 miles OR Day off	36-49
Week 2	Long run: 8-10 miles	Easy run: 4-8 miles, then 8 × 100-meter strides	Progression run: 2-mile warm-up; 4 miles continuous, starting at 35 seconds per mile slower than 10K pace, increasing pace 5-10 seconds per mile after each mile; 1-mile cool-down	Easy run: 7-8 miles	Regular run: 5-7 miles, then 8 × 100-meter strides	Hills: 2-mile warm-up; 8 × 400-meter hill at 5K effort; jog down for recovery; 1-mile cool-down	Easy to regular run: 1-4 miles OR Day off	38-51
Week 3	Long run: 8-12 miles	Easy run: 4-8 miles, then 8 × 100-meter strides	Tempo intervals: 2-mile warm-up; 4 × 1 mile at 10K pace with 800-meter jog between; 1-mile cool-down	Easy run: 7-8 miles	Regular run: 5-8 miles, then 8 × 100-meter strides	Intervals: 2-mile warm-up; 8 × 400 meters at 10K pace with 200-meter jog between; 1-mile cool-down	Easy to regular run: 1-4 miles OR Day off	38-54

	Sunday	Monday	Tuesday	Wednesday	Thursday	Friday	Saturday	Week's mileage
Week 4	Long run: 10-14 miles	Easy run: 4-8 miles, then 8 × 100-meter strides	Tempo run: 2-mile warm-up; 4-5 miles continuous at half-marathon pace; 1-mile cool-down	Easy run: 7-8 miles	Regular run: 5-8 miles, then 8 × 100-meter strides	Hills: 2-mile warm-up; 8 × 400-meter hill at 5K effort; jog down for recovery; 1-mile cool-down	Easy to regular run: 1-4 miles OR Day off	40-57
Week 5	Long run: 10-14 miles	Easy run: 4-8 miles, then 8 × 100-meter strides	Progression run: 2-mile warm-up; 4-6 miles continuous starting at marathon pace and increasing pace 3-5 seconds per mile after each mile; 1-mile cool-down	Easy run: 7-8 miles	Regular run: 5-8 miles, then 8 × 100-meter strides	Intervals: 2-mile warm-up; 1 mile at 10K pace; 1 mile at marathon pace; 1,200 meters at 10K pace; 1 mile at marathon pace; 800 meters at 5K pace; 1 mile at marathon pace; 400 meters at mile pace; 200-meter jog between all intervals; 1-mile cool-down	Easy to regular run: 1-4 miles OR Day off	42-60
Week 6	Long run: 10-14 miles	Easy run: 4-8 miles, then 8 × 100-meter strides	Tempo run: 2-mile warm-up; 5-6 miles continuous, starting a little slower than and working into half-marathon pace for final 3 miles; 1-mile cool-down	Easy run: 7-8 miles	Regular run: 5-8 miles, then 8 × 100-meter strides	Hills: 2-mile warm-up; 8 × 600-meter hill at 5K effort; jog down for recovery; 1-mile cool-down	Easy to regular run: 1-4 miles OR Day off	43-60

(continued)

12-Week 15K–Half-Marathon Schedule: Up to 60 Miles per Week (continued)

	Sunday	Monday	Tuesday	Wednesday	Thursday	Friday	Saturday	Week's mileage
Week 7	Long run: 10-14 miles	Easy run: 4-8 miles, then 8 × 100-meter strides	Tempo run: 2-mile warm-up; 4-6 miles continuous at half-marathon pace; 1-mile cool-down	Easy run: 7-8 miles	Regular run: 5-8 miles, then 8 × 100-meter strides	Intervals: 2-mile warm-up; 8 × 400 meters at 10K pace with 200-meter jog between; 1-mile cool-down	Easy to regular run: 1-4 miles OR Day off	39-57
Week 8	Long run: 12-14 miles	Easy run: 5-7 miles, then 8 × 100-meter strides	Regular run: 6-8 miles, then 8 × 100-meter strides	Easy run: 4-6 miles	Regular run: 4-6 miles, then 8 × 100-meter strides	Tempo run: 2-mile warm-up; 4-5 miles continuous at half-marathon pace; 1-mile cool-down	Easy to regular run: 1-4 miles OR Day off	38-53
Week 9	Long run: 10-14 miles	Easy run: 4-6 miles, then 8 × 100-meter strides	Tempo run: 2-mile warm-up; 4-5 miles continuous at half-marathon pace; 800-meter jog; 4 × 400 meters at 5K pace with 200-meter jog between; 1-mile cool-down	Easy run: 7-8 miles	Regular run: 5-8 miles, then 8 × 100-meter strides	If racing tomorrow: Easy to regular run: 1-4 miles OR If not racing tomorrow: Hills: 2-mile warm-up; 8 × 400-meter hill at 5K effort; jog down for recovery; 1-mile cool-down	Race: 10K or shorter OR Easy to regular run: 1-4 miles	41-57

	Sunday	Monday	Tuesday	Wednesday	Thursday	Friday	Saturday	Week's mileage
Week 10	Long run: 9-12 miles	Easy run: 6-8 miles, then 8 × 100-meter strides	If raced previous Saturday: Easy run: 6-8 miles OR If didn't race previous Saturday: Tempo intervals: 2-mile warm-up; 4-6 × 1 mile at half-marathon pace with 400-meter jog between; 1-mile cool-down	Easy run: 7-8 miles	Regular run: 5-7 miles, then 8 × 100-meter strides	Intervals: 2-mile warm-up; 8 × 400 meters at 10K pace with 200-meter jog between; 1-mile cool-down	Easy to regular run: 1-4 miles OR Day off	39-55
Week 11	Long run: 8-10 miles	Easy run: 5-7 miles, then 8 × 100-meter strides	Intervals: 2-mile warm-up; 4 × 1 mile at 10K pace with 400-meter jog between; 1-mile cool-down	Easy run: 4-6 miles	Regular run: 4-6 miles, then 8 × 100-meter strides	Tempo run: 2-mile warm-up; 4-6 miles continuous at half-marathon pace; 1-mile cool-down	Easy to regular run: 1-4 miles OR Day off	36-51
Week 12	Long run: 6-8 miles	Easy run: 4-6 miles, then 8 × 100-meter strides	Tempo intervals: 2-mile warm-up; 5 × 800 meters at half-marathon pace with 400-meter jog between; 1-mile cool-down	Easy run: 3-5 miles, then 8 × 100-meter strides	Easy run: 2-4 miles OR Day off	Easy run: 2-4 miles	Race 15K to half-marathon OR Easy run: 2-4 miles (for Sunday 15K to half-marathon)	22-34 (not including race)

12-Week 15K–Half-Marathon Schedule: 35-70 Miles per Week

	Sunday	Monday	Tuesday	Wednesday	Thursday	Friday	Saturday	Week's mileage
Week 1	Long run: 8-10 miles	Easy run: 6-8 miles, then 8 × 100-meter strides	Tempo run: 2-mile warm-up; 4-6 miles continuous at half-marathon pace; 1-mile cool-down	Easy run: 7-10 miles	Regular run: 5-7 miles, then 8 × 100-meter strides	Intervals: 2-mile warm-up; 8 × 400 meters at 10K pace with 200-meter jog between; 1-mile cool-down	Easy run: 4-6 miles	43-56
Week 2	Long run: 8-12 miles	Easy run: 6-8 miles, then 8 × 100-meter strides	Progression run: 2-mile warm-up; 4-6 miles continuous, starting at 35 seconds per mile slower than 10K pace, increasing pace 5-10 seconds per mile after each mile; 1-mile cool-down	Easy run: 7-10 miles	Regular run: 5-7 miles, then 8 × 100-meter strides	Hills: 2-mile warm-up; 8 × 400-meter hill at 5K effort; jog down for recovery; 1-mile cool-down	Easy to regular run: 4-6 miles	44-60
Week 3	Long run: 10-12 miles	Easy run: 6-8 miles, then 8 × 100-meter strides	Tempo intervals: 2-mile warm-up; 4-6 × 1 mile at 10K pace with 800-meter jog between; 1-mile cool-down	Easy run: 7-10 miles	Regular run: 5-8 miles, then 8 × 100-meter strides	Intervals: 2-mile warm-up; 10 × 400 meters at 10K pace with 200-meter jog between; 1-mile cool-down	Easy to regular run: 4-6 miles	47-62

	Sunday	Monday	Tuesday	Wednesday	Thursday	Friday	Saturday	Week's mileage
Week 4	Long run: 12-14 miles	Easy run: 6-8 miles, then 8 × 100-meter strides	Tempo run: 2-mile warm-up; 4-6 miles continuous at half-marathon pace; 1-mile cool-down	Easy run: 7-10 miles	Regular run: 5-8 miles, then 8 × 100-meter strides	Hills: 2-mile warm-up; 8 × 600- to 800-meter hill at 5K effort; jog down for recovery; 1-mile cool-down	Easy to regular run: 4-8 miles OR Day off	46-68
Week 5	Long run: 13-15 miles	Easy run: 6-8 miles, then 8 × 100-meter strides	Progression run: 2-mile warm-up; 5-7 miles continuous, starting at marathon pace and increasing pace 3-5 seconds per mile after each mile; 1-mile cool-down	Easy run: 7-10 miles	Regular run: 5-8 miles, then 8 × 100-meter strides	Intervals: 2-mile warm-up; 1 mile at 10K pace; 1 mile at marathon pace; 1,200 meters at 10K pace; 1 mile at marathon pace; 800 meters at 5K pace; 1 mile at marathon pace; 400 meters at mile pace; 200-meter jog between all intervals; 1-mile cool-down	Easy to regular run: 4-8 miles	53-69
Week 6	Long run: 13-16 miles	Easy run: 4-8 miles, then 8 × 100-meter strides	Tempo run; 2-mile warm-up; 5-8 miles continuous, starting a little slower than and working into half-marathon pace for final 3 miles; 1-mile cool-down	Easy run: 7-10 miles	Regular run: 5-8 miles, then 8 × 100-meter strides	Hills: 2-mile warm-up; 8 × 600-meter hill at 5K effort; jog down for recovery; 1-mile cool-down	Easy to regular run: 4-8 miles	50-70

(continued)

12-Week 15K–Half-Marathon Schedule: 35-70 Miles per Week *(continued)*

	Sunday	Monday	Tuesday	Wednesday	Thursday	Friday	Saturday	Week's mileage
Week 7	Long run: 13-16 miles	Easy run: 4-8 miles, then 8 × 100-meter strides	Tempo run: 2-mile warm-up; 4-6 miles continuous at half-marathon pace; 1-mile cool-down	Easy run: 7-10 miles	Regular run: 5-8 miles, then 8 × 100-meter strides	Intervals: 2-mile warm-up; 10 × 400 meters at 10K pace with 200-meter jog between; 1-mile cool-down	Easy to regular run: 4-8 miles	49-68
Week 8	Long run: 13-16 miles	Easy run: 5-7 miles, then 8 × 100-meter strides	Regular run: 6-8 miles, then 8 × 100-meter strides	Easy run: 6-8 miles	Regular run: 4-6 miles, then 8 × 100-meter strides	Tempo run: 2-mile warm-up; 4-6 miles continuous at half-marathon pace; 1-mile cool-down	Easy to regular run: 2-6 miles OR Day off	41-60
Week 9	Long run: 13-16 miles	Easy run: 4-6 miles, then 8 × 100-meter strides	Tempo run: 2-mile warm-up; 4-6 miles continuous at half-marathon pace; 800-meter jog; 6 × 400 meters at 5K pace with 200-meter jog between; 1-mile cool-down	Easy run: 7-10 miles	Regular run: 5-8 miles, then 8 × 100-meter strides	If racing tomorrow: Easy to regular run: 1-4 miles OR If not racing tomorrow: Hills: 2-mile warm-up; 8 × 600-meter hill at 5K effort; jog down for recovery; 1-mile cool-down	Race: 10K or shorter OR Easy to regular run: 4-6 miles	44-66

	Sunday	Monday	Tuesday	Wednesday	Thursday	Friday	Saturday	Week's mileage
Week 10	Long run: 11-13 miles	Easy run: 6-8 miles, then 8 × 100-meter strides	If raced previous Saturday: Easy run: 6-8 miles OR If didn't race previous Saturday: Tempo intervals: 2-mile warm-up; 6-8 × 1 mile at half-marathon pace with 400-meter jog between; 1-mile cool-down	Easy run: 7-10 miles	Regular run: 5-7 miles, then 8 × 100-meter strides	Intervals: 2-mile warm-up; 8 × 400 meters at 10K pace with 200-meter jog between; 1-mile cool-down	Easy to regular run: 4-6 miles	45-63
Week 11	Long run: 8-12 miles	Easy run: 5-7 miles, then 8 × 100-meter strides	Intervals: 2-mile warm-up; 4-6 × 1 mile at 10K pace with 400-meter jog between; 1-mile cool-down	Easy run: 6-8 miles	Regular run: 4-6 miles, then 8 × 100-meter strides	Tempo run: 2-mile warm-up; 4-6 miles continuous at half-marathon pace; 1-mile cool-down	Easy to regular run: 2-6 miles OR Day off	38-58
Week 12	Long run: 6-10 miles	Easy run: 4-6 miles, then 8 × 100-meter strides	Tempo intervals: 2-mile warm-up; 6 × 800 meters at half-marathon pace with 400-meter jog between; 1-mile cool-down	Easy run: 4-6 miles, then 8 × 100-meter strides	Easy run: 2-4 miles OR Day off	Easy run: 2-4 miles	Race 15K to half-marathon OR Easy run: 2-4 miles (for Sunday 15K to half-marathon)	23-41 (not including race)

12-Week 15K–Half-Marathon Schedule: 45+ Miles per Week

	Sunday	Monday	Tuesday	Wednesday	Thursday	Friday	Saturday	Week's mileage
Week 1	Long run: 10-12 miles	Easy run: 6-8 miles, then 8 × 100-meter strides	Tempo run: 2- to 3-mile warm-up; 4-6 miles continuous at half-marathon pace; 1- to 2-mile cool-down	Easy run: 7-10 miles	Regular run: 6-9 miles, then 8 × 100-meter strides	Intervals: 2- to 3-mile warm-up; 8 × 400 meters at 10K pace with 200-meter jog between; 1- to 2-mile cool-down	Easy run: 4-6 miles	46-64
Week 2	Long run: 10-14 miles	Easy run: 6-8 miles, then 8 × 100-meter strides	Progression run: 2- to 3-mile warm-up; 4-6 miles continuous, starting at 35 seconds per mile slower than 10K pace, increasing pace 5-10 seconds per mile after each mile; 1- to 2-mile cool-down	Easy run: 7-10 miles	Regular run: 6-9 miles, then 8 × 100-meter strides	Hills: 2- to 3-mile warm-up; 8 × 400-meter hill at 5K effort; jog down for recovery; 1- to 2-mile cool-down	Easy to regular run: 4-6 miles	47-67
Week 3	Long run: 12-14 miles	Easy run: 6-8 miles, then 8 × 100-meter strides	Tempo intervals: 2- to 3-mile warm-up; 4-6 × 1 mile at 10K pace with 800-meter jog between; 1- to 2-mile cool-down	Easy run: 7-10 miles	Regular run: 6-10 miles, then 8 × 100-meter strides	Intervals: 2- to 3-mile warm-up; 10-12 × 400 meters at 10K pace with 200-meter jog between; 1- to 2-mile cool-down	Easy to regular run: 4-6 miles	51-70

	Sunday	Monday	Tuesday	Wednesday	Thursday	Friday	Saturday	Week's mileage
Week 4	Long run: 14-16 miles	Easy run: 6-8 miles, then 8 × 100-meter strides	Tempo run: 2- to 3-mile warm-up; 4-6 miles continuous at half-marathon pace; 1- to 2-mile cool-down	Easy run: 7-10 miles	Regular run: 6-10 miles, then 8 × 100-meter strides	Hills: 2- to 3-mile warm-up; 8 × 600- to 800-meter hill at 5K effort; jog down for recovery; 1- to 2-mile cool-down	Easy to regular run: 4-8 miles OR Day off	49-74
Week 5	Long run: 15-18 miles	Easy run: 6-8 miles, then 8 × 100-meter strides	Progression run: 2- to 3-mile warm-up; 6-8 miles continuous, starting at marathon pace and increasing pace 3-5 seconds per mile after each mile; 1- to 2-mile cool-down	Easy run: 7-10 miles	Regular run: 6-10 miles, then 8 × 100-meter strides	Intervals: 2- to 3-mile warm-up; 1 mile at 10K pace; 1 mile at marathon pace; 1,200 meters at 10K pace; 1 mile at marathon pace; 800 meters at 5K pace; 1 mile at marathon pace; 400 meters at mile pace; 200-meter jog between all intervals; 1- to 2-mile cool-down	Easy to regular run: 4-8 miles	56-78
Week 6	Long run: 15-18 miles	Easy run: 4-8 miles, then 8 × 100-meter strides	Tempo run: 2- to 3-mile warm-up; 5-8 miles continuous, starting a little slower than and working into half-marathon pace for final 3 miles; 1- to 2-mile cool-down	Easy run: 7-10 miles	Regular run: 6-10 miles, then 8 × 100-meter strides	Hills: 2- to 3-mile warm-up; 8 × 600-meter hill at 5K effort; jog down for recovery; 1- to 2-mile cool-down	Easy to regular run: 4-8 miles	53-78

(continued)

12-Week 15K–Half-Marathon Schedule: 45+ Miles per Week (continued)

	Sunday	Monday	Tuesday	Wednesday	Thursday	Friday	Saturday	Week's mileage
Week 7	Long run: 15-18 miles	Easy run: 4-8 miles, then 8 × 100-meter strides	Tempo run: 2- to 3-mile warm-up; 4-6 miles continuous at half-marathon pace; 1- to 2-mile cool-down	Easy run: 7-10 miles	Regular run: 6-10 miles, then 8 × 100-meter strides	Intervals: 2- to 3-mile warm-up; 10-12 × 400 meters at 10K pace with 200-meter jog between; 1- to 2-mile cool-down	Easy to regular run: 4-8 miles	50-75
Week 8	Long run: 15-18 miles	Easy run: 5-7 miles, then 8 × 100-meter strides	Regular run: 6-8 miles, then 8 × 100-meter strides	Easy run: 6-8 miles	Regular run: 5-7 miles, then 8 × 100-meter strides	Tempo run: 2- to 3-mile warm-up; 4-6 miles continuous at half-marathon pace; 1- to 2-mile cool-down	Easy to regular run: 2-6 miles OR Day off	46-65
Week 9	Long run: 15-18 miles	Easy run: 4-6 miles, then 8 × 100-meter strides	Tempo run: 2- to 3-mile warm-up; 4-6 miles continuous at half-marathon pace; 800-meter jog; 6 × 400 meters at 5K pace with 200-meter jog between; 1- to 2-mile cool-down	Easy run: 7-10 miles	Regular run: 6-10 miles, then 8 × 100-meter strides	If racing tomorrow: Easy to regular run: 1-4 miles OR If not racing tomorrow: Hills: 2- to 3-mile warm-up; 8 × 600-meter hill at 5K effort; jog down for recovery; 1- to 2-mile cool-down	Race: 10K or shorter OR Easy to regular run: 4-6 miles	50-75

	Sunday	Monday	Tuesday	Wednesday	Thursday	Friday	Saturday	Week's mileage
Week 10	Long run: 13-15 miles	Easy run: 6-8 miles, then 8 × 100-meter strides	If raced previous Saturday: Easy run: 6-8 miles OR If didn't race previous Saturday: Tempo intervals: 2- to 3-mile warm-up; 6-8 × 1 mile at half-marathon pace with 400-meter jog between; 1- to 2-mile cool-down	Easy run: 7-10 miles	Regular run: 6-9 miles, then 8 × 100-meter strides	Intervals: 2- to 3-mile warm-up; 8 × 400 meters at 10K pace with 200-meter jog between; 1- to 2-mile cool-down	Easy to regular run: 4-6 miles	48-68
Week 11	Long run: 10-14 miles	Easy run: 5-7 miles, then 8 × 100-meter strides	Intervals: 2- to 3-mile warm-up: 4-6 × 1 mile at 10K pace with 400-meter jog between; 1- to 2-mile cool-down	Easy run: 6-8 miles	Regular run: 5-7 miles, then 8 × 100-meter strides	Tempo run: 2- to 3-mile warm-up; 4-6 miles continuous at half-marathon pace; 1- to 2-mile cool-down	Easy to regular run: 2-6 miles OR Day off	41-65
Week 12	Long run: 8-12 miles	Easy run: 4-6 miles, then 8 × 100-meter strides	Tempo intervals: 2- to 3-mile warm-up; 6 × 800 meters at half-marathon pace with 400-meter jog between; 1- to 2-mile cool-down	Easy run: 4-6 miles, then 8 × 100-meter strides	Easy run: 2-4 miles OR Day off	Easy run: 2-4 miles	Race 15K to half-marathon OR Easy run: 2-4 miles (for Sunday 15K to half-marathon)	25-41 (not including race)

16-Week 15K–Half-Marathon Schedule: Up to 60 Miles per Week

	Sunday	Monday	Tuesday	Wednesday	Thursday	Friday	Saturday	Week's mileage
Week 1	Long run: 6-8 miles	Easy run: 4-6 miles	Regular run: 4-6 miles	Regular run: 4-6 miles	Regular run: 4-6 miles	Intervals: 2-mile warm-up; 6-8 × 400 meters at 10K pace with 200-meter recovery; 1-mile cool-down	Easy run: 1-4 miles OR Day off	27-42
Week 2	Long run: 6-8 miles	Easy run: 4-6 miles, then 8 × 100-meter strides	Tempo run: 2-mile warm-up; 3-4 miles continuous at half-marathon goal pace; 1-mile cool-down	Easy run: 4-6 miles	Regular run: 4-6 miles	Intervals: 2-mile warm-up; 4-6 × 800 meters at 10K pace with 400-meter jog between; 1-mile cool-down	Day off	30-40
Week 3	Long run: 6-8 miles	Easy run: 5-7 miles, then 8 × 100-meter strides	Hilly run: 6-8 miles on hilly course at regular run pace; if hills not available, run 10 seconds per mile faster than regular run pace	Easy run: 4-6 miles	Regular run: 4-6 miles, then 8 × 100-meter strides	Intervals: 2-mile warm-up; 3-4 × 1 mile at half-marathon pace with 400-meter jog between; 1-mile cool-down	Easy run: 1-6 miles OR Day off	32-49
Week 4	Long run: 6-8 miles	Easy run: 5-7 miles, then 8 × 100-meter strides	Tempo run: 2-mile warm-up; 4-6 miles continuous at half-marathon pace; 1-mile cool-down	Easy run: 5-7 miles	Regular run: 5-7 miles then 8 × 100-meter strides	Intervals: 2-mile warm-up; 8-10 × 400 meters at 10K pace with 200-meter jog between; 1-mile cool-down	Easy run: 1-6 miles OR Day off	34-50
Week 5	Long run: 6-10 miles	Easy run: 6-7 miles, then 8 × 100-meter strides	Progression run: 2-mile warm-up, 4-6 miles continuous, starting at marathon pace, increasing pace 5 seconds per mile after each mile; 1-mile cool-down	Easy run: 5-7 miles	Regular run: 6-8 miles, then 8 × 100-meter strides	Hills: 2-mile warm-up; 6-8 × 600-meter hill at 5K effort; jog down for recovery; 1-mile cool-down	Easy run: 1-6 miles OR Day off	37-56

	Sunday	Monday	Tuesday	Wednesday	Thursday	Friday	Saturday	Week's mileage
Week 6	Long run: 6-10 miles	Easy run: 6-7 miles, then 8 × 100-meter strides	Tempo run: 2-mile warm-up; 4-6 miles continuous at half-marathon pace; 1-mile cool-down	Easy run: 5-7 miles	Regular run: 6-8 miles, then 8 × 100-meter strides	Intervals: 2-mile warm-up; 6-8 × 800 meters at 10K pace with 400-meter jog between; 1-mile cool-down	Easy run: 1-6 miles OR Day off	37-55
Week 7	Long run: 8-12 miles	Easy run: 6-7 miles	Tempo intervals: 2-mile warm-up; 4-6 × 1 mile at half-marathon pace with 800-meter jog between; 1-mile cool-down	Easy run: 5-7 miles	Regular run: 6-8 miles	Intervals: 2-mile warm-up; 1 mile at 10K pace; 1 mile at marathon pace; 1,200 meters at 10K pace, 1 mile at marathon pace; 800 meters at 5K pace; 1 mile at marathon pace; 400 meters at mile pace; 200-meter jog after all intervals; 1-mile cool-down	Easy run: 1-4 miles OR Day off	42-56
Week 8	Long run: 8-12 miles	Easy run: 4-6 miles, then 8 × 100-meter strides	Tempo run: 2-mile warm-up; 6-8 miles continuous at marathon pace; 1-mile cool-down	Easy run: 5-7 miles	Regular run: 6-8 miles, then 8 × 100-meter strides	Hills: 2-mile warm-up; 6-8 × 600- to 800-meter hill at 5K effort; jog down for recovery; 1-mile cool-down	Easy run: 1-6 miles OR Day off	38-61
Week 9	Long run: 8-12 miles OR 6-8 miles if racing on following Saturday	Easy run: 6-8 miles, then 8 × 100-meter strides	Progression run: 2-mile warm-up, 6-8 miles continuous, starting at marathon pace, increasing pace 5 seconds per mile after each mile; 1-mile cool-down	Easy run: 5-7 miles	Regular run: 6-8 miles, then 8 × 100-meter strides	If racing tomorrow: Easy to regular run: 1-4 miles OR If not racing tomorrow: Intervals: 2-mile warm-up; 4-6 × 1 mile at half-marathon pace with 400-meter jog between; 1-mile cool-down	Race: 10K or shorter OR Easy run: 1-6 miles	40-60

(continued)

16-Week 15K–Half-Marathon Schedule: Up to 60 Miles per Week (continued)

	Sunday	Monday	Tuesday	Wednesday	Thursday	Friday	Saturday	Week's mileage
Week 10	Long run: 8-12 miles	Easy run: 6-8 miles, then 8 × 100-meter strides	Hilly run: 6-8 miles on hilly course at a little faster than regular run pace; if hills not available, run 10 seconds per mile faster than regular run pace	Easy run: 5-7 miles	Regular run: 6-8 miles, then 8 × 100-meter strides	Intervals: 2-mile warm-up; 8-10 × 400 meters at 10K pace with 200-meter jog between; 1-mile cool-down	Easy run: 1-6 miles OR Day off	37-55
Week 11	Long run: 8-13 miles	Easy run: 6-7 miles	Tempo intervals: 2-mile warm-up; 2-3 × 2 miles at half-marathon pace with 800-meter jog between; 1-mile cool-down	Easy run: 5-7 miles	Easy run: 5-7 miles	Hills: 2-mile warm-up; 6-8 × 400-meter hill at 5K effort; jog down for recovery; 1-mile cool-down	Easy run: 1-6 miles OR Day off	40-60
Week 12	Long run: 9-13 miles	Easy run: 6-7 miles then 8 × 100-meter strides	Tempo run: 2-mile warm-up; 6-8 miles at marathon pace; 1-mile cool-down	Easy run: 5-7 miles	Regular run: 5-7 miles, then 8 × 100-meter strides	Intervals: 2-mile warm-up; 2 × set of 800 meters at 10K pace, 1 mile at half-marathon pace, and 800 meters at 10K pace; 400-meter jog between intervals and 800-meter jog between sets; 1-mile cool-down	Easy run: 1-6 miles OR Day off	42-59
Week 13	Long run: 8-10 miles	Easy run: 5-7 miles, then 8 × 100-meter strides	Tempo run: 2-mile warm-up; 3-6 miles continuous at half-marathon pace; 800-meter jog; 6 × 400 meters at mile pace with 200-meter jog between; 1-mile cool-down	Easy run: 5-7 miles	Regular run: 5-7 miles, then 8 × 100-meter strides	Intervals: 2-mile warm-up; 6-8 × 800 meters at 10K pace with 400-meter jog between; 1-mile cool-down	Easy run: 1-4 miles OR Day off	39-55

	Sunday	Monday	Tuesday	Wednesday	Thursday	Friday	Saturday	Week's mileage
Week 14	Long run: 8-10 miles, last 2 miles 5-10 seconds per mile faster than marathon pace	Easy run: 4-6 miles, then 8 × 100-meter strides	Tempo run: 2-mile warm-up; 3 miles continuous at 25 seconds per mile slower than 10K pace; 1-mile cool-down	Easy run: 4-6 miles	Regular run: 4-6 miles, then 8 × 100-meter strides	Intervals: 2-mile warm-up; 8 × 400 meters at 5K pace with 200-meter jog between; 1-mile cool-down	Easy run: 1-4 miles OR Day off	32-44
Week 15	Long run: 6-8 miles	Easy: 1-4 miles OR Day off	Tempo intervals: 2-mile warm-up; 2-3 × 1.5 miles at half-marathon pace with 1-mile jog between; 1-mile cool-down	Easy run: 4-6 miles	Regular run: 4-6 miles, then 8 × 100-meter strides	Intervals: 2-mile warm-up; 4-6 × 800 meters at 10K pace with 400-meter jog between; 1-mile cool-down	Easy run: 1-4 miles OR Day off	26-42
Week 16	Long run: 6-8 miles	Day off	Intervals: 2-mile warm-up; 6-8 × 400 meters at 10K pace with 200-meter jog between; 1-mile cool-down	Easy run: 3-4 miles	Easy run: 1-4 miles, then 6 × 100-meter strides OR Day off	Easy run: 2-4 miles	Race 15K to half-marathon OR Easy run: 2-4 miles (for Sunday 15K to half-marathon)	16-26 (not including race)

16-Week 15K–Half-Marathon Schedule: 35-70 Miles per Week

	Sunday	Monday	Tuesday	Wednesday	Thursday	Friday	Saturday	Week's mileage
Week 1	Long run: 8-10 miles	Easy run: 4-6 miles	Regular run: 4-6 miles	Regular run: 5-7 miles	Regular run: 4-6 miles	Intervals: 2-mile warm-up; 8 × 400 meters at 10K pace with 200-meter jog between; 1-mile cool-down	Easy run: 4 miles	35-45
Week 2	Long run: 8-10 miles	Easy run: 4-6 miles, then 8 × 100-meter strides	Tempo run: 2-mile warm-up; 3-4 miles continuous at half-marathon pace; 1-mile cool-down	Easy run: 5-7 miles	Regular run: 4-6 miles	Intervals: 2-mile warm-up; 4-6 × 800 meters at 10K pace with 400-meter jog between; 1-mile cool-down	Day off	33-43
Week 3	Long run: 10-12 miles	Easy run: 5-7 miles, then 8 × 100-meter strides	Hilly run: 6-8 miles on hilly course at regular run pace; if hills not available, run 10 seconds per mile faster than regular run pace	Easy run: 5-7 miles	Regular run: 4-6 miles, then 8 × 100-meter strides	Intervals: 2-mile warm-up; 3-4 × 1 mile at half-marathon pace with 400-meter jog between; 1-mile cool-down	Easy run: 3-6 miles	38-51
Week 4	Long run: 10-12 miles	Easy run: 5-7 miles, then 8 × 100-meter strides	Tempo run: 2-mile warm-up; 5-6 miles continuous at half-marathon pace; 1-mile cool-down	Easy run: 5-7 miles	Regular run: 5-7 miles, then 8 × 100-meter strides	Intervals: 2-mile warm-up; 10 × 400 meters at 10K pace with 200-meter jog between; 1-mile cool-down	Easy run: 3-6 miles	43-55
Week 5	Long run: 10-14 miles	Easy run: 6-7 miles, then 8 × 100-meter strides	Progression run: 2-mile warm-up; 5-6 miles continuous, starting at marathon pace, increasing pace 5-10 seconds per mile after each mile; 1-mile cool-down	Easy run: 7-8 miles	Regular run: 6-9 miles, then 8 × 100-meter strides	Hills: 2-mile warm-up; 8 × 600-meter hill at 5K effort; jog down for recovery; 1-mile cool-down	Easy run: 1-6 miles OR Day off	46-62

	Sunday	Monday	Tuesday	Wednesday	Thursday	Friday	Saturday	Week's mileage
Week 6	Long run: 10-14 miles	Easy run: 6-8 miles, then 8 × 100-meter strides	Tempo run: 2-mile warm-up; 6-8 miles continuous at half-marathon pace; 1-mile cool-down	Easy run: 7-8 miles	Regular run: 6-9 miles, then 8 × 100-meter strides	Intervals: 2-mile warm-up; 6-8 × 800 meters at 10K pace with 400-meter jog between; 1-mile cool-down	Easy run: 3-6 miles	48-64
Week 7	Long run: 12-16 miles	Easy run: 6-8 miles	Tempo intervals: 2-mile warm-up; 6 × 1 mile at half-marathon pace with 800-meter jog between; 1-mile cool-down	Easy run: 7-9 miles	Regular run: 6-9 miles	Intervals: 2-mile warm-up; 1 mile at 10K pace; 1 mile at marathon pace; 1,200 meters at 10K pace; 1 mile at marathon pace; 800 meters at 5K pace; 1 mile at marathon pace; 400 meters at mile pace; 200-meter jog between all intervals; 1-mile cool-down	Easy run: 1-4 miles OR Day off	52-67
Week 8	Long run: 12-16 miles	Easy run: 4-6 miles, then 8 × 100-meter strides	Tempo run: 2-mile warm-up; 6-8 miles at marathon pace; 1-mile cool-down	Easy run: 7-9 miles	Regular run: 6-9 miles, then 8 × 100-meter strides	Hills: 2-mile warm-up; 8 × 600- to 800-meter hill at 5K effort; jog down for recovery; 1-mile cool-down	Easy run: 3-6 miles	50-68
Week 9	Long run: 12-16 miles OR 6-8 miles if racing on following Saturday	Easy run: 6-8 miles, then 8 × 100-meter strides	Progression run: 2-mile warm-up; 6-8 miles continuous, starting at marathon pace, increasing each pace 5-10 seconds per mile after each mile; 1-mile cool-down	Easy run: 7-9 miles	Regular run: 6-9 miles, then 8 × 100-meter strides	If racing tomorrow: Easy to regular run: 1-4 miles OR If not racing tomorrow: Intervals: 2-mile warm-up; 4-6 × 1 mile at half-marathon pace with 400-meter jog between; 1-mile cool-down	Race: 10K or shorter OR Easy run: 4-6 miles	42-69

35-70 Miles per Week
16-Week 15K–Half-Marathon Schedule

(continued)

16-Week 15K–Half-Marathon Schedule: 35-70 Miles per Week (continued)

	Sunday	Monday	Tuesday	Wednesday	Thursday	Friday	Saturday	Week's mileage
Week 10	Long run: 12-16 miles	Easy run: 6-8 miles, then 8 × 100-meter strides	Hilly run: 8-10 miles on hilly course at a little faster than regular training pace; if no hills available, run 10 seconds per mile faster than regular run pace	Easy run: 7-9 miles	Regular run: 7-9 miles, then 8 × 100-meter strides	Intervals: 2-mile warm-up; 8-10 × 400 meters at 10K pace with 200-meter jog between; 1-mile cool-down	Easy run: 3-6 miles	49-63
Week 11	Long run: 10-14 miles	Easy run: 6-8 miles	Tempo intervals: 2-mile warm-up; 3 × 2 miles at half-marathon pace with 800-meter jog between; 1-mile cool-down	Easy run: 7-9 miles	Easy run: 6-8 miles	Hills: 2-mile warm-up: 8-10 × 400-meter hill at 5K effort; jog down for recovery; 1-mile cool-down	Easy run: 3-6 miles	49-63
Week 12	Long run: 12-15 miles	Easy run: 6-8 miles, then 8 × 100-meter strides	Tempo run: 2-mile warm-up; 6-8 miles at marathon pace; 1-mile cool-down	Easy run: 7-9 miles	Regular run: 6-8 miles, then 8 × 100-meter strides	Intervals: 2-mile warm-up; 2 × sets of 800 meters at 10K pace, 1 mile at half-marathon pace, 800 meters at 10K pace; 400-meter jog between intervals and 800-meter jog between sets; 1-mile cool-down	Easy run: 1-6 miles OR Day off	47-65
Week 13	Long run: 10-14 miles	Easy run: 5-7 miles, then 8 × 100-meter strides	Tempo run: 2-mile warm-up; 4-6 miles continuous at half-marathon pace; 800-meter jog; 6 × 400 meters at mile pace with 200-meter jog between; 1-mile cool-down	Easy run: 5-7 miles	Regular run: 6-8 miles, then 8 × 100-meter strides	Intervals: 2-mile warm-up; 8 × 800 meters at 10K pace with 400-meter jog between; 1-mile cool-down	Easy run 1-6 miles OR Day off	44-62

	Sunday	Monday	Tuesday	Wednesday	Thursday	Friday	Saturday	Week's mileage
Week 14	Long run: 10-13 miles, with the last 2 miles at 5-10 seconds per mile faster than marathon pace	Easy run: 4-6 miles, then 8 × 100-meter strides	Tempo run: 2-mile warm-up; 3 miles continuous at 25 seconds per mile slower than 10K pace; 1-mile cool-down	Easy run: 4-6 miles	Regular run: 5-7 miles, then 8 × 100-meter strides	Intervals: 2-mile warm-up; 8 × 400 meters at 5K pace with 200-meter jog between; 1-mile cool-down	Easy run: 2-4 miles	37-50
Week 15	Long run: 8-12 miles	Easy run: 1-4 miles OR Day off	Tempo intervals: 2-mile warm-up; 3 × 2 miles at half-marathon pace with 1-mile jog between; 1-mile cool-down	Easy run: 4-8 miles	Regular run: 5-7 miles, then 8 × 100-meter strides	Intervals: 2-mile warm-up; 6 × 800 meters at 10K pace with 400-meter jog between; 1-mile cool-down	Easy run: 1-6 miles OR Day off	35-55
Week 16	Long run: 8-10 miles	Day off	Intervals: 2-mile warm-up; 8 × 400 meters at 10K pace with 200-meter jog between; 1-mile cool-down	Easy run: 3-5 miles	Easy run: 3-5 miles, then 6 × 100-meter strides OR Day off	Easy run: 2-4 miles	Race 15K to half-marathon OR Easy run: 2-4 miles (for Sunday 15K to half-marathon)	19-30 (not including race)

16-Week 15K–Half-Marathon Schedule: 35+ Miles per Week

	Sunday	Monday	Tuesday	Wednesday	Thursday	Friday	Saturday	Week's mileage
Week 1	Long run: 8-10 miles	Easy run: 4-6 miles	Regular run: 4-6 miles	Regular run: 5-7 miles	Regular run: 4-6 miles	Intervals: 2- to 3-mile warm-up; 8 × 400 meters at 10K pace with 200-meter jog between; 1- to 2-mile cool-down	Easy run: 4 miles	35-47
Week 2	Long run: 8-10 miles	Easy run: 4-6 miles, then 8 × 100-meter strides	Tempo run: 2- to 3-mile warm-up; 3-4 miles continuous at half-marathon pace; 1- to 2-mile cool-down	Easy run: 5-7 miles	Regular run: 4-6 miles	Intervals: 2- to 3-mile warm-up; 4-6 × 800 meters at 10K pace with 400-meter jog between; 1- to 2-mile cool-down	Day off	33-47
Week 3	Long run: 10-12 miles	Easy run: 5-7 miles, then 8 × 100-meter strides	Hilly run: 6-8 miles on hilly course at regular run pace; if no hills available, run 10 seconds per mile faster than regular run pace	Easy run: 5-7 miles	Regular run: 4-6 miles, then 8 × 100-meter strides	Intervals: 2- to 3-mile warm-up; 3-4 × 1 mile at half-marathon pace with 400-meter jog between; 1- to 2-mile cool-down	Easy run: 4-6 miles	41-56
Week 4	Long run: 10-12 miles	Easy run: 5-7 miles, then 8 × 100-meter strides	Tempo run: 2- to 3-mile warm-up; 5-6 miles continuous at half-marathon pace; 1- to 2-mile cool-down	Easy run: 6-8 miles	Regular run: 5-7 miles, then 8 × 100-meter strides	Intervals: 2- to 3-mile warm-up; 10-12 × 400 meters at 10K pace with 200-meter jog between; 1- to 2-mile cool-down	Easy run: 4-6 miles	45-62
Week 5	Long run: 12-14 miles	Easy run: 6-7 miles, then 8 × 100-meter strides	Progression run: 2- to 3-mile warm-up; 5-6 miles continuous, starting at marathon pace, increasing pace 5-10 seconds per mile after each mile; 1- to 2-mile cool-down	Easy run: 7-9 miles	Regular run: 6-9 miles, then 8 × 100-meter strides	Hills: 2- to 3-mile warm-up; 8 × 600-meter hill at 5K effort; jog down for recovery; 1- to 2-mile cool-down	Easy run: 1-6 miles OR Day off	48-67

	Sunday	Monday	Tuesday	Wednesday	Thursday	Friday	Saturday	Week's mileage
Week 6	Long run: 12-14 miles	Easy run: 6-8 miles, then 8 × 100-meter strides	Tempo run: 2- to 3-mile warm-up; 6-8 miles continuous at half-marathon pace; 1- to 2-mile cool-down	Easy run: 7-9 miles	Regular run: 6-9 miles, then 8 × 100-meter strides	Intervals: 2- to 3-mile warm-up; 6-8 × 800 meters at 10K pace with 400-meter jog between; 1- to 2-mile cool-down	Easy run: 4-6 miles	51-70
Week 7	Long run: 14-16 miles	Easy run: 6-8 miles	Tempo intervals: 2- to 3-mile warm-up; 6-8 × 1 mile at half-marathon pace with 800-meter jog between; 1- to 2-mile cool-down	Easy run: 7-10 miles	Regular run: 6-9 miles	Intervals: 2- to 3-mile warm-up; 1 mile at 10K pace; 1 mile at marathon pace; 1,200 meters at 10K pace; 1 mile at marathon pace; 800 meters at 5K pace; 1 mile at marathon pace; 400 meters at mile pace; 200-meter jog between all intervals; 1- to 2-mile cool-down	Easy run: 1-4 miles OR Day off	54-74
Week 8	Long run: 14-16 miles	Easy run: 4-6 miles, then 8 × 100-meter strides	Tempo run: 2- to 3-mile warm-up; 6-8 miles continuous at marathon pace; 1- to 2-mile cool-down	Easy run: 7-10 miles	Regular run: 6-9 miles, then 8 × 100-meter strides	Hills: 2- to 3-mile warm-up; 8 × 600- to 800-meter hill at 5K effort; jog down for recovery; 1- to 2-mile cool-down	Easy run: 4-6 miles	53-77
Week 9	Long run: 15-18 miles OR 6-8 miles if racing on following Saturday	Easy run: 6-8 miles, then 8 × 100-meter. strides	Progression run: 2- to 3-mile warm up, 8-10 miles continuous, starting at marathon pace, increasing pace 5-10 seconds per mile after each mile; 1- to 2-mile cool-down	Easy run: 7-10 miles	Regular run: 6-9 miles, then 8 × 100-meter strides	If racing tomorrow: Easy to regular run: 1-4 miles OR If not racing tomorrow: Intervals: 2- to 3-mile warm-up; 4-6 × 1 mile at half-marathon pace with 400-meter jog between; 1- to 2-mile cool-down	Race: 10K or shorter OR Easy run: 4-6 miles	40-77

(continued)

16-Week 15K–Half-Marathon Schedule: 35+ Miles per Week (continued)

	Sunday	Monday	Tuesday	Wednesday	Thursday	Friday	Saturday	Week's mileage
Week 10	Long run: 15-18 miles	Easy run: 6-8 miles, then 8 × 100-meter strides	Hilly run: 8-10 miles on hilly course at a little faster than regular run pace; if no hills available, run 10 seconds per mile faster than regular run pace	Easy run: 7-10 miles	Regular run: 7-9 miles, then 8 × 100-meter strides	Intervals: 2- to 3-mile warm-up; 8-10 × 400 meters at 10K pace with 200-meter jog between; 1- to 2-mile cool-down	Easy run: 4-6 miles	53-70
Week 11	Long run: 12-15 miles	Easy run: 6-8 miles	Tempo intervals: 2- to 3-mile warm-up; 3 × 2 miles at half-marathon pace with 800-meter jog between; 1- to 2-mile cool-down	Easy run: 7-10 miles	Easy run: 6-8 miles	Hills: 2- to 3-mile warm-up; 8-10 × 400-meter hill at 5K effort; jog down for recovery; 1- to 2-mile cool-down	Easy run: 4-6 miles	52-69
Week 12	Long run: 15-18 miles	Easy run: 6-8 miles, then 8 × 100-meter strides	Tempo run: 2- to 3-mile warm-up; 6-8 miles continuous at marathon pace; 1- to 2-mile cool-down	Easy run: 7-10 miles	Regular run: 6-8 miles, then 8 × 100-meter strides	Intervals: 2- to 3-mile warm-up; 2 × sets of 800 meters at 10K pace, 1 mile at half-marathon pace, another 1 mile at half-marathon pace, 800 meters at 10K pace; 400-meter jog between intervals and 800-meter jog between sets; 1- to 2-mile cool-down	Easy run: 1-6 miles OR Day off	51-73
Week 13	Long run: 14-18 miles	Easy run: 6-8 miles, then 8 × 100-meter strides	Tempo run: 2- to 3-mile warm-up; 4-6 miles continuous at half-marathon pace; 800-meter jog; 6 × 400 meters at mile pace with 200-meter jog between; 1- to 2-mile cool-down	Easy run: 6-8 miles	Regular run: 6-8 miles, then 8 × 100-meter strides	Intervals: 2- to 3-mile warm-up; 8 × 800 meters at 10K pace with 400-meter jog between; 1- to 2-mile cool-down	Easy run 1-6 miles OR Day off	49-71

	Sunday	Monday	Tuesday	Wednesday	Thursday	Friday	Saturday	Week's mileage
Week 14	Long run: 12-15 miles, last 2 miles 5-10 seconds per mile faster than marathon pace	Easy run: 4-6 miles, then 8 × 100-meter strides	Tempo run: 2- to 3-mile warm-up; 3 miles continuous at 25 seconds per mile slower than 10K pace; 1- to 2-mile cool-down	Easy run: 4-6 miles	Regular run: 6-8 miles, then 8 × 100-meter strides	Intervals: 2- to 3-mile warm-up; 8 × 400 meters at 5K pace with 200-meter jog between; 1- to 2-mile cool-down	Easy run: 2-4 miles	40-55
Week 15	Long run: 10-12 miles	Easy run: 1-4 miles OR Day off	Tempo intervals: 2- to 3-mile warm-up; 3 × 2 miles at half-marathon pace with 1-mile jog between; 1- to 2-mile cool-down	Easy run: 6-8 miles	Regular run: 6-8 miles, then 8 × 100-meter strides	Intervals: 2- to 3-mile warm-up; 6 × 800 meters at 10K pace with 400-meter jog between; 1- to 2-mile cool-down	Easy run: 1-6 miles OR Day off	40-60
Week 16	Long run: 8-10 miles	Day off	Intervals: 2- to 3-mile warm-up; 8 × 400 meters at 10K pace with 200-meter jog between; 1- to 2-mile cool-down	Easy run: 4-6 miles	Easy run: 3-5 miles, then 6 × 100-meter strides OR Day off	Easy run: 2-4 miles	Race 15K to half-marathon OR Easy run: 2-4 miles (for Sunday 15K to half-marathon)	20-33 (not including race)

12

Training for and Racing the Marathon

This chapter will prepare you for the marathon, which is perhaps the most revered and feared distance in running (26.2 miles or 42.2 kilometers).

A complete guide to everything connected with marathon training and racing is outside the scope of the book. If you want to fully understand the event, I recommend *Advanced Marathoning*, by Pete Pfitzinger and Scott Douglas.

Following are six marathon schedules, three that are 12 weeks long and three that are 16 weeks long. The weekly mileage ranges for the 12-week schedules are up to 60, 35 to 70, and 45 or more. The weekly mileage ranges for the 16-week schedules are up to 65, 40 to 75, and 35 or more. As I said in chapter 7, there are many variables to consider when deciding which schedule to follow. Refer there for more details.

A Brief Guide to Following the Schedules

Each day's training in the schedules is described using the main types of runs I described at length in chapter 7. You'll want to refresh your memory occasionally by rereading those descriptions during your buildup. For quick reference, here are the types of runs you'll encounter in these schedules, and what I mean by each. Note that there are marathon-specific tweaks to some of these types of runs.

• *Easy run:* Done the day after your longest and hardest runs. Don't worry about pace. Just run at a comfortable, conversational effort level—no hard breathing, no bearing down. You should finish feeling energized for the next day's training.

• *Regular run:* A little faster or more effortful than an easy run, but still at a conversational pace. These are what you might think of as your getting-in-the-miles runs. It's okay to push things a little in the last few miles if you're feeling good.

• *Easy to regular run:* Start these runs as if they're a recovery run. If you're tired and want to stay at that gentle effort level for the whole run, that's fine. If you feel like going a little harder once you're warmed up, that's fine. But don't force yourself to go faster just because you think you "should" hit a certain pace.

• *Tempo run:* A sustained run at a "comfortably hard" effort level that requires concentration. In these schedules, you'll do some tempo runs at half-marathon pace and some at marathon pace. The shorter tempos tend to be at half-marathon pace. To gauge the right effort for those tempo runs, imagine I were riding a bike alongside and asked you a question. You should be able to answer in a complete sentence, but you shouldn't be able to carry on an in-depth conversation as on an easy or regular run. For marathon-pace runs, you should be even more able to speak in complete sentences, but it's likely that toward the end of them you'll need to concentrate a bit to do so.

• *Progression run:* A sustained run at an increasingly fast pace. Progression runs accomplish much of what conventional tempo runs do while also helping you practice increasing your effort as fatigue mounts. They tend to be a little longer than tempo runs because you start at a slower pace.

• *Intervals:* Repeats, usually between 400 meters and one mile long, usually run between mile and 10K race pace. You can do these on a track for precision and a uniform running surface, but you can also do them on roads or elsewhere with good footing. It's okay to roughly convert the distances stated in the training schedules to timed segments off the track, such as running at 5K effort for three minutes if the schedules prescribe 800-meter repeats at 5K pace.

• *Hill workout:* Running at 5K effort—not pace!—up a moderately steep hill, and jogging down for recovery. Ideally, the hill will be steep enough to make the climbing noticeable, but not so steep that it's difficult to maintain good upright running form with quick turnover.

• *Long run:* Your longest run of the week, done at a conversational pace. Start at a gentle effort and gradually increase intensity to that of a regular run as your body warms up. Don't rush it—you've got plenty of time to get in a good rhythm for the second half of the run. Some of the long runs incorporate stints at marathon pace toward the end. This is great practice at maintaining a strong effort despite cumulative fatigue.

• *Strides:* Short (100 meters or so) bouts of fast running at around mile race pace, usually done either after an easy run or before a hard workout or race. Concentrate on maintaining good running form and staying relaxed while running fast. Strides should feel good and be fun; you'll usually feel better after doing them than you did before. Do strides on a flat, level surface with reliable footing.

Maintain Moderation in Marathon Training

It's tempting to think that more is always better when you're marathon training. You're getting ready for such a demanding race, so training super hard has to be the way to go, right?

My marathon history says otherwise. I hope you'll learn from mistakes I made before two really important marathons.

The first was in my buildup for the 1996 Olympic Marathon. I recovered quickly after making the team in February. I ran some solid races in the spring, including just missing my 10,000-meter best on the track. These races boosted my confidence given that I ran them off of marathon, rather than track-specific, training.

Three weeks before the Olympic Marathon, I ran the Utica Boilermaker 15K. I placed 11th against a strong international field and was the top American finisher. My time was a solid 44:15 for a hilly course on a hot day. I should have been content with the morning's work and what it told me about my fitness, especially because I hadn't cut back before the 15K. Instead, I thought, "I have the Olympic

Marathon coming up—I should be training like I've never trained before." So I did a 10-mile cool-down after the race.

Mistake! I started feeling worn down later that week. I told myself I'd feel better once I really started tapering for the marathon. That didn't happen. The Olympic race was a slog almost from the start. I was already out of contention once the serious racing started in the second half. I finished 41st in 2:20:27, almost eight minutes behind the winner.

The second concerns the 1997 New York City Marathon. I was eager to run well in my first marathon since the Olympic disappointment. The challenging New York course, where place is more important than time, played to my strengths as a good cross-country runner.

Training for the race was going well. Five weeks before the marathon I ran a half-marathon PR of 1:03:08. Unfortunately, I adopted that more-is-better mindset I had before the Olympics. I got on a schedule of doing a hard workout on Fridays, a long run on Saturdays, easy on Sunday, and then attacking a hilly rollercoaster loop on Mondays. I ignored my body's signals that three hard sessions in four days was too much, and I got increasingly tired.

In New York, I felt flat and lost touch with the lead pack almost immediately and ran most of the race by myself. I placed 18th in 2:20:41. Pete Julian, who was one of my training partners then and is now a leading coach, coined the term "Big Apple Monday" for overdoing it in training. Pete and I still joke about it, telling each other, "I think I pulled a Big Apple Monday" when we realize we should have stopped someone we coach from finishing their workout rather than let them run themselves into the ground.

In contrast, earlier in my marathon career I trained a little more conservatively. I went into races like the Pan American Games and Olympic Marathon Trials going in the right direction, still on the up part of the curve, instead of having gone over the top and heading down the backside of the hill.

A challenge here is that as you get fitter from marathon training, it's easier to feel like you've become invincible. So you push things a little more in the belief that you don't need to take recovery as seriously as you used to. You start to think that something like constant low-level fatigue or heavy legs won't come back to bite you. The problem is that, as with Olympic Marathon buildup, you often don't realize you messed up until it's too late.

The training schedules in this chapter have the proper amount of recovery built in. Don't sabotage them by adding miles or pushing the pace on easy days. Constantly running on tired legs will hurt your chances before the start, not prepare you for the final 10K of the marathon.

Ration Your Prerace Resources

You'll put in a lot of hard work over the 12 or 16 weeks of your marathon training. Don't blow it on race weekend by spending a long time walking around a massive expo on hard cement floors. Get in, get your number, and get out. Conserve your energy for the race. (Unless I'm giving a talk or signing books!)

Along the same lines, save the sightseeing for after your race. Try to find acceptable restaurants close to where you're staying that won't require long waits to be seated. You're there on a mission, not as a tourist.

How to Race the Marathon

It's often said that the marathon doesn't really start until 20 miles. I agree that most of the hard work happens in the final 10K. But you still have to run the first 20 miles! I said elsewhere that you can't win a distance race in the first 400 meters, but you can lose it then. One challenge in the marathon is remembering that "the first 400 meters" in this case means something more like "the first 10 miles."

That's a long time to be patient but absolutely the right approach. If you go out too fast in a 5K or 10K, you'll slow by a matter of seconds per mile toward the end. Running too aggressively early in the marathon can mean slowing more than a minute per mile for the final several miles.

Running even pace is your best bet if you're mostly focused on time. Some people advise running slightly faster than goal pace for the first half, to account for the inevitable slowing in the final few miles. I don't think it helps to put too much time in the bank like that. The risk of going too fast early on and then having to slow more than you planned is high.

Of course, your pace is likely to fluctuate some, because of things like uphill and downhill stretches, turns, wind direction, navigating to get drinks, and the reality that few of us are metronomes. If a mile split is suddenly 10 seconds slower than what you've been running, don't freak out. Stay confident and stay on task. If that last mile had a hill or headwind, then you're likely to make up that time later on a downhill or when the wind is at your back.

If in the second half of the race, you're consistently slower than goal pace, don't let it destroy your willpower. It can be hard to think clearly once you start to get really tired. My first marathon was at Boston in 1994. I was running really well up through around 22 miles. Then deep fatigue set in. I ran a 5:30 mile after averaging a little over 5:00 per mile, or 2:12 marathon pace, until then. I panicked. "5:30? That's like 2:25 pace. Am I going to run 2:25?" Obviously, I wasn't going to lose more than 10 minutes in the last few miles. But I was so tired that I didn't immediately realize that, and I went negative in my head. That hurt me because I lost some of that drive to bear down as best I could the rest of the way. I still ran decently—2:13:24, the second fastest marathon of my career—but I might have been able to run 2:12 if I'd quickly realized my math error and stayed positive.

If you do a great job of pacing yourself early on, the first 18 or so miles shouldn't be a strain. Hopefully you'll just feel like you're running under control, doing occasional body checks to keep your form relaxed, and staying upbeat with lots of positive self-talk. Somewhere between 18 and 20 miles you're probably going to start getting tired. Dehydration and depletion will start to be issues, and you might start feeling a little muscle damage.

The best thing you can do from this point, when the free ride of the early miles is undeniably over, is to have prepared for it mentally. Visualize this crucial spot before the race. Tell yourself, "I know I'm going to be tired around 18. I'm not going to freak out and think, '8 miles to go?!' That's where I'm going to remind myself of all the hard work I did to get here and remind myself why this is important to me. I'm going to stay on top of it and stay positive no matter how badly it hurts."

Then take the rest of the race one mile at a time. You'll be able to run stronger and stay more positive if you just concentrate on running your current mile the best you can. Don't fall into the trap of thinking about the total distance that remains and how long that might take you. Your energy level and enthusiasm will likely fluctuate in the final miles. Don't assume that a bad patch will stay bad the rest of the way. If you can weather those patches, soon you'll be able to tell yourself something like "just one more mile" or "just 15 more minutes." Then bear down and complete the job the best you can.

Race-Day Nutrition

Pro marathoners have it easier than everyday runners when it comes to marathon fueling. The standard during my marathons was elite-only tables with our personalized fluids every 5K. For me that meant grabbing a bottle approximately every 15 minutes and being able to take my time getting in four to six ounces of sport drink.

Mimic that routine the best you can with what's available at your marathon. Drinking four to six ounces three to four times an hour is close to the maximum your GI system can process when you're running at marathon pace. You really want to maximize sport drink intake early in the race, before your stomach starts to get wonky.

Take the same approach with gels and other edible sport nutrition products. Elite marathoners who use gels generally take one or two in the first 18 miles. They time it so that they finish the gel soon before they'll get fluids. Taking gels later in the race can cause stomach problems.

Do your homework before your marathon to know exactly when fluids will be available, and then practice your planned routine on long runs. It's especially valuable to practice drinking a fair amount of sport drink on your long runs that involve stretches at marathon pace, or on some of your longer tempo runs. It's one thing to get down a few ounces of liquid at an easy pace, and quite another to consistently take in four to six ounces when you're running harder.

Late in the race, especially if your stomach is bothering you, you can get some of the benefit of sport drink by rinsing your mouth with it and then spitting it out. You'll often see elite marathoners doing this as late as the 40-kilometer mark. This trick works because sensors in your mouth will tell your brain that carbs are on the way. You'll then get a little psychological burst and will feel better. The process is the same as when you get home from a long run and eat or drink carbs and immediately feel revived, even though there hasn't been time for what you ate or drank to get to your muscles.

Endurance Sports Nutrition by Suzanne Girard Eberle and *Advanced Marathoning* have comprehensive information about on-the-run fueling.

Race-Day Shoes

The other thing besides drinking to get comfortable with during training is the shoes you'll wear in the marathon. Many people going for a PR will wear high-stack, carbon-plated "super shoes." They don't have great durability, so you probably don't want to wear them too often before your marathon. Two long runs, such as three weeks before and one week before, plus one of the workouts incorporating half-marathon or marathon pace, should be enough to know if they'll work for you on race day.

Lessons From Coach Coogan's Marathons

Marathons are tough to get right. One of my more memorable bad ones is the 1998 Chicago Marathon.

The problem for me at that race was that there was a very elite group up front who planned to set out at world-record pace, which I was never close to being able to run. There were also a lot of guys with personal bests around 2:20, which was too slow for my plans. Rod DeHaven, who would go on to run the 2000 Olympic Marathon, and I were sort of stuck in no-man's-land in terms of pace. We decided to run 2:11 pace (5:00 per mile) for as long as we could. Rod and I were good friends and occasional training partners, and we agreed to take turns pacing, alternating who led every mile.

Rod and I took turns doing this for the first 18 or so miles. In a perfect world I would never be the person trying to keep the pace at 5:00 a mile. I would hope to be able to just sit in a pack and run at a pace that seems comfortable and manageable. When I made the Olympic team two years earlier, that's exactly what I did. (More on that shortly.)

Rod's and my 5:00-per-mile goal pace may have felt comfortable that day if I didn't have to be the one making sure we stayed on it every other mile. But with just the two of us, it became increasingly difficult to move in front of Rod and reliably hit 5:00 pace. Sometimes a mile would be into the wind or have a few turns in it.

I think by leading every other mile I used up lots of my willpower and mental strength early in the race. I became tired too early in the race. The last 10K was a disaster. I became negative in my head, my body was running out of energy, and I bonked. I think I ran the last few miles at 6:30-per-mile pace. I finished 20th in 2:15:33, two and a half minutes slower than my PR, and more than four minutes slower than what Rod and I had hoped to run.

If I did this race again, I wouldn't try to run 2:11, even though that's what I think I was capable of running. Leading every other mile at 2:11 pace might be like running 2:08 pace in the back of a pack. I was not a 2:08 guy! If I ran the race today, I would probably suggest to Rod that we run 2:15 pace for the first 20 miles, and then do a body check and see if we could pick the pace up the last few miles. I paid the price by forcing the issue in the race. I didn't relax and run in a zone that would have been successful for me. I forced the issue, and the marathon won. Sometimes it's best not to get so caught up on time and just race. If I had done so that year in Chicago, it would have been a more enjoyable experience, and I would have wound up running faster.

The 1996 Olympic Marathon Trials was one of the best and most rewarding races I ran at any distance. I set myself up to succeed in that February 1996 race by what I did in 1995. In March 1995, I won the silver medal in the marathon at the Pan American Games. I quickly switched to track-racing mode. That June, I finished second at the U.S. 5,000-meter championship, which qualified me for the World Championships in August 1995. After worlds, I began my Olympic Trials buildup in the fall.

I visualized a lot that fall and winter. I was trying to see myself making the team and racing smart. The field was full of great runners, including former 10K world-record holder Arturo Barrios, 1993 world marathon champion Mark Plaatjes, and Ed Eyestone and Bob Kempainen, who had been on the 1992 Olympic Marathon team. (Ed was also on the 1988 Olympic squad in the event.)

I felt that Bob was the favorite after his 2:08 at Boston in 1994. I told myself that Bob always ran smart and wouldn't make a stupid mistake. When the race started, I fell into the lead pack and kept track of where Bob and a few other top guys were. One person who wasn't really a favorite shot out to a decent lead early on, which made me a little nervous, because I didn't know who he was. I just kept telling myself, "You're good, he'll come back, just stay with the lead pack."

Eventually we caught the early leader, and the race was on. Somewhere around 17 or 18 miles, Bob put in a surge that probably lasted about 800 meters. I immediately said to myself, "Give it a mile to reel him in; you're okay, Mark." Once I got back up with Bob, he made another move, and I knew I had to match it because it was time to make the Olympic team. After 20 miles, Bob, Keith Brantly, and I were clear of everyone else. Bob threw in a 4:42 23rd mile, which is flying that late in the race. It took everything I had mentally and physically to hold on. Bob eventually pulled away in the 24th mile—while throwing up!—and held the lead to the finish. So much for my track times giving me the edge over Bob late in the race.

Keith and I knew we were going to make the team and ran together until about half a mile to go. I kicked to claim second place and a lifetime best of 2:13:05.

I ran really smart in this race and stuck to my game plan. I knew it would get tough, and I was where I wanted to be when Bob made his move to win. All the visualization I'd done of that scenario was a big help, because when it happened in reality, I had already experienced it and knew what I was going to do.

Sometimes, things fall your way; you should try to capitalize on those opportunities. The Trials marathon was on a hilly course on a cold day, and I thrive on hills and love the cold. Also, I got all my beverages during the race, and I never felt in danger of bonking. All these factors contributed to staying mentally positive the entire race and running the best marathon of my life.

What About Boston?

The schedules have as their default that your marathon is held on a Saturday. You'll see in the final week how to tweak things if you're instead racing on a Sunday.

And then there's the Boston Marathon, famously held on a Monday.

If you're running Boston, follow the adjustments for a Sunday marathon, and run an easy two to four miles on the day before the race. If you want to take that Saturday off, you have my blessing. I'd much rather have you skip a run two days before the race than the day before.

Be happy that you're getting an extra day during the weekend to prepare mentally and physically for the run from Hopkinton to Boston. Just sit back, relax, and enjoy your time in Boston. (But not too much! See "Ration Your Prerace Resources" earlier in this chapter.)

12-Week Marathon Schedule: Up to 60 Miles per Week

	Sunday	Monday	Tuesday	Wednesday	Thursday	Friday	Saturday	Week's mileage
Week 1	Long run: 8-12 miles	Easy run: 1-4 miles OR Day off	Tempo run: 2-mile warm-up; 4-5 miles continuous at half-marathon pace; 1-mile cool-down	Easy run: 5-7 miles	Regular run: 4-6 miles, then 8 × 100-meter strides	Intervals: 2-mile warm-up; 8 × 400 meters at 10K pace, with 200-meter jog recovery between intervals; 1-mile cool-down	Easy run: 1-4 miles OR Day off	29-47
Week 2	Long run: 10-14 miles	Easy run: 1-4 miles OR Day off	Progression run: 2-mile warm-up; 4-5 miles continuous starting at 35 seconds slower than 10K pace, increasing pace 5-10 seconds per mile after each mile; 1-mile cool-down	Easy run: 5-7 miles	Regular run: 4-6 miles, then 8 × 100-meter strides	Hills repeats: 2-mile warm-up; 8 × 400- to 500-meter hill at 5K effort; jog down for recovery; 1-mile cool-down	Easy to regular run: 3-4 miles	36-50
Week 3	Long run: 12-14 miles	Easy run: 1-4 miles OR Day off	Tempo intervals: 2-mile warm-up; 3 × 1.5 miles at marathon pace with 800-meter jog between; 1-mile cool-down	Easy run: 5-7 miles	Regular run: 4-6 miles, then 8 × 100-meter strides	Intervals: 2-mile warm-up; 10 × 400 meters at 10K pace with 200-meter jog recovery; 1-mile cool-down	Easy to regular run: 1-4 miles OR Day off	36-50
Week 4	Long run: 13-16 miles	Easy run: 1-4 miles OR Day off	Tempo run: 2-mile warm-up; 6-8 miles continuous at marathon pace; 1-mile cool-down	Easy run: 3-5 miles	Regular run: 4 miles	Hills: 2-mile warm-up; 6-8 × 600- to 800-meter hill at 5K effort; jog down for recovery; 1-mile cool-down	Easy to regular run: 1-4 miles OR Day off	36-55

(continued)

12-Week Marathon Schedule: Up to 60 Miles per Week (continued)

	Sunday	Monday	Tuesday	Wednesday	Thursday	Friday	Saturday	Week's mileage
Week 5	Long run: 14-18 miles	Easy run: 1-4 miles OR Day off	Progression run: 2-mile warm-up; 6-8 miles continuous starting at marathon pace and increasing pace 3-5 seconds per mile after each mile; 1-mile cool-down	Easy run: 7-10 miles	Regular run: 4-6 miles, then 8 × 100-meter strides	Intervals: 2-mile warm-up; 1 mile at 10K pace; 1 mile at marathon pace; 1,200 meters at 10K pace; 1 mile at marathon pace; 800 meters at 5K pace; 1 mile at marathon pace; 400 meters at mile pace; 200-meter jog between all intervals; 1-mile cool-down	Easy run: 1-4 miles OR Day off	43-62
Week 6	Long run with pace work: 15-18 miles; last 5 miles at marathon pace	Easy run: 1-4 miles OR Day off	Tempo run: 2-mile warm-up; 8-10 miles starting a little slower than and working into marathon pace; 1-mile cool-down	Easy run: 7-10 miles	Regular run: 6-9 miles, then 8 × 100-meter strides	Hills: 2-mile warm-up; 8 × 600- to 800-meter hill at 5K effort; jog down for recovery; 1-mile cool-down	Easy to regular run: 1-4 miles OR Day off	46-67
Week 7	Long run with pace work: 17-20 miles; last 2 miles at marathon pace	Easy run: 1-4 miles OR Day off	Tempo run: No warm-up jog; 10-13 miles; over the last 5 miles gradually increase pace to run last mile at marathon pace; 1-mile cool-down	Easy run: 4-6 miles	Regular run: 4-6 miles, then 8 × 100-meter strides	Intervals: 2-mile warm-up; 2 sets of 4 × 800 meters at a little slower than 10K pace; 400-meter jog between intervals and 800-meter jog between sets (i.e., 800-meter jog after the fourth repeat); 1-mile cool-down	Easy to regular run: 1-6 miles OR Day off	42-62
Week 8	Long run: 18-22 miles	Easy run: 1-4 miles OR Day off	Regular run: 6-8 miles	Easy run: 4-6 miles	Regular run: 4-6 miles	Tempo run: 2-mile warm-up; 8-10 miles continuous at marathon pace; 1-mile cool-down	Easy to regular run: 1-4 miles OR Day off	43-63

	Sunday	Monday	Tuesday	Wednesday	Thursday	Friday	Saturday	Week's mileage
Week 9	Long run with pace work: 16-18 miles; last 4 miles at marathon pace	Easy run: 1-4 miles OR Day off	Tempo run: 2-mile warm-up; 6-8 miles continuous at 3-5 seconds per mile faster than marathon pace; 800-meter jog; then 6 × 400 meters at 5K pace with 200-meter jog between; 1-mile cool-down	Easy run: 7-10 miles	Regular run: 6-9 miles, then 8 × 100-meter strides	If racing tomorrow: Easy to regular run: 1-4 miles OR If not racing tomorrow: Hills: 2-mile warm-up; 6-8 × 600- to 800-meter hill at 5K effort; jog down for recovery; 1-mile cool-down	Race: 10 miles or shorter OR Easy to regular run: 1-4 miles	48-66
Week 10	Long run: 12-15 miles	Easy run: 1-4 miles OR Day off	If raced previous Saturday: Easy run: 6-8 miles If didn't race previous Saturday: Tempo run: 2-mile warm-up; 8 miles continuous at marathon pace; 1-mile cool-down	Easy run: 7-10 miles	Regular run: 6-9 miles, then 8 × 100-meter strides	Intervals: 2-mile warm-up; 8 × 400 meters at 10K pace with 200-meter jog recovery; 1-mile cool-down	Easy to regular run: 1-6 miles OR Day off	37-61
Week 11	Long run: 10-14 miles	Easy run: 1-4 miles OR Day off	Intervals: 2-mile warm-up; 3 × 3 miles with 800-meter jog between each set; 1st and 3rd interval at marathon pace; 2nd interval at half-marathon pace; 1-mile cool-down	Day off	Regular run: 5-7 miles, then 8 × 100-meter strides	Tempo run: 2-mile warm-up, 4-6 miles at marathon pace; 1-mile cool-down	Easy to regular run: 1-6 miles OR Day off	35-53
Week 12	Long run: 8-12 miles	Easy run: 1-4 miles OR Day off	Intervals: 2-mile warm-up; 6 × 800 meters at half-marathon pace with a 400-meter jog between; 1-mile cool-down	Easy run: 4-6 miles, then 8 × 100-meter strides	Easy run: 1-4 miles OR Day off	Easy run: 2-4 miles	Race marathon OR Easy run: 2-4 miles (for Sunday marathon)	21-37 (not including race)

12-Week Marathon Schedule: 35-70 Miles per Week

	Sunday	Monday	Tuesday	Wednesday	Thursday	Friday	Saturday	Week's mileage
Week 1	Long run: 8-12 miles	Easy run: 4-6 miles, then 8 × 100-meter strides	Tempo run: 2-mile warm-up; 4-5 miles continuous at half-marathon pace; 1-mile cool-down	Easy run: 5-7 miles	Regular run: 4-6 miles, then 8 × 100-meter strides	Intervals: 2-mile warm-up; 8 × 400 meters at 10K pace with 200-meter jog recovery; 1-mile cool-down	Easy run: 3-4 miles	37-49
Week 2	Long run: 10-14 miles	Easy run: 4-6 miles, then 8 × 100-meter strides	Progression run: 2-mile warm-up; 4-5 miles continuous starting at 35 seconds slower than 10K pace, increasing pace 5-10 seconds per mile after each mile; 1-mile cool-down	Easy run: 5-7 miles	Regular run: 4-6 miles, then 8 × 100-meter strides	Hills: 2-mile warm-up; 8 × 400-meter hill at 5K effort; jog down for recovery; 1-mile cool-down	Easy to regular run: 3-4 miles	40-51
Week 3	Long run: 12-14 miles	Easy run: 4-6 miles, then 8 × 100-meter strides	Tempo intervals: 2-mile warm-up; 3-4 × 1.5 miles at marathon pace with 800-meter jog between; 1-mile cool-down	Easy run: 5-7 miles	Regular run: 4-6 miles, then 8 × 100-meter strides	Intervals: 2-mile warm-up; 10 × 400 meters at 10K pace with 200-meter recovery jog between intervals; 1-mile cool-down	Easy to regular run: 2-4 miles	43-54
Week 4	Long run: 13-16 miles	Easy run: 4 miles	Tempo run: 2-mile warm-up; 6-8 miles continuous at marathon pace; 1-mile cool-down	Easy run: 3-5 miles	Regular run: 4 miles	Hills: 2-mile warm-up; 6-8 × 600-meter hill at 5K effort; jog down for recovery; 1-mile cool-down	Easy to regular run: 1-4 miles OR Day off	40-53

	Sunday	Monday	Tuesday	Wednesday	Thursday	Friday	Saturday	Week's mileage
Week 5	Long run: 14-18 miles	Easy run: 4 miles, then 8 × 100-meter strides	Progression run: 2-mile warm-up; 6-8 miles continuous starting at marathon pace increasing pace 3-5 seconds per mile after each mile; 1-mile cool-down	Easy run: 7-10 miles	Regular run: 4-6 miles, then 8 × 100-meter strides	Intervals: 2-mile warm-up; 1 mile at 10K pace; 1 mile at marathon pace; 1,200 meters at 10K pace; 1 mile at marathon pace; 800 meters at 5K pace; 1 mile at marathon pace; 400 meters at mile pace; 200-meter jog after all intervals; 1-mile cool-down	Easy to regular run: 1-6 miles OR Day off	49-66
Week 6	Long run with pace work: 15-18 miles; last 5 miles at marathon pace	Easy run: 4 miles	Tempo run: 2-mile warm-up; 8-10 miles starting a little slower than and working into marathon pace; 1-mile cool-down	Easy run: 7-10 miles	Regular run: 6-9 miles, then 8 × 100-meter strides	Hills: 2-mile warm-up; 8 × 600- to 800-meter hill at 5K effort; jog down for recovery; 1-mile cool-down	Easy to regular run: 4-6 miles	55-71
Week 7	Long run: 17-20 miles; last 2 miles at marathon pace	Easy run: 2-4 miles	Tempo run: No warm-up jog; 10-13 miles; over the last 5 miles gradually increase pace to run last mile at marathon pace; 1-mile cool-down	Easy run: 4-6 miles	Regular run: 4-6 miles, then 8 × 100-meter strides	Intervals: 2-mile warm-up; 2 sets of 4 × 800 meters at a little slower than 10K pace; 400-meter jog between intervals and 800-meter jog between the sets; 1-mile cool-down	Easy to regular run: 4-6 miles	50-64
Week 8	Long run: 18-22 miles	Easy run: 1-4 miles OR Day off	Regular run: 6-8 miles	Easy run: 4-6 miles	Regular run: 4-6 miles	Tempo run: 2-mile warm-up; 8-10 miles at marathon pace; 1-mile cool-down	Easy to regular run: 1-4 miles OR Day off	43-63

(continued)

210

12-Week Marathon Schedule: 35-70 Miles per Week (continued)

	Sunday	Monday	Tuesday	Wednesday	Thursday	Friday	Saturday	Week's mileage
Week 9	Long run: 16-18 miles; last 2 miles a little faster than marathon pace	Easy run: 4-6 miles, then 8 × 100-meter strides	Tempo run: 2-mile warm-up; 6-8 miles continuous at 3-5 seconds per mile faster than marathon pace; 800-meter jog; 6 × 400 meters at 5K pace with 200-meter jog between; 1-mile cool-down	Easy run: 7-10 miles	Regular run: 6-9 miles, then 8 × 100-meter strides	If racing tomorrow: Easy to regular run: 1-4 miles OR If not racing tomorrow: Hills: 2-mile warm-up; 6-8 × 600- to 800-meter hill at 5K effort; jog down for recovery; 1-mile cool-down	Race: 10 miles or shorter OR Easy to regular run: 1-4 miles	54-71
Week 10	Long run: 12-15 miles	Easy run: 6-8 miles, then 8 × 100-meter strides	If raced previous Saturday: Easy run: 6-8 miles If didn't race previous Saturday: Tempo run: 2-mile warm-up; 8 miles continuous at marathon pace; 1-mile cool-down	Easy run: 7-10 miles	Regular run: 6-9 miles, then 8 × 100-meter strides	Intervals: 2-mile warm-up; 8 × 400 meters at 10K pace with 200-meter jog between; 1-mile cool-down	Easy to regular run: 1-6 miles OR Day off	43-65
Week 11	Long run: 10-14 miles	Easy run: 5-7 miles	Intervals: 2-mile warm-up; 3 × 3 miles with 800-meter jog between sets; 1st and 3rd interval at marathon pace, 2nd at half-marathon pace; 1-mile cool-down	Easy run: 6-8 miles	Regular run: 5-7 miles, then 8 × 100-meter strides	Tempo run: 2-mile warm-up; 4-6 miles at marathon pace; 1-mile cool-down	Easy to regular run: 1-6 miles OR Day off	45-64
Week 12	Long run: 8-12 miles	Easy run: 4-6 miles	Intervals: 2-mile warm-up; 6 × 800 meters at half-marathon pace with 400-meter jog between; 1-mile cool-down	Easy run: 4-6 miles, then 8 × 100-meter strides	Easy run: 1-4 miles OR Day off	Easy run: 2-4 miles	Race marathon OR Easy run: 2-4 miles (for Sunday marathon)	25-39 (not including race)

12-Week Marathon Schedule: 45+ Miles per Week

	Sunday	Monday	Tuesday	Wednesday	Thursday	Friday	Saturday	Week's mileage
Week 1	Long run: 10-12 miles	Easy run: 6-8 miles, then 8 × 100-meter strides	Tempo run: 2- to 3-mile warm-up; 4-6 miles continuous at pace; 1- to 2-mile cool-down	Easy run: 7-9 miles	Regular run: 7-9 miles, then 8 × 100-meter strides	Intervals: 2- to 3-mile warm-up; 8 × 400 meters at 10K pace with 200-meter jog between; 1- to 2-mile cool-down	Easy run: 4-6 miles	47-63
Week 2	Long run: 10-14 miles	Easy run: 6-8 miles, then 8 × 100-meter strides	Progression run: 2- to 3-mile warm-up; 4-6 miles continuous, starting at 35 seconds slower than 10K pace, increasing pace 5-10 seconds per mile after each mile; 1- to 2-mile cool-down	Easy run: 7-9 miles	Regular run: 7-9 miles, then 8 × 100-meter strides	Hills: 2- to 3-mile warm-up; 8 × 400- to 500-meter hill at 5K effort; jog down for recovery; 1- to 2-mile cool-down	Easy to regular run: 4-6 miles	48-64
Week 3	Long run: 12-14 miles	Easy run: 6-8 miles, then 8 × 100-meter strides	Tempo intervals: 2- to 3-mile warm-up; 4 × 1.5 miles at marathon pace with 800-meter jog between; 1- to 2-mile cool-down	Easy run: 7-10 miles	Regular run: 7-9 miles, then 8 × 100-meter strides	Intervals: 2- to 3-mile warm-up; 10-12 × 400 meters at 10K pace with 200-meter jog between; 1- to 2-mile cool-down	Easy to regular run: 4-6 miles	53-69
Week 4	Long run: 14-16 miles	Easy run: 6-8 miles	Tempo run: 2- to 3-mile warm-up; 6-8 miles continuous at marathon pace; 1- to 2-mile cool-down	Easy run: 7-10 miles	Regular run: 6-9 miles	Hills: 2- to 3-mile warm-up; 8 × 600- to 800-meter hill at 5K effort; jog down for recovery; 1- to 2-mile cool-down	Easy to regular run: 1-4 miles OR Day off	49-73

(continued)

12-Week Marathon Schedule: 45+ Miles per Week (continued)

	Sunday	Monday	Tuesday	Wednesday	Thursday	Friday	Saturday	Week's mileage
Week 5	Long run: 15-18 miles	Easy run: 6-8 miles, then 8 × 100-meter strides	Progression run: 2- to 3-mile warm-up; 6-8 miles continuous starting at marathon pace and increasing pace 3-5 seconds per mile after each mile; 1- to 2-mile cool-down	Easy run: 7-10 miles	Regular run: 6-9 miles, then 8 × 100-meter strides	Intervals: 2- to 3-mile warm-up; 1 mile at 10K pace; 1 mile at marathon pace; 1,200 meters at 10K pace; 1 mile at marathon pace; 800 meters at 5K pace; 1 mile at marathon pace; 400 meters at mile pace; 200-meter jog between intervals; 1- to 2-mile cool-down	Easy to regular run: 4-6 miles	55-73
Week 6	Long run with pace work: 15-18 miles; last 5 miles at marathon pace	Easy run: 4-8 miles	Tempo run; 2- to 3-mile warm-up; 8-10 miles starting a little slower than and working into marathon pace; 1- to 2-mile cool-down	Easy run: 7-10 miles	Regular run: 6-9 miles, then 8 × 100-meter strides	Hills: 2- to 3-mile warm-up; 8 × 600- to 800-meter hill at 5K effort; jog down for recovery; 1- to 2-mile cool-down	Easy to regular run: 4-6 miles	56-79
Week 7	Long run: 18-20 miles; last 2 miles at marathon pace	Easy run: 4-8 miles	Tempo run: No warm-up jog; 13 miles, gradually increase pace over the last 5 miles to run last mile at marathon pace; 1- to 2-mile cool-down	Easy run: 7-10 miles	Regular run: 6-9 miles, then 8 × 100-meter strides	Intervals: 2- to 3-mile warm-up; 2 sets of 4 × 800 meters at a little slower than 10K pace; 400-meter jog between intervals and 800-meter jog between the two sets; 1- to 2-mile cool-down	Easy to regular run: 4-6 miles	61-77

	Sunday	Monday	Tuesday	Wednesday	Thursday	Friday	Saturday	Week's mileage
Week 8	Long run: 20-22 miles	Easy run: 5-7 miles	Regular run: 6-8 miles, then 8 × 100-meter strides	Easy run: 6-8 miles	Regular run: 5-7 miles	Tempo run: 2- to 3-mile warm-up; 8-10 miles continuous at marathon pace; 1- to 2-mile cool-down	Easy to regular run: 1-4 miles OR Day off	53-71
Week 9	Long run with pace work: 16-18 miles, last 4 miles a little faster than marathon pace	Easy run: 4-6 miles, then 8 × 100-meter strides	Tempo run: 2- to 3-mile warm-up; 6-8 miles continuous at 3-5 seconds per mile faster than marathon pace; 800-meter jog; 6 × 400 meters at 5K pace with 200-meter jog between; 1- to 2-mile cool-down	Easy run: 7-10 miles	Regular run: 6-9 miles, then 8 × 100-meter strides	If racing tomorrow: Easy to regular run: 1-4 miles OR If not racing tomorrow: Hills: 2- to 3-mile warm-up; 8 × 600- to 800-meter hill at 5K effort; jog down for recovery; 1- to 2-mile cool-down	Race: 10 miles or shorter OR Easy to regular run: 4-6 miles	54-75
Week 10	Long run: 13-15 miles	Easy run: 6-8 miles, then 8 × 100-meter strides	If raced previous Saturday: Easy run: 6-8 miles OR If didn't race previous Saturday: Tempo run: 2- to 3-mile warm-up; 8 miles continuous at marathon pace; 1- to 2-mile cool-down	Easy run: 7-10 miles	Regular run: 6-9 miles, then 8 × 100-meter strides	Intervals: 2- to 3-mile warm-up; 8 × 400 meters at 10K pace with 200-meter jog between; 1- to 2-mile cool-down	Easy to regular run: 4-6 miles	48-69

(continued)

45+ Miles per Week
12-Week Marathon Schedule

12-Week Marathon Schedule: 45+ Miles per Week (continued)

	Sunday	Monday	Tuesday	Wednesday	Thursday	Friday	Saturday	Week's mileage
Week 11	Long run: 12-14 miles	Easy run: 5-7 miles	Intervals: 2- to 3-mile warm-up; 3 × 3 miles with 800-meter jog between sets; 1st and 3rd interval at marathon pace, 2nd at half-marathon pace; 1- to 2-mile cool-down	Easy run: 6-8 miles	Regular run: 5-7 miles, then 8 × 100-meter strides	Tempo run: 2- to 3-mile warm-up; 4-6 miles continuous at marathon pace; 1- to 2-mile cool-down	Easy to regular run: 1-6 miles OR Day off	46-68
Week 12	Long run: 8-12 miles	Easy run: 4-6 miles	Intervals: 2- to 3-mile warm-up; 6 × 800 meters at half-marathon pace with 400-meter jog between; 1- to 2-mile cool-down	Easy run: 4-6 miles, then 8 × 100-meter strides	Easy run: 1-4 miles OR Day off	Easy run: 2-4 miles	Race marathon OR Easy run: 2-4 miles (for Sunday marathon)	25-41 (not including race)

16-Week Marathon Schedule: Up to 65 Miles per Week

	Sunday	Monday	Tuesday	Wednesday	Thursday	Friday	Saturday	Week's mileage
Week 1	Long run: 8-10 miles	Easy run: 4-6 miles	Regular run: 4-6 miles	Day off	Regular run: 4-6 miles	Intervals: 2-mile warm-up; 8 × 400 meters at 10K pace with 200-meter jog recovery; 1-mile cool-down	Easy run: 1-4 miles OR Day off	26-38
Week 2	Long run: 8-10 miles	Easy run: 4-6 miles, then 6-8 × 100-meter strides	Tempo run: 2-mile warm-up; 3-4 miles continuous at half-marathon pace; 1-mile cool-down	Day off	Regular run: 4-6 miles	Intervals: 2-mile warm-up; 4-5 × 800 meters at 10K pace with 400-meter jog recovery; 1-mile cool-down	Easy run: 1-4 miles OR Day off	28-40
Week 3	Long run: 10-12 miles	Easy run: 5-7 miles, then 6-8 × 100-meter strides	Hilly run: 6-8 miles on hilly course at regular run pace; if no hills available, run 10 seconds per mile faster than regular run pace	Day off	Regular run: 4-6 miles, then 6-8 × 100-meter strides	Intervals: 2-mile warm-up; 3 × 1 mile at half-marathon pace with 400-meter jog recovery; 1-mile cool-down	Easy run: 1-4 miles OR Day off	32-44
Week 4	Long run: 10-12 miles	Easy run: 5-7 miles, then 6-8 × 100-meter strides	Tempo run: 2-mile warm-up; 5-6 miles continuous at half-marathon pace; 1-mile cool-down	Day off	Regular run: 5-7 miles, then 6-8 × 100-meter strides	Intervals: 2-mile warm-up; 8 × 400 meters at 10K pace with 200-meter jog recovery; 1-mile cool-down	Easy run: 1-4 miles OR Day off	34-45

(continued)

16-Week Marathon Schedule: Up to 65 Miles per Week (continued)

	Sunday	Monday	Tuesday	Wednesday	Thursday	Friday	Saturday	Week's mileage
Week 5	Long run: 12-14 miles	Easy run: 6-7 miles, then 8 × 100-meter strides	Progression run: 2-mile warm-up; 6-8 miles continuous starting at marathon pace, increasing each pace 3-5 seconds per mile after each mile; 1-mile cool-down	Day off	Regular run: 6-9 miles, then 8 × 100-meter strides	Hills: 2-mile warm-up; 8 × 400-meter hill at 5K effort; jog down for recovery, 1-mile cool-down	Easy run: 1-4 miles OR Day off	40-52
Week 6	Long run: 12-14 miles	Easy run: 6-8 miles, then 8 × 100-meter strides	Tempo run: 2-mile warm-up, 6-8 miles continuous at marathon pace; 1-mile cool-down	Day off	Regular run: 6-9 miles, then 8 × 100-meter strides	Intervals: 2-mile warm-up; 6 × 800 meters at 10K pace with 400-meter jog recovery; 1-mile cool-down	Easy run: 1-4 miles OR Day off	40-53
Week 7	Long run: 14-16 miles	Easy run: 4-6 miles	Tempo intervals: 2-mile warm-up; 4 × 1.5 miles at marathon pace with 800-meter jog between; 1-mile cool-down	Day off	Regular run: 6-9 miles	Intervals: 2-mile warm-up; 1 mile at 10K pace; 1 mile at marathon pace; 1,200 meters at 10K pace; 1 mile at marathon pace; 800 meters at 5K pace; 1 mile at marathon pace; 400 meters at mile pace; 200-meter jog between all intervals; 1-mile cool-down	Easy run: 1-4 miles OR Day off	43-54

	Sunday	Monday	Tuesday	Wednesday	Thursday	Friday	Saturday	Week's mileage
Week 8	Long run: 14-16 miles	Easy run: 4-6 miles, then 8 × 100-meter strides	Tempo run: 2-mile warm-up; 8-10 miles at marathon pace; 1-mile cool-down	Day off	Regular run: 6-9 miles, then 8 × 100-meter strides	If racing tomorrow: Easy run: 2-4 miles OR If not racing tomorrow: Hills: 2-mile warm-up; 8 × 400-meter hill at 5K effort; jog down for recovery; 1-mile cool-down	Race: 10K to half-marathon OR Easy run: 1-4 miles	47-65
Week 9	If raced 15K or longer: Easy run: 6-8 miles OR If didn't race or raced 10K: Long run: 15-18 miles	Easy run: 4-6 miles, then 8 × 100-meter strides	If raced 15K or longer previous Saturday: Regular run: 8-10 miles OR If didn't race or raced 10K: Progression run: 2-mile warm-up; 8-10 miles continuous, starting at marathon pace and increasing pace 3-5 seconds per mile after each mile; 1-mile cool-down	Day off	Regular run: 6-9 miles, then 8 × 100-meter strides	Intervals: 2-mile warm-up; 4-6 × 1 mile at marathon pace or a little faster with 400-meter jog between; 1-mile cool-down	Easy run: 1-4 miles OR Day off	32-60
Week 10	Long run: 15-18 miles	Easy run: 4-6 miles, then 8 × 100-meter strides	Hilly run: 10-12 miles on hilly course at regular run pace; if no hills available, run 10 seconds per mile faster than regular run pace	Day off	Regular run: 7-9 miles, then 8 × 100-meter strides	Intervals: 2-mile warm-up; 8 × 400 meters at 10K pace with 200-meter jog between; 1-mile cool-down	Easy run: 1-4 miles OR Day off	42-55

(continued)

16-Week Marathon Schedule: Up to 65 Miles per Week (continued)

	Sunday	Monday	Tuesday	Wednesday	Thursday	Friday	Saturday	Week's mileage
Week 11	Long run 12-14 miles	Easy run: 4-6 miles	Tempo intervals: 2-mile warm-up; 4 × 2 miles at marathon pace with 800-meter jog between; 1-mile cool-down	Day off	Easy run: 6-8 miles	If racing tomorrow: Easy run: 2-4 miles OR If not racing tomorrow: Hills: 2-mile warm-up; 8 × 400-meter hill at 5K effort; jog down for recovery; 1-mile cool-down	Race: 10K to half-marathon OR Day off	47-64
Week 12	If raced 15K or longer: Easy run: 6-10 miles OR If didn't race or raced 10K: Long run: 18-20 miles	Easy run: 3-6 miles, then 8 × 100-meter strides	If raced 15K or longer previous Saturday: Regular run: 8-10 miles OR If didn't race or raced 10K: Tempo run: 2-mile warm-up; 6-8 miles at marathon pace; 1-mile cool-down	Day off	Regular run: 6-8 miles, then 8 × 100-meter strides	Intervals: 2-mile warm-up; 800 meters at 10K pace; 1 mile at half-marathon pace; 800 meters at 10K pace; 1 mile at half-marathon pace; 400-meter jog between intervals; 1-mile cool-down	Day off	30-52
Week 13	Long run: 20-22 miles	Easy run: 3-8 miles, then 8 × 100-meter strides	Tempo run: 2-mile warm-up; 4-6 miles continuous at half-marathon pace; 800-meter jog; 6 × 400 meters at mile pace with 200-meter jog between; 1-mile cool-down	Day off	Regular run: 6-8 miles, then 8 × 100-meter strides	Intervals: 2-mile warm-up; 8 × 800 meters at 10K pace with 400-meter jog between; 1-mile cool-down	Easy run: 1-4 miles OR Day off	47-62

	Sunday	Monday	Tuesday	Wednesday	Thursday	Friday	Saturday	Week's mileage
Week 14	Long run: 15-18 miles, last 2 miles faster than marathon pace	Easy run: 4-6 miles, then 6 × 100-meter strides	Tempo run: 2-mile warm-up; 4-6 miles continuous at marathon pace; 1-mile cool-down	Day off	Regular run: 6-8 miles, then 6 × 100-meter strides	Intervals: 2-mile warm-up; 8 × 400 meters at 10K pace with 200-meter jog between; 1-mile cool-down	Easy run: 1-4 miles OR Day off	40-53
Week 15	Long run: 10-12 miles	Easy run: 1-4 miles OR Day off	Tempo intervals: 2-mile warm-up; 2 × 3 miles continuous at marathon pace with 1-mile jog between; 1-mile cool-down	Day off	Regular run: 6-8 miles, then 8 × 100-meter strides	Tempo run: 2-mile warm-up; 4-6 miles continuous at marathon pace; 1-mile cool-down	Easy run: 1-4 miles OR Day off	33-47
Week 16	Long run: 8-10 miles	Day off	Intervals: 2-mile warm-up; 8 × 400 meters at 10K pace with 200-meter jog between; 1-mile cool-down	Easy run: 2-4 miles	Easy run: 1-4 miles OR Day off	Easy run: 2-4 miles	Race marathon OR Easy run: 2-4 miles (for Sunday marathon)	18-28 (not including race)

16-Week Marathon Schedule: 40-75 Miles per Week

	Sunday	Monday	Tuesday	Wednesday	Thursday	Friday	Saturday	Week's mileage
Week 1	Long run: 8-10 miles	Easy run: 4-6 miles	Regular run: 4-6 miles	Regular run: 5-7 miles	Regular run: 4-6 miles	Intervals: 2-mile warm-up; 8 × 400 meters at 10K pace with 200-meter jog recovery; 1-mile cool-down	Easy run: 1-4 miles OR Day off	31-45
Week 2	Long run: 8-10 miles	Easy run: 4-6 miles, then 6 × 100-meter strides	Tempo run: 2-mile warm-up; 3-4 miles continuous at half-marathon pace; 1-mile cool-down	Easy run: 5-7 miles	Regular run: 4-6 miles, then 6 × 100-meter strides	Intervals: 2-mile warm-up; 4-5 × 800 meters at 10K pace with 400-meter jog recovery between intervals; 1-mile cool-down	Easy run: 1-4 miles OR Day off	33-47
Week 3	Long run: 10-12 miles	Easy run: 5-7 miles, then 6-8 × 100-meter strides	Hilly run: 6-8 miles on hilly course at regular run pace; if hills not available, run 10 seconds per mile faster than regular run pace	Easy run: 5-7 miles	Regular run: 4-6 miles, then 6-8 × 100-meter strides	Intervals: 2-mile warm-up; 3 × 1 mile at half-marathon pace with 400-meter jog between; 1-mile cool-down	Easy run: 1-4 miles OR Day off	36-50
Week 4	Long run: 10-12 miles	Easy run: 5-7 miles, then 6-8 × 100-meter strides	Tempo run: 2-mile warm-up; 5-6 miles continuous at half-marathon pace; 1-mile cool-down	Easy run: 6-8 miles	Regular run: 5-7 miles, then 6-8 × 100-meter strides	Intervals: 2-mile warm-up; 8-10 × 400 meters at 10K pace with 200-meter jog recovery; 1-mile cool-down	Easy run: 1-4 miles OR Day off	40-54
Week 5	Long run: 12-14 miles	Easy run: 6-7 miles, then 8 × 100-meter strides	Progression run: 2-mile warm-up; 6-8 miles continuous starting at marathon pace, increasing pace 3-5 seconds per mile after each mile; 1-mile cool-down	Easy run: 7-9 miles	Regular run: 6-9 miles, then 8 × 100-meter strides	Hills: 2-mile warm-up; 8 × 600-meter hill at 5K effort; jog down for recovery; 1-mile cool-down	Easy run: 1-4 miles OR Day off	48-61

	Sunday	Monday	Tuesday	Wednesday	Thursday	Friday	Saturday	Week's mileage
Week 6	Long run: 12-14 miles	Easy run: 6-8 miles, then 8 × 100-meter strides	Tempo run: 2-mile warm-up; 6-8 miles continuous at marathon pace; 1-mile cool-down	Easy run: 7-9 miles	Regular run: 6-9 miles, then 8 × 100-meter strides	Intervals: 2-mile warm-up; 6-8 × 800 meters at 10K pace with 400-meter jog recovery; 1-mile cool-down	Easy run: 1-4 miles OR Day off	47-64
Week 7	Long run: 14-16 miles	Easy run: 6-8 miles	Tempo intervals: 2-mile warm-up; 4 × 1.5 miles at marathon pace with 800-meter jog between; 1-mile cool-down	Easy run: 7-10 miles	Regular run: 6-9 miles	Intervals: 2-mile warm-up; 1 mile at 10K pace; 1 mile at marathon pace; 1,200 meters at 10K pace; 1 mile at marathon pace; 800 meters at 5K pace; 1 mile at marathon pace; 400 meters at mile pace; 200-meter jog between intervals; 1-mile cool-down	Easy run: 1-4 miles OR Day off	52-66
Week 8	Long run: 14-16 miles	Easy run: 4-6 miles, then 8 × 100-meter strides	Tempo run: 2-mile warm-up; 8-10 miles at marathon pace; 1-mile cool-down	Easy run: 7-10 miles	Regular run: 6-9 miles, then 8 × 100-meter strides	If racing tomorrow: Easy run: 2-4 miles OR If not racing tomorrow: Hills: 2-mile warm-up; 6-8 × 600- to 800-meter hill at 5K effort; jog down for recovery; 1-mile cool-down	Race: 10K to half-marathon OR Easy run: 1-4 miles	50-75

(continued)

221

16-Week Marathon Schedule: 40-75 Miles per Week (continued)

	Sunday	Monday	Tuesday	Wednesday	Thursday	Friday	Saturday	Week's mileage
Week 9	If raced 15K or longer: Easy run: 6-8 miles OR If didn't race or raced 10K: Long run: 15-18 miles	Easy run: 4-6 miles, then 8 × 100-meter strides	If raced 15K or longer previous Saturday: Regular run: 8-10 miles OR If didn't race or raced 10K: Progression run: 2-mile warm-up; 8-10 miles continuous, starting at marathon pace and increasing pace 3-5 seconds per mile after each mile; 1-mile cool-down	Easy run: 7-10 miles	Regular run: 6-9 miles, then 8 × 100-meter strides	Intervals: 2-mile warm-up; 6-8 × 1 mile at marathon pace or a little faster with 400-meter jog between; 1-mile cool-down	Easy run: 1-4 miles OR Day off	41-73
Week 10	Long run: 15-18 miles	Easy run: 6-8 miles, then 8 × 100-meter strides	Hilly run: 10-12 miles on hilly course at regular run pace; if no hills available, run 10 seconds per mile faster than regular run pace	Easy run: 7-10 miles	Regular run: 7-9 miles, then 8 × 100-meter strides	Intervals: 2-mile warm-up; 8-10 × 400 meters at 10K pace with 200-meter jog between; 1-mile cool-down	Easy run: 1-4 miles OR Day off	51-68
Week 11	Long run: 12-14 miles	Easy run: 6-8 miles	Tempo intervals: 2-mile warm-up; 4 × 2 miles at marathon pace with 800-meter jog between; 1-mile cool-down	Easy run: 7-10 miles	Easy run: 6-8 miles	If racing tomorrow: Easy run: 2-4 miles OR If not racing tomorrow: Hills: 2-mile warm-up; 8-10 × 400-meter hill at 5K effort; jog down for recovery; 1-mile cool-down	Race: 10K to half-marathon OR Easy run: 1-4 miles	50-74

	Sunday	Monday	Tuesday	Wednesday	Thursday	Friday	Saturday	Week's mileage
Week 12	If raced 15K or longer or longer Easy run: 6-10 miles OR If didn't race or raced 10K: Long run: 18-20 miles	Easy run: 4-6 miles, then 8 × 100-meter strides	If raced 15K or longer previous Saturday: Regular run: 8-10 miles OR If didn't race or raced 10K: Tempo run: 2-mile warm-up; 6-8 miles at marathon pace; 1-mile cool-down	Easy run: 7-10 miles	Regular run: 6-8 miles, then 8 × 100-meter strides	Intervals: 2-mile warm-up; 2 × set of 800 meters at 10K pace, 1 mile at half-marathon pace, 800 meters at 10K pace; 400-meter jog between intervals and 800-meter jog between sets; 1 mile cool-down	Easy run: 1-4 miles OR Day off	42-70
Week 13	Long run: 20-22 miles	Easy run: 4-6 miles	Tempo run: 2-mile warm-up; 4-6 miles continuous at half-marathon pace; 800-meter jog; 6 × 400 meters at mile pace with 200-meter jog between; 1-mile cool-down	Easy run: 6-8 miles	Regular run: 6-8 miles, then 8 × 100-meter strides	Intervals: 2-mile warm-up; 8 × 800 meters at 10K pace with 400-meter jog between; 1-mile cool-down	Easy run: 1-4 miles OR Day off	54-68
Week 14	Long run: 15-18 miles, last 2 miles faster than marathon goal pace	Easy run: 4-6 miles, then 6 × 100-meter strides	Tempo run: 2-mile warm-up; 4-6 miles continuous at marathon pace; 1-mile cool-down	Easy run: 4-6 miles	Regular run: 6-8 miles, then 6 × 100-meter strides	Intervals: 2-mile warm-up; 8 × 400 meters at 10K pace with 200-meter jog between; 1-mile cool-down	Easy run: 1-4 miles OR Day off	42-57

(continued)

16-Week Marathon Schedule: 40-75 Miles per Week (continued)

	Sunday	Monday	Tuesday	Wednesday	Thursday	Friday	Saturday	Week's mileage
Week 15	Long run: 10-12 miles	Easy run: 1-4 miles OR Day off	Tempo intervals: 2-mile warm-up; 2 × 3 miles continuous at marathon pace with 1-mile jog between; 1-mile cool-down	Easy run: 6-8 miles	Regular run: 6-8 miles, then 8 × 100-meter strides	Tempo run: 2-mile warm-up; 4-6 miles continuous at marathon pace; 1-mile cool-down	Easy run: 1-4 miles OR Day off	39-57
Week 16	Long run: 8-10 miles	Day off	Intervals: 2-mile warm-up; 8 × 400 meters at 10K pace with 200-meter jog between; 1-mile cool-down	Easy run: 2-6 miles	Easy run: 1-4 miles OR Day off	Easy run: 2-4 miles	Race marathon OR Easy run: 2-4 miles (for Sunday marathon)	18-30 (not including race)

16-Week Marathon Schedule: 35+ Miles per Week

	Sunday	Monday	Tuesday	Wednesday	Thursday	Friday	Saturday	Week's mileage
Week 1	Long run: 8-10 miles	Easy run: 4-6 miles	Regular run: 4-6 miles	Regular run: 5-7 miles	Regular run: 4-6 miles	Intervals: 2- to 3-mile warm-up; 8 × 400 meters at 10K pace with 200-meter jog between intervals; 1- to 2-mile cool-down	Easy run: 4 miles	35-47
Week 2	Long run: 8-10 miles	Easy run: 4-6 miles, then 8 × 100-meter strides	Tempo run: 2- to 3-mile warm-up; 3-4 miles continuous at half-marathon pace; 1- to 2-mile cool-down	Easy run: 5-7 miles	Regular run: 4-6 miles	Intervals: 2- to 3-mile warm-up; 4-5 × 800 meters at 10K pace with 400-meter jog recovery; 1- to 2-mile cool-down	Easy run: 1-4 miles OR Day off	33-51
Week 3	Long run: 10-12 miles	Easy run: 5-7 miles, then 8 × 100-meter strides	Hilly run: 6-8 miles on hilly course at regular run pace; if hills not available, run 10 seconds per mile faster than regular run pace	Easy run: 5-7 miles	Regular run: 4-6 miles, then 8 × 100-meter strides	Intervals: 2- to 3-mile warm-up; 3 × 1 mile at half-marathon pace with 400-meter jog between; 1- to 2-mile cool-down	Easy run: 4-6 miles	41-53
Week 4	Long run: 10-12 miles	Easy run: 5-7 miles, then 8 × 100-meter strides	Tempo run: 2- to 3-mile warm-up; 5-6 miles continuous at half-marathon pace; 1- to 2-mile cool-down	Easy run: 6-8 miles	Regular run: 5-7 miles then 8 × 100-meter strides	Intervals: 2- to 3-mile warm-up; 10-12 × 400 meters at 10K pace with 200-meter jog recovery; 1- to 2-mile cool-down	Easy run: 4-6 miles	45-61

(continued)

16-Week Marathon Schedule: 35+ Miles per Week (*continued*)

	Sunday	Monday	Tuesday	Wednesday	Thursday	Friday	Saturday	Week's mileage
Week 5	Long run: 12-14 miles	Easy run: 6-7 miles, then 8 × 100-meter strides	Progression run: 2- to 3-mile warm-up; 6-8 miles continuous starting at marathon pace, increasing each pace 3-5 seconds per mile after each mile; 1- to 2-mile cool-down	Easy run: 7-9 miles	Regular run: 6-9 miles, then 8 × 100-meter strides	Hills: 2- to 3-mile warm-up; 8 × 600-meter hill at 5K effort; jog down for recovery; 1- to 2-mile cool-down	Easy run: 1-6 miles OR Day off	49-68
Week 6	Long run: 12-14 miles	Easy run: 6-8 miles, then 8 × 100-meter strides	Tempo run: 2- to 3-mile warm-up; 6-8 miles continuous at marathon pace; 1- to 2-mile cool-down	Easy run: 7-9 miles	Regular run: 6-9 miles, then 8 × 100-meter strides	Intervals: 2- to 3-mile warm-up; 6-8 × 800 meters at 10K pace with 400-meter jog recovery; 1- to 2-mile cool-down	Easy run: 4-6 miles	51-73
Week 7	Long run: 14-16 miles	Easy run: 6-8 miles	Tempo intervals: 2- to 3-mile warm-up; 4 × 1.5 miles at marathon pace with 800-meter jog between; 1- to 2-mile cool-down	Easy run 7-10 miles	Regular run: 6-9 miles	Intervals: 2- to 3-mile warm-up; 1 mile at 10K pace; 1 mile at marathon pace; 1,200 meters at 10K pace; 1 mile at marathon pace; 800 meters at 5K pace; 1 mile at marathon pace; 400 meters at mile pace; 200-meter jog between all intervals; 1- to 2-mile cool-down	Easy run: 1-4 miles OR Day off	52-70

	Sunday	Monday	Tuesday	Wednesday	Thursday	Friday	Saturday	Week's mileage
Week 8	Long run: 14-16 miles	Easy run: 4-6 miles, then 8 × 100-meter strides	Tempo run: 2- to 3-mile warm-up; 8-10 miles continuous at marathon pace; 1- to 2-mile cool-down	Easy run: 7-10 miles	Regular run: 6-9 miles, then 8 × 100-meter strides	If racing tomorrow: Easy run: 2-4 miles OR If not racing tomorrow: Hills: 2- to 3-mile warm-up; 8 × 600- to 800-meter hill at 5K effort; jog down for recovery; 1- to 2-mile cool-down	Race: 10K to half-marathon OR Easy run: 4-6 miles	56-74
Week 9	If raced 15K or longer: Easy run: 6-8 miles OR If didn't race or raced 10K: Long run: 15-18 miles	Easy run: 6-8 miles, then 8 × 100-meter strides	If raced 15K or longer previous Saturday: Regular run: 8-10 miles OR If didn't race or raced 10K: Progression run: 2- to 3-mile warm-up; 8-10 miles continuous, starting at marathon pace and increasing pace 3-5 seconds per mile after each mile; 1- to 2-mile cool-down	Easy run: 7-10 miles	Regular run: 6-9 miles, then 8 × 100-meter strides	Intervals: 2- to 3-mile warm-up; 6-8 × 1 mile at marathon pace or a little faster with 400-meter jog between; 1- to 2-mile cool-down	Easy run: 1-6 miles	45-81
Week 10	Long run: 15-18 miles	Easy run: 6-8 miles, then 8 × 100-meter strides	Hilly run: 10-12 miles on hilly course at regular run pace; if hills not available, run 10 seconds per mile faster than regular run pace	Easy run: 7-10 miles	Regular run: 7-9 miles, then 8 × 100-meter strides	Intervals: 2- to 3-mile warm-up; 8-10 × 400 meters at 10K pace with 200-meter jog between; 1- to 2-mile cool-down	Easy run: 4-6 miles	55-72

(continued)

16-Week Marathon Schedule: 35+ Miles per Week (continued)

	Sunday	Monday	Tuesday	Wednesday	Thursday	Friday	Saturday	Week's mileage
Week 11	Long run: 12-14 miles	Easy run: 6-8 miles	Tempo intervals: 2- to 3-mile warm-up; 4 × 2 miles at marathon pace with 800-meter jog between; 1- to 2-mile cool-down	Easy run: 7-10 miles	Easy run: 6-8 miles	If racing tomorrow: Easy run: 2-4 miles OR If not racing tomorrow: Hills: 2- to 3-mile warm-up; 8-10 × 400-meter hill at 5K effort; jog down for recovery; 1- to 2-mile cool-down	Race: 10K to half-marathon OR Easy run: 4-6 miles	56-73
Week 12	If raced 15K or longer: Easy run: 6-10 miles OR If didn't race or raced 10K: Long run: 18-20 miles	Easy run: 6-8 miles, then 8 × 100-meter strides	If raced 15K or longer previous Saturday: Regular run: 8-10 miles OR If didn't race or raced 10K: Tempo run: 2- to 3-mile warm-up; 6-8 miles continuous at marathon pace; 1- to 2-mile cool-down	Easy run: 7-10 miles	Regular run: 6-8 miles, then 8 × 100-meter strides	Intervals: 2- to 3-mile warm-up; 2 × set of 800 meters at 10K pace, 1 mile at half-marathon pace, 1 mile at half-marathon pace, 800 meters at 10K pace; 400-meter jog between intervals and 800-meter jog between sets; 1- to 2-mile cool-down	Easy run: 1-6 miles OR Day off	45-80
Week 13	Long run: 20-22 miles	Easy run: 6-8 miles, then 8 × 100-meter strides	Tempo run: 2- to 3-mile warm-up; 4-6 miles continuous at half-marathon pace; 800-meter jog; 6 × 400 meters at mile pace with 200-meter jog between; 1- to 2-mile cool-down	Easy run: 6-8 miles	Regular run: 6-8 miles, then 8 × 100-meter strides	Intervals: 2- to 3-mile warm-up; 8 × 800 meters at 10K pace with 400-meter jog between; 1- to 2-mile cool-down	Easy run: 1-6 miles OR Day off	56-77

	Sunday	Monday	Tuesday	Wednesday	Thursday	Friday	Saturday	Week's mileage
Week 14	Long run: 15-18 miles, last 2 miles faster than marathon goal pace	Easy run: 4-6 miles, then 8 × 100-meter strides	Tempo run: 2- to 3-mile warm-up; 4-6 miles continuous at marathon pace; 1- to 2-mile cool-down	Easy run: 4-6 miles	Regular run: 6-8 miles, then 8 × 100-meter strides	Intervals: 2- to 3-mile warm-up; 8 × 400 meters at 10K pace with 200-meter jog between; 1- to 2-mile cool-down	Easy run: 2-4 miles	45-61
Week 15	Long run: 12-14 miles	Easy run: 1-4 miles OR Day off	Tempo intervals: 2- to 3-mile warm-up; 2 × 3 miles continuous at marathon pace with 1-mile jog between; 1- to 2-mile cool-down	Easy run: 6-8 miles	Regular run: 6-8 miles, then 8 × 100-meter strides	Tempo run: 2- to 3-mile warm-up; 4-6 miles continuous at marathon pace; 1- to 2-mile cool-down	Easy run: 1-6 miles OR Day off	41-63
Week 16	Long run: 9-12 miles	Day off	Intervals: 2- to 3-mile warm-up; 8 × 400 meters at 10K pace with 200-meter jog between; 1- to 2-mile cool-down	Easy run: 2-6 miles	Easy run: 1-4 miles OR Day off	Easy run: 2-4 miles	Race marathon OR Easy run: 2-4 miles (for Sunday marathon)	19-34 (not including race)

13

Training for and Racing Many Events in a Short Period

The schedules in the previous five chapters are for when you have a goal race at a specific distance and are willing to commit several weeks to focusing on that event. Here, the underlying approach is different. The schedules in this chapter are for the common scenario of doing many races of varying distance in a relatively short time. What races you run—how far and how often—is up to you. The exception is that I'm assuming you won't include a marathon among them; I created the schedules for races between the mile and the half-marathon.

Following are six schedules, all of them eight weeks long. The first three schedules cover an eight-week block of just training before a period of frequent racing. The weekly mileage ranges for these schedules are up to 45, 35 to 55, and 45 or more. The second three schedules cover an eight-week period in which you'll be racing frequently. The weekly mileage ranges for these schedules are up to 45, 35 to 55, and 40 or more.

I've capped the frequent-racing schedules at eight weeks because you're best off regrouping after a lot of racing in a short time. Of course, you don't have to follow those schedules for eight weeks—you might target four races in six weeks, for example, and call it a season. If you want to do another block of compressed racing soon after your first one, take at least a week of just easy runs, then repeat one of the training-only schedules for at least a month.

As I said in chapter 7, there are many variables to consider when deciding which schedule to follow. Refer there for more details. Be especially realistic with yourself about the proper weekly mileage when deciding which frequent-racing schedule to follow. If you plan to race at least every other week during those eight weeks, you don't want to also aim to maintain an arbitrary minimum weekly mileage you set for yourself. Save your physical and mental energy for the races.

A Brief Guide to Following the Schedules

Each day's training in the schedules is described using the main types of runs I described at length in chapter 7. You'll want to refresh your memory occasionally by rereading those descriptions during your buildup. For quick reference, here are the types of runs you'll encounter in these schedules, and what I mean by each.

- *Easy run:* Done the day after your longest and hardest runs. Don't worry about pace. Just run at a comfortable, conversational effort level—no hard breathing, no bearing down. You should finish feeling energized for the next day's training.

- *Regular run:* A little faster or more effortful than an easy run, but still at a conversational pace. These are what you might think of as your getting-in-the-miles runs. It's okay to push things a little in the last few miles if you're feeling good.

- *Tempo run:* A sustained run at a "comfortably hard" effort level that requires concentration. To gauge the right effort for those tempo runs, imagine I were riding a bike alongside and asked you a question. You should be able to answer in a complete sentence, but you shouldn't be able to carry on an in-depth conversation as on an easy or regular run. The tempo runs in the training-only schedules are to be done at half-marathon pace. The tempo runs in the frequent-racing schedules are to be done a little slower than that—the goal with these is to maintain your high-end aerobic fitness without taxing you much. You'll do these more moderate tempos only during weeks when you're not racing.

- *Progression run:* A sustained run at an increasingly fast pace. Progression runs accomplish much of what conventional tempo runs do while also helping you practice increasing your effort as fatigue mounts. They tend to be a little longer than tempo runs because you start at a slower pace. For the progression run in the training-only schedule, you'll start at marathon pace and go five seconds per mile faster after each mile.

- *Intervals:* Repeats between 200 meters and one mile long, run between mile and 10K race pace. You can do these on a track for precision and a uniform running surface, but you can also do them on roads or elsewhere with good footing. It's okay to roughly convert the distances stated in the training schedules to timed segments off the track, such as running at 5K effort for three minutes if the schedules prescribe 800-meter repeats at 5K pace.

- *Hill workout:* Running at 5K effort—not pace!—up a moderately steep hill, and jogging down for recovery. Ideally, the hill will be steep enough to make the climbing noticeable, but not so steep that it's difficult to maintain good upright running form with quick turnover.

- *Long run:* Your longest run of the week, done at a conversational pace. Start at a gentle effort and gradually increase intensity to that of a regular run as your body warms up. Don't rush it—you've got plenty of time to get in a good rhythm for the second half of the run. The long runs in the frequent-racing schedules have a larger range than in other schedules in this book. There's great variance among runners in how they feel the day after a race; plus, you're probably going to be more fatigued the day after a 10-mile race than after a 5K. See Adapting the Schedules for more guidance on long runs when you're racing a lot.

- *Strides:* Short (100 meters or so) bouts of fast running at around mile race pace, usually done either after an easy run or before a hard workout or race. Concentrate on maintaining good running form and staying relaxed while running fast. Strides should feel good and be fun; you'll usually feel better after doing them than you did before. Do strides on a flat, level surface with reliable footing.

Adapting the Schedules

The 8-week frequent-racing schedules accommodate racing or not racing on each of its weekends. For the most part, the week's workouts are the same through Thursday. Then you'll see options for what to do Friday and Saturday, depending on whether you're racing that Saturday.

There are many other variables to account for, such as races occurring on Sunday, how far you're racing, how often you're racing, and how quickly you tend to recover after racing. Here's some general guidance on tweaking the schedules:

- *If you're racing on Sunday:* On Friday, do a two- to three-mile warm-up, then four to six 200-meter repeats at 1-mile to 5K race pace with a 200-meter jog between. Finish with a one- to two-mile cool-down. On Saturday, do the prerace session called for on Fridays in the schedules. The goal here is to feel good and not get fatigued so you can have a successful race on Sunday.

- *If you're racing a 10K or shorter on Sunday:* Do the long run scheduled for Sunday on the Monday of that week, and do the easy run scheduled for Monday on that Tuesday. Then resume the normal schedule on Wednesday.

- *If you're racing 15K or longer on Saturday or Sunday:* Do the long run scheduled for Sunday on the Monday of that week, and do the easy run scheduled for Monday on that Tuesday. (If this longer race was on Saturday, do a short, easy run on Sunday, or take the day off.) Then resume the normal schedule on Wednesday.

- *If you've raced 15K or longer:* I recommend not racing the following weekend. Let your body recover from the race and let your mind recharge. Choose a long run distance from the lower end of the prescribed range.

Lessons From Coach Coogan's Periods of Frequent Racing

Some people will say it's a bad idea to race frequently. I don't fall into that category. You just need to be aware of what you're doing and that you can't do it all the time.

In my career, I often raced a lot. "I don't train to train; I train to race" was what I said to myself. Races on the calendar always gave me good incentive to get out the door. The anticipation of a race always put a little bit of a pop in my step.

Living in the Boston area or in Boulder, Colorado, the weather was often trying; having a race in a better environment was always something to look forward to.

Racing a lot can also help you get callused a bit. You better know what that feeling is when you step to the line to race—you know you can really suck it up. You can deliver. I love that feeling of "bring on the pain; today I am ready for it." Racing frequently helped me get that feeling.

Being race-sharp will help you race well and at your upper limits. If you've run a shorter race recently, then the pace in longer races should seem more comfortable and doable. I always liked racing a 5K a couple of weeks before a big 10K or a road race a few weeks before a marathon. Running well in one race can help you with your confidence going into your next one. If you run a PR in the 5K one weekend, you might be super excited to beat that time the next weekend.

Frequent races can help you run better week after week. This happened to me when I ran a fast 5K on the Boston University indoor track a couple of weeks before I made the Olympic marathon team. You might not think running a 5K soon before a marathon would be beneficial, but to me it was. I felt I needed to race, just to go through my warm-up routine. I also wanted to make sure nothing was bugging me if I went faster than marathon race pace. Running in the 13:40s told me no one was going to outkick me in the Olympic Trials race. So I gained some needed confidence jumping in that 5K and winning it.

There are a few drawbacks to racing too much. The biggest problem is that at some point you'll start to lose fitness. If you want to race often, then something in the training will have to go, like a regular long run or a hard session during the week.

I also noticed after a series of many races that my mind would start to get tired. I was getting mentally exhausted because it became too tough to keep getting pumped up for races. Once you're tired mentally, races will not go as well as they could have. When I was racing a lot in Europe, I would almost always run my best race in my first or second meet. When I think back now, I feel it's because I let my fitness deteriorate. I wasn't getting in a long run, just a lot of short recovery runs. I should have done more maintenance runs of 10 or 12 miles to keep my endurance up.

After the summer track season, I would often head to my parents' beach house and run the Falmouth Road Race on Cape Cod. I don't think I ever had a good Falmouth race, because I had lost my fitness racing in Europe or Falmouth was my last race of the season and I was mentally tired. Olympian Todd Williams and I use to joke about how hard Falmouth was and how we usually died in that race. Todd and I would say how we could sometimes hear the helicopter following the lead women in the race. Hearing the helicopter made us refocus and try to run hard to the finish line.

Bottom line: If you're going to race frequently, then you must realize that after a month or two you'll eventually lose fitness and your races will not be your best performances. If you have frequent races planned, make sure you still get in some decent longer runs midweek. It seems like it takes a long time get fit, but a fairly short time to lose your fitness.

8-Week Prep for Frequent Racing Schedule: Up to 45 Miles per Week

	Sunday	Monday	Tuesday	Wednesday	Thursday	Friday	Saturday	Week's mileage
Week 1	Long run: 7-10 miles	Easy run: 3-5 miles, then 8 × 100-meter strides	Intervals: 2-mile warm-up; 8 × 400 meters at 5K pace with 200-meter jog between; 1-mile cool-down	Easy run: 6 miles	Regular run: 3-5 miles, then 8 × 100-meter strides	Tempo run: 2-mile warm-up; 4 miles continuous at half-marathon pace; 1-mile cool-down	Easy run: 1-3 miles OR Day off	32-42
Week 2	Long run: 7-10 miles	Easy run: 3-5 miles, then 8 × 100-meter strides	Intervals: 2-mile warm-up; 6 × 800 meters at 5K pace with 400-meter jog between; 1-mile cool-down	Easy run: 6 miles	Regular run: 3-5 miles, then 8 × 100-meter strides	Hills: 2-mile warm-up; 6-8 × 400-meter hill at 5K effort; jog down for recovery; 1-mile cool-down	Easy run: 1-3 miles OR Day off	33-44
Week 3	Long run: 7-10 miles	Easy run: 3-5 miles, then 8 × 100-meter strides	Intervals: 2-mile warm-up; 4 × 400 meters at mile pace with 200-meter jog between; 2 × 800 meters at 5K pace with 400-meter jog between; 4 × 200 meters at mile pace with 200-meter jog between; 1-mile cool-down	Easy run: 6 miles	Regular run: 3-5 miles, then 8 × 100-meter strides	Intervals and tempo run: 2-mile warm-up; 4 × 400 meters at 5K pace with 200-meter jog between; 2 miles continuous at 25 seconds per mile slower than 10K pace; 400-meter jog; 2 × 400 meters at mile pace with 200-meter jog between; 1-mile cool-down	Easy run: 1-3 miles OR Day off	33-43
Week 4	Long run: 7-10 miles	Easy run: 3-5 miles, then 8 × 100-meter strides	Intervals: 2-mile warm-up; 10-12 × 200 meters at mile pace with 200-meter jog between; 1-mile cool-down	Easy run: 6 miles	Regular run: 3-5 miles, then 8 × 100-meter strides	Tempo run: 2-mile warm-up; 4 miles continuous at half-marathon pace; 1-mile cool-down	Easy run: 1-3 miles OR Day off	31-42

	Sunday	Monday	Tuesday	Wednesday	Thursday	Friday	Saturday	Week's mileage
Week 5	Long run: 7-10 miles	Easy run: 3-5 miles, then 8 × 100-meter strides	Intervals: 2-mile warm-up; 3-4 × 1 mile at 10K pace with 400-meter jog between; 1-mile cool-down	Easy run: 6 miles	Regular run: 3-5 miles, then 8 × 100-meter strides	Hills: 2-mile warm-up; 8 × 400-meter hill at 5K effort; jog down for recovery; 1-mile cool-down	Easy run: 1-3 miles OR Day off	33-44
Week 6	Long run: 7-10 miles	Easy run: 3-5 miles, then 8 × 100-meter strides	Intervals: 2-mile warm-up; 4-5 × set of 800 meters at 10K pace, 200-meter jog, 200 meters at mile pace, 400-meter jog; 1-mile cool-down	Easy run: 6 miles	Regular run: 3-5 miles, then 8 × 100-meter strides	Progression run: 2-mile warm-up; 5 miles continuous, starting at marathon pace, increasing pace 5 seconds per mile after each mile; 1-mile cool-down	Easy run: 1-3 miles OR Day off	34-45
Week 7	Long run: 7-10 miles	Easy run: 3-5 miles, then 8 × 100-meter strides	Intervals: 2-mile warm-up; 8 × 400 meters at 5K pace with 200-meter jog between; 1-mile cool-down	Easy run: 6 miles	Regular run: 3-5 miles, then 8 × 100-meter strides	Tempo run and intervals: 2-mile warm-up; 3 miles continuous at half-marathon pace; 800-meter jog; 4 × 400 meters at mile pace with 200-meter jog between; 1-mile cool-down	Easy run: 1-3 miles OR Day off	33-43
Week 8	Long run: 7-10 miles	Easy run: 3-5 miles, then 8 × 100-meter strides	Intervals: 2-mile warm-up; 6 × 800 meters at 5K pace with 400-meter jog between intervals; 1-mile cool-down	Easy run: 6 miles	Regular run: 3-5 miles, then 8 × 100-meter strides	Tempo run: 2-mile warm-up; 4 miles continuous at half-marathon pace; 1-mile cool-down	Easy run: 1-3 miles OR Day off	33-43

8-Week Prep for Frequent Racing Schedule: 35-55 Miles per Week

	Sunday	Monday	Tuesday	Wednesday	Thursday	Friday	Saturday	Week's mileage
Week 1	Long run: 8-12 miles	Easy run: 5-8 miles, then 8 × 100-meter strides	Intervals: 2-mile warm-up; 8 × 400 meters at 5K pace with 200-meter jog between; 1-mile cool-down	Easy run: 6-8 miles	Regular run: 5-8 miles, then 8 × 100-meter strides	Tempo run: 2-mile warm-up; 4 miles continuous at half-marathon pace; 1-mile cool-down	Easy run: 3-5 miles	40-54
Week 2	Long run: 8-12 miles	Easy run: 5-8 miles, then 8 × 100-meter strides	Intervals: 2-mile warm-up; 6 × 800 meters at 5K pace with 400-meter jog between; 1-mile cool-down	Easy run: 6-8 miles	Regular run: 5-8 miles, then 8 × 100-meter strides	Hills: 2-mile warm-up; 6-8 × 400-meter hill at 5K effort; jog down for recovery; 1-mile cool-down	Easy run: 3-5 miles OR Day off	37-55
Week 3	Long run: 8-12 miles	Easy run: 5-8 miles, then 8 × 100-meter strides	Intervals: 2-mile warm-up; 4 × 400 meters at mile pace with 200-meter jog between; 3 × 800 meters at 5K pace with 400-meter jog between; 4 × 200 meters at mile pace with 200-meter jog between; 1-mile cool-down	Easy run: 6-8 miles	Regular run: 5-8 miles, then 8 × 100-meter strides	Intervals and tempo run: 2-mile warm-up; 4 × 400 meters at 5K pace with 200-meter jog between; 2 miles continuous at 25 seconds per mile slower than 10K pace; 400-meter jog; 2 × 400 meters at mile pace with 200-meter jog between; 1-mile cool-down	Easy run: 3-5 miles	42-56
Week 4	Long run: 8-12 miles	Easy run: 5-8 miles, then 8 × 100-meter strides	Intervals: 2-mile warm-up; 10-12 × 200 meters at mile pace with 200-meter jog between; 1-mile cool-down	Easy run: 6-8 miles	Regular run: 5-8 miles, then 8 × 100-meter strides	Tempo run: 2-mile warm-up; 4 miles continuous at half-marathon pace; 1-mile cool-down	Easy run: 3-5 miles OR Day off	36-54

	Sunday	Monday	Tuesday	Wednesday	Thursday	Friday	Saturday	Week's mileage
Week 5	Long run: 8-12 miles	Easy run: 5-8 miles, then 8 × 100-meter strides	Intervals: 2-mile warm-up; 3-4 × 1 mile at 10K pace with 400-meter jog between; 1-mile cool-down	Easy run: 6-8 miles	Regular run: 5-8 miles, then 8 × 100-meter strides	Hills: 2-mile warm-up; 8 × 400-meter hill at 5K effort; jog down for recovery; 1-mile cool-down	Easy run: 3-5 miles	41-56
Week 6	Long run: 8-12 miles	Easy run: 5-8 miles, then 8 × 100-meter strides	Intervals: 2-mile warm-up; 4-6 × set of 800 meters at 10K pace, 200-meter jog, 200 meters at mile pace, 400-meter jog; 1-mile cool-down	Easy run: 6-8 miles	Regular run: 5-8 miles, then 8 × 100-meter strides	Progression run: 2-mile warm-up; 5 miles continuous, starting at marathon pace, increasing pace 5 seconds per mile after each mile; 1-mile cool-down	Easy run: 3-5 miles OR Day off	39-58
Week 7	Long run: 8-12 miles	Easy run: 5-8 miles, then 8 × 100-meter strides	Intervals: 2-mile warm-up; 8 × 400 meters at 5K pace with 200-meter jog between; 1-mile cool-down	Easy run: 6-8 miles	Regular run: 5-8 miles, then 8 × 100-meter strides	Tempo run and intervals: 2-mile warm-up; 3 miles continuous at half-marathon pace; 800-meter jog; 4 × 400 meters at mile pace with 200-meter jog between; 1-mile cool-down	Easy run: 3-5 miles	41-55
Week 8	Long run: 8-12 miles	Easy run: 5-8 miles, then 8 × 100-meter strides	Intervals: 2-mile warm-up; 6 × 800 meters at 5K pace with 400-meter jog between; 1-mile cool-down	Easy run: 6-8 miles	Regular run: 5-8 miles, then 8 × 100-meter strides	Tempo run: 2-mile warm-up; 4 miles continuous at half-marathon pace; 1-mile cool-down	Easy run: 3-5 miles OR Day off	39-56

8-Week Prep for Frequent Racing Schedule: 45+ Miles per Week

	Sunday	Monday	Tuesday	Wednesday	Thursday	Friday	Saturday	Week's mileage
Week 1	Long run: 12-15 miles	Easy run: 6-8 miles, then 8 × 100-meter strides	Intervals: 2- to 3-mile warm-up; 8-10 × 400 meters at 5K pace with 200-meter jog between; 1- to 2-mile cool-down	Easy run: 8-10 miles	Regular run: 6-8 miles, then 8 × 100-meter strides	Tempo run: 2- to 3-mile warm-up; 4 miles continuous at half-marathon pace; 1- to 2-mile cool-down	Easy run: 4-6 miles	49-65
Week 2	Long run: 12-15 miles	Easy run: 6-8 miles, then 8 × 100-meter strides	Intervals: 2- to 3-mile warm-up; 6 × 800 meters at 5K pace with 400-meter jog between; 1- to 2-mile cool-down	Easy run: 8-10 miles	Regular run: 6-8 miles, then 8 × 100-meter strides	Hills: 2- to 3-mile warm-up; 8 × 400-meter hill at 5K effort; jog down for recovery; 1- to 2-mile cool-down	Easy run: 4-6 miles OR Day off	46-65
Week 3	Long run: 12-15 miles	Easy run: 6-8 miles, then 8 × 100-meter strides	Intervals: 2- to 3-mile warm-up; 4 × 400 meters at mile pace with 200-meter jog between; 4 × 800 meters at 5K pace with 400-meter jog between; 4 × 200 meters at mile pace with 200-meter jog between; 1- to 2-mile cool-down	Easy run: 8-10 miles	Regular run: 6-8 miles, then 8 × 100-meter strides	Intervals and tempo run: 2- to 3-mile warm-up; 4 × 400 meters at 5K pace with 200-meter jog between; 3-4 miles continuous at 25-30 seconds per mile slower than 10K pace; 400-meter jog; 2 × 400 meters at mile pace with 200-meter jog between; 1- to 2-mile cool-down	Easy run: 4-6 miles	52-68
Week 4	Long run: 12-15 miles	Easy run: 6-8 miles, then 8 × 100-meter strides	Intervals: 2- to 3-mile warm-up; 12 × 200 meters at mile pace with 200-meter jog between; 1- to 2-mile cool-down	Easy run: 8-10 miles	Regular run: 6-8 miles, then 8 × 100-meter strides	Tempo run: 2- to 3-mile warm-up; 4 miles continuous at half-marathon pace; 1- to 2-mile cool-down	Easy run: 4-6 miles OR Day off	45-64

	Sunday	Monday	Tuesday	Wednesday	Thursday	Friday	Saturday	Week's mileage
Week 5	Long run: 12-15 miles	Easy run: 6-8 miles, then 8 × 100-meter strides	Intervals: 2- to 3-mile warm-up; 4-6 × 1 mile at 10K pace with 400-meter jog between; 1- to 2-mile cool-down	Easy run: 8-10 miles	Regular run: 6-8 miles, then 8 × 100-meter strides	Hills: 2- to 3-mile warm-up; 8 × 400-meter hill at 5K effort; jog down for recovery; 1- to 2-mile cool-down	Easy run: 4-6 miles	51-68
Week 6	Long run: 12-15 miles	Easy run: 6-8 miles, then 8 × 100-meter strides	Intervals: 2- to 3-mile warm-up; 6 × set of 800 meters at 10K pace, 200-meter jog, 200 meters at mile pace, 400-meter jog; 1- to 2-mile cool-down	Easy run: 8-10 miles	Regular run: 6-8 miles, then 8 × 100-meter strides	Progression run: 2- to 3-mile warm-up; 5 miles continuous, starting at marathon pace, increasing pace 5 seconds per mile after each mile; 1- to 2-mile cool-down	Easy run: 4-6 miles OR Day off	49-68
Week 7	Long run: 12-15 miles	Easy run: 6-8 miles, then 8 × 100-meter strides	Intervals: 2- to 3-mile warm-up; 8-10 × 400 meters at 5K pace with 200-meter jog between; 1- to 2-mile cool-down	Easy run: 8-10 miles	Regular run: 6-8 miles, then 8 × 100-meter strides	Tempo run and intervals: 2- to 3-mile warm-up; 4 miles continuous at half-marathon pace; 800-meter jog; 4 × 400 meters at mile pace with 200-meter jog between; 1- to 2-mile cool-down	Easy run: 4-6 miles	51-66
Week 8	Long run: 12-15 miles	Easy run: 6-8 miles, then 8 × 100-meter strides	Intervals: 2- to 3-mile warm-up; 6 × 800 meters at 5K pace with 400-meter jog between; 1- to 2-mile cool-down	Easy run: 8-10 miles	Regular run: 6-8 miles, then 8 × 100-meter strides	Tempo run: 2- to 3-mile warm-up; 4-5 miles continuous at half-marathon pace; 1- to 2-mile cool-down	Easy run: 4-6 miles OR Day off	46-66

8-Week Frequent Racing Schedule: Up to 45 Miles per Week

	Sunday	Monday	Tuesday	Wednesday	Thursday	Friday	Saturday	Week's mileage
Week 1	Long run: 7-8 miles	Easy run: 3-5 miles, then 6 × 100-meter strides	Intervals: 2-mile warm-up; 8 × 400 meters at 5K pace with 200-meter jog between; 1-mile cool-down	Easy run: 4-6 miles	Regular run: 4-5 miles, then 6 × 100-meter strides	If racing tomorrow: Easy run: 2-4 miles, then 6 × 100-meter strides OR If not racing tomorrow: Tempo run: 2-mile warm-up; 3-4 miles continuous at 25-30 seconds per mile slower than 10K pace; 1-mile cool-down	Race OR Easy run: 3-4 miles	32-45
Week 2	Long run: 7-8 miles	Easy run: 3-5 miles, then 6 × 100-meter strides	Intervals: 2-mile warm-up; 4-6 × 800 meters at 10-20 seconds per mile faster than 10K pace with 400-meter jog between; 1-mile cool-down	Easy run: 4-6 miles	Regular run: 4-5 miles, then 6 × 100-meter strides	If racing tomorrow: Easy run: 2-4 miles, then 6 × 100-meter strides OR If not racing tomorrow: Tempo run: 2-mile warm-up; 3-4 miles continuous at 25-30 seconds per mile slower than 10K pace; 1-mile cool-down	Race OR Easy run: 3-4 miles	32-45
Week 3	Long run: 7-8 miles	Easy run: 3-5 miles, then 6 × 100-meter strides	Intervals: 2-mile warm-up; 2-4 × 800 meters at 5K pace; 2 × 400 meters at mile pace; 400-meter jog after all intervals; 1-mile cool-down	Easy run: 4-6 miles	Regular run: 4-5 miles, then 6 × 100-meter strides	If racing tomorrow: Easy run: 2-4 miles, then 6 × 100-meter strides OR If not racing tomorrow: Tempo run: 2-mile warm-up; 3-4 miles continuous at 25-30 seconds per mile slower than 10K pace; 1-mile cool-down	Race OR Easy run: 3-4 miles	31-45

	Sunday	Monday	Tuesday	Wednesday	Thursday	Friday	Saturday	Week's mileage
Week 4	Long run: 7-8 miles	Easy run: 3-5 miles, then 6 × 100-meter strides	Intervals: 2-mile warm-up; 6-8 × 400 meters at 5K pace with 200-meter jog between; 1-mile cool-down	Easy run: 4-6 miles	Regular run: 4-5 miles, then 6 × 100-meter strides	If racing tomorrow: Easy run: 2-4 miles, then 6 × 100-meter strides OR If not racing tomorrow: Tempo run: 2-mile warm-up; 3-4 miles continuous at 25-30 seconds per mile slower than 10K pace; 1-mile cool-down	Race OR Easy run: 3-4 miles	31-45
Week 5	Long run: 7-8 miles	Easy run: 3-5 miles, then 6 × 100 meters	Intervals: 2-mile warm-up; 3-5 × 800 meters at 10-20 seconds per mile faster than 10K pace with 400-meter jog between; 1-mile cool-down	Easy run: 4-6 miles	Regular run: 4-5 miles, then 6 × 100-meter strides	If racing tomorrow: Easy run: 2-4 miles, then 6 × 100-meter strides OR If not racing tomorrow: Tempo run: 2-mile warm-up; 3-4 miles continuous at 25-30 seconds per mile slower than 10K pace; 1-mile cool-down	Race OR Easy run: 3-4 miles	31-45
Week 6	Long run: 7-8 miles	Easy run: 3-5 miles, then 6 × 100 meters	Intervals: 2-mile warm-up; 6-8 × 400 meters at 5K pace with 200-meter jog between; 1-mile cool-down	Easy run: 4-6 miles	Easy run: 4-5 miles, then 6 × 100-meter strides	If racing tomorrow: Easy run: 2-4 miles, then 6 × 100-meter strides OR If not racing tomorrow: Tempo run: 2-mile warm-up; 3-4 miles continuous at 25-30 seconds per mile slower than 10K pace; 1-mile cool-down	Race OR Easy run: 3-4 miles	31-45

241

8-Week Frequent Racing Schedule: Up to 45 Miles per Week *(continued)*

	Sunday	Monday	Tuesday	Wednesday	Thursday	Friday	Saturday	Week's mileage
Week 7	Long run: 7-8 miles	Easy run: 3-5 miles, then 6 × 100 meters	Intervals: 2-mile warm-up; 2-4 × 800 meters at 5K pace; 2 × 400 meters at mile pace; 400-meter jog after all intervals; 1-mile cool-down	Easy run: 4-6 miles	Easy run: 4-5 miles, then 6 × 100-meter strides	If racing tomorrow: Easy run: 2-4 miles, then 6 × 100-meter strides OR If not racing tomorrow: Tempo run: 2-mile warm-up; 3-4 miles continuous at 25-30 seconds per mile slower than 10K pace; 1-mile cool-down	Race OR Easy run: 3-4 miles	31-45
Week 8	Long run: 7-8 miles	Easy run: 3-5 miles, then 6 × 100 meters	Intervals: 2-mile warm-up; 6-8 × 400 meters at 5K pace with 200-meter jog between; 1-mile cool-down	Easy run: 4-6 miles	Easy run: 4-5 miles, then 6 × 100-meter strides	If racing tomorrow: Easy run: 2-4 miles, then 6 × 100-meter strides OR If not racing tomorrow: Tempo run: 2-mile warm-up; 3-4 miles continuous at 25-30 seconds per mile slower than 10K pace; 1-mile cool-down	Race OR Easy run: 3-4 miles	31-45

8-Week Frequent Racing Schedule: 35-55 Miles per Week

	Sunday	Monday	Tuesday	Wednesday	Thursday	Friday	Saturday	Week's mileage
Week 1	Long run: 7-14 miles	Easy run: 5-7 miles, then 8 × 100-meter strides	Intervals: 2-mile warm-up; 6-8 × 400 meters at 5K pace with 200-meter jog between; 1-mile cool-down	Easy run: 6-8 miles	Regular run: 4-5 miles, then 6 × 100-meter strides	If racing tomorrow: Easy run: 2-4 miles, then 6 × 100-meter strides OR If not racing tomorrow: Tempo run: 2-mile warm-up; 3-5 miles continuous at 25-30 seconds per mile slower than 10K pace; 1-mile cool-down	Race OR Easy run: 3-6 miles	35-55
Week 2	Long run: 7-14 miles	Easy run: 5-7 miles, then 8 × 100-meter strides	Intervals: 2-mile warm-up; 4-6 × 800 meters at 10-20 seconds per mile faster than 10K pace with 400-meter jog between intervals; 1-mile cool-down	Easy run: 6-8 miles	Regular run: 4-5 miles, then 6 × 100-meter strides	If racing tomorrow: Easy run: 2-4 miles, then 6 × 100-meter strides OR If not racing tomorrow: Tempo run: 2-mile warm-up; 3-5 miles continuous at 25-30 seconds per mile slower than 10K pace; 1-mile cool-down	Race OR Easy run: 3-6 miles	35-55
Week 3	Long run: 7-14 miles	Easy run: 5-7 miles, then 8 × 100-meter strides	Intervals: 2-mile warm-up; 2-4 × 800 meters at 5K pace; 2 × 400 meters at mile pace; 400-meter jog after all intervals; 1-mile cool-down	Easy run: 6-8 miles	Regular run: 4-5 miles, then 6 × 100-meter strides	If racing tomorrow: Easy run: 2-4 miles, then 6 × 100-meter strides OR If not racing tomorrow: Tempo run: 2-mile warm-up; 3-5 miles continuous at 25-30 seconds per mile slower than 10K pace; 1-mile cool-down	Race OR Easy run: 3-6 miles	35-55

8-Week Frequent Racing Schedule: 35-55 Miles per Week *(continued)*

	Sunday	Monday	Tuesday	Wednesday	Thursday	Friday	Saturday	Week's mileage
Week 4	Long run: 7-14 miles	Easy run: 5-7 miles, then 8 × 100-meter strides	Intervals: 2-mile warm-up; 6-8 × 400 meters at 5K pace with 200-meter jog between; 1-mile cool-down	Easy run: 6-8 miles	Regular run: 4-5 miles, then 6 × 100-meter strides	If racing tomorrow: Easy run: 2-4 miles, then 6 × 100-meter strides OR If not racing tomorrow: Tempo run: 2-mile warm-up; 3-5 miles continuous at 25-30 seconds per mile slower than 10K pace; 1-mile cool-down	Race OR Easy run: 3-6 miles	35-55
Week 5	Long run: 7-14 miles	Easy run: 5-7 miles, then 8 × 100 meters	Intervals: 2-mile warm-up; 3-6 × 800 meters at 10-20 seconds per mile faster than 10K pace with 400-meter jog between; 1-mile cool-down	Easy run: 6-8 miles	Regular run: 4-5 miles, then 6 × 100-meter strides	If racing tomorrow: Easy run: 2-4 miles, then 6 × 100-meter strides OR If not racing tomorrow: Tempo run: 2-mile warm-up; 3-5 miles continuous at 25-30 seconds per mile slower than 10K pace; 1-mile cool-down	Race OR Easy run: 3-6 miles	35-55
Week 6	Long run: 7-14 miles	Easy run: 5-7 miles, then 8 × 100 meters	Intervals: 2-mile warm-up; 6-8 × 400 meters at 5K pace with 200-meter jog between; 1-mile cool-down	Easy run: 6-8 miles	Easy run: 4-5 miles, then 6 × 100-meter strides	If racing tomorrow: Easy run: 2-4 miles, then 6 × 100-meter strides OR If not racing tomorrow: Tempo run: 2-mile warm-up; 3-5 miles continuous at 25-30 seconds per mile slower than 10K pace; 1-mile cool-down	Race OR Easy run: 3-6 miles	35-55

	Sunday	Monday	Tuesday	Wednesday	Thursday	Friday	Saturday	Week's mileage
Week 7	Long run: 7-14 miles	Easy run: 5-7 miles, then 8 × 100 meters	Intervals: 2-mile warm-up; 3-5 × 800 meters at 5K pace; 2 × 400 meters at mile pace; 400-meter jog after all intervals; 1-mile cool-down	Easy run: 6-8 miles	Easy run: 4-5 miles, then 6 × 100-meter strides	If racing tomorrow: Easy run: 2-4 miles, then 6 × 100-meter strides OR If not racing tomorrow: Tempo run: 2-mile warm-up; 3-5 miles continuous at 25-30 seconds per mile slower than 10K pace; 1-mile cool-down	Race OR Easy run: 3-6 miles	35-55
Week 8	Long run: 7-14 miles	Easy run: 5-7 miles, then 8 × 100 meters	Intervals: 2-mile warm-up; 6-8 × 400 meters at 5K pace with 200-meter jog between; 1-mile cool-down	Easy run: 6-8 miles	Easy run: 4-5 miles, then 6 × 100-meter strides	If racing tomorrow: Easy run: 2-4 miles, then 6 × 100-meter strides OR If not racing tomorrow: Tempo run: 2-mile warm-up; 3-5 miles continuous at 25-30 seconds per mile slower than 10K pace; 1-mile cool-down	Race OR Easy run: 3-6 miles	35-55

8-Week Frequent Racing Schedule: 40+ Miles per Week

	Sunday	Monday	Tuesday	Wednesday	Thursday	Friday	Saturday	Week's mileage
Week 1	Long run: 8-16 miles	Easy run: 5-8 miles, then 8 × 100-meter strides	Intervals: 2-mile warm-up; 6-10 × 400 meters at 5K pace with 200-meter jog between; 1- to 2-mile cool-down	Easy run: 6-10 miles	Regular run: 4-6 miles, then 8 × 100-meter strides	If racing tomorrow: Easy run: 2-4 miles, then 6 × 100-meter strides OR If not racing tomorrow: Tempo run: 2-mile warm-up; 3-5 miles continuous at 25-30 seconds per mile slower than 10K pace; 1- to 2-mile cool-down	Race OR Easy run: 4-8 miles	40-70
Week 2	Long run: 8-16 miles	Easy run: 5-8 miles, then 8 × 100-meter strides	Intervals: 2-mile warm-up; 4-8 × 800 meters at 10-20 seconds per mile faster than 10K pace with 400-meter jog between; 1- to 2-mile cool-down	Easy run: 6-10 miles	Regular run: 4-6 miles, then 8 × 100-meter strides	If racing tomorrow: Easy run: 2-4 miles, then 6 × 100-meter strides OR If not racing tomorrow: Tempo run: 2-mile warm-up; 3-5 miles continuous at 25-30 seconds per mile slower than 10K pace; 1- to 2-mile cool-down	Race OR Easy run: 4-8 miles	40-70
Week 3	Long run: 8-16 miles	Easy run: 5-8 miles, then 8 × 100-meter strides	Intervals: 2-mile warm-up; 3-6 × 800 meters at 5K pace; 2 × 400 meters at mile pace; 400-meter jog after all intervals; 1- to 2-mile cool-down	Easy run: 6-10 miles	Regular run: 4-6 miles, then 8 × 100-meter strides	If racing tomorrow: Easy run: 2-4 miles, then 6 × 100-meter strides OR If not racing tomorrow: Tempo run: 2-mile warm-up; 3-5 miles continuous at 25-30 seconds per mile slower than 10K pace; 1- to 2-mile cool-down	Race OR Easy run: 4-8 miles	40-70

	Sunday	Monday	Tuesday	Wednesday	Thursday	Friday	Saturday	Week's mileage
Week 4	Long run: 8-16 miles	Easy run: 5-8 miles, then 8 × 100-meter strides	Intervals: 2-mile warm-up; 6-8 × 400 meters at 5K pace with 200-meter jog between; 1- to 2-mile cool-down	Easy run: 6-10 miles	Regular run: 4-6 miles, then 8 × 100-meter strides	If racing tomorrow: Easy run: 2-4 miles, then 6 × 100-meter strides OR If not racing tomorrow: Tempo run: 2-mile warm-up; 3-5 miles continuous at 25-30 seconds per mile slower than 10K pace; 1- to 2-mile cool-down	Race OR Easy run: 4-8 miles	40-70
Week 5	Long run: 8-16 miles	Easy run: 5-8 miles, then 8 × 100 meters	Intervals: 2-mile warm-up; 4-8 × 800 meters at 10-20 seconds per mile faster than 10K pace with 400-meter jog between; 1- to 2-mile cool-down	Easy run: 6-10 miles	Regular run: 4-6 miles, then 8 × 100-meter strides	If racing tomorrow: Easy run: 2-4 miles, then 6 × 100-meter strides OR If not racing tomorrow: Tempo run: 2-mile warm-up; 3-5 miles continuous at 25-30 seconds per mile slower than 10K pace; 1- to 2-mile cool-down	Race OR Easy run: 4-8 miles	40-70
Week 6	Long run: 8-16 miles	Easy run: 5-8 miles, then 8 × 100 meters	Intervals: 2-mile warm-up; 6-10 × 400 meters at 5K pace with 200-meter jog between; 1- to 2-mile cool-down	Easy run: 6-10 miles	Easy run: 4-6 miles, then 8 × 100-meter strides	If racing tomorrow: Easy run: 2-4 miles, then 6 × 100-meter strides OR If not racing tomorrow: Tempo run: 2-mile warm-up; 3-5 miles continuous at 25-30 seconds per mile slower than 10K pace; 1- to 2-mile cool-down	Race OR Easy run: 4-8 miles	40-70

(continued)

40+ Miles per Week
8-Week Frequent Racing Schedule

8-Week Frequent Racing Schedule: 40+ Miles per Week *(continued)*

	Sunday	Monday	Tuesday	Wednesday	Thursday	Friday	Saturday	Week's mileage
Week 7	Long run: 8-16 miles	Easy run: 5-8 miles, then 8 × 100 meters	Intervals: 2-mile warm-up; 3-6 × 800 meters at 5K pace; 2 × 400 meters at mile pace; 400-meter jog after all intervals; 1- to 2-mile cool-down	Easy run: 6-10 miles	Easy run: 4-6 miles, then 8 × 100-meter strides	If racing tomorrow: Easy run: 2-4 miles, then 6 × 100-meter strides OR If not racing tomorrow: Tempo run: 2-mile warm-up; 3-5 miles continuous at 25-30 seconds per mile slower than 10K pace; 1- to 2-mile cool-down	Race OR Easy run: 4-8 miles	40-70
Week 8	Long run: 8-16 miles	Easy run: 5-8 miles, then 8 × 100 meters	Intervals: 2-mile warm-up at 5K pace; 6-8 × 400 meters at 5K pace with 200-meter jog between; 1- to 2-mile cool-down	Easy run: 6-10 miles	Easy run: 4-6 miles, then 8 × 100-meter strides	If racing tomorrow: Easy run: 2-4 miles, then 6 × 100-meter strides OR If not racing tomorrow: Tempo run: 2-mile warm-up; 3-5 miles continuous at 25-30 seconds per mile slower than 10K pace; 1- to 2-mile cool-down	Race OR Easy run: 4-8 miles	40-70

14

Training for a Quick Transition From One Race Distance to Another

This final chapter is for when you've completed a long race (either a marathon or one in the 15K-to-half-marathon range) and want to run well at a much shorter race soon after. This quick-turn scenario isn't as extreme as it might sound. I know, because I successfully did it more than once in my career. It's possible to emerge from a long race feeling relatively fresh. Instead of taking a full recovery and losing some of your hard-won fitness, you can take a little downtime and then hop right back into formal training. You'll still be able to draw on the endurance gained during your half-marathon or marathon training. Combine that with some race-specific workouts for a much shorter event, and you'll have an unbeatable combination of strength and speed.

Following are training schedules for three scenarios: transitioning from the marathon to 5K, transitioning from the marathon to 10K, and transitioning from a 15K or half-marathon (or similar distance) to the mile or 5K. All of the schedules are eight weeks long, ending with the race at your shorter goal distance, with three mileage ranges for each schedule.

For the marathon-to-5K schedules, the mileage ranges are up to 45 miles per week, 25 to 55 miles per week, and 35 or more miles per week. For the marathon-to-10K schedules, the mileage ranges are up to 45 miles per week, 30 to 55 miles per week, and 30 or more miles per week. For the 15K–half-marathon-to-mile-or-5K schedules, the ranges are up to 45 miles per week, 25 to 50 miles per week, and 30 or more miles per week.

My Assumptions for You
Following One of These Schedules

I'm not saying you *have* to quickly target a shorter race after a long buildup to a longer one; I'm saying you *can*, and you might surprise yourself with how well you do. But there are caveats.

The biggest one is that you should feel good physically and mentally after your longer race. If you finessed your way through a minor injury during your half-marathon or marathon training, focus on getting fully healthy before targeting another race at any distance. Similarly, if you got beaten up more than usual during your race, prioritize being able to walk and run normally.

You should also not feel mentally drained from training for and racing the longer race. Don't force yourself to start serious training by an arbitrary date. Wait until you feel that inner urge to chase a goal again. Be honest with yourself about whether you can again commit the time and mental energy to a block of training so soon after your previous race.

Put a lot of thought into which mileage range to target. These schedules start immediately or almost immediately after you've completed a long race. You'll need to balance continuing to recover from that race with doing the necessary training to run well at a much shorter distance. In the second week of each schedule, you'll do one workout. For the next six weeks, you'll do two workouts, plus a long run. In the final week, you'll do a light workout early in the week and end with your race. When in doubt, err toward a lower mileage range than your norm. I'd rather you be able to do the weekly workouts and long runs well than compromise those elements just to hit a weekly mileage goal. If you realize partway through your schedule that you're struggling to hit its weekly mileage range, it's okay to switch to one of the shorter-mileage schedules. The race-specific workouts will be the same, just sometimes with a little less volume.

For the marathon-to-10K schedules, I'm assuming you've taken the first week after the marathon off from running. That continues one or more days into the first week of those schedules. The marathon-to-5K schedules assume one week off from running between your marathon and the first week of the schedule. If you like to do a little jogging during that week, that's up to you. But remember, you'll soon be back to pretty serious training. It's better to end that first week after your marathon eager to get going than wishing you had taken another few days to recover.

For the 15K–half-marathon-to-mile-or-5K schedules, I'm assuming no time off after your longer race. The first week of those schedules counts as a recovery week. Your first hard workout in it won't be until a week and a half after the longer race.

A Brief Guide to Following the Schedules

Each day's training in the schedules is described using the main types of runs I described at length in chapter 7. You'll want to refresh your memory occasionally by rereading those descriptions during your buildup. For quick reference, here are the types of runs you'll encounter in these schedules, and what I mean by each.

- *Easy run:* Done the day after your longest and hardest runs. Don't worry about pace. Just run at a comfortable, conversational effort level—no hard breathing, no bearing down. You should finish feeling energized for the next day's training.

- *Regular run:* A little faster or more effortful than an easy run, but still at a conversational pace. These are what you might think of as your getting-in-the-miles runs. It's okay to push things a little in the last few miles if you're feeling good.

- *Tempo run:* A sustained run at a "comfortably hard" effort level that requires concentration. To gauge the right effort for those tempo runs, imagine I were riding a bike alongside and asked you a question. You should be able to answer in a complete sentence, but you shouldn't be able to carry on an in-depth conversation as on an easy or regular run. The tempo runs in these schedules are at a moderate pace of 25 to 30 seconds per mile slower than 10K pace. The goal with these is to maintain your high-end aerobic fitness without taxing you much.

- *Progression run:* A sustained run at an increasingly fast pace. Progression runs accomplish much of what conventional tempo runs do while also helping you practice increasing your effort as fatigue mounts. They tend to be a little longer than tempo runs because you start at a slower pace.

- *Intervals:* Repeats between 200 meters and one mile long, run between mile and 5K race pace. You can do these on a track for precision and a uniform running surface, but you can also do them on roads or elsewhere with good footing. It's okay to roughly convert the distances stated in the training schedules to timed segments off the track, such as running at 5K effort for three minutes if the schedules prescribe 800-meter repeats at 5K pace.

- *Long run:* Your longest run of the week, done at a conversational pace. Start at a gentle effort and gradually increase intensity to that of a regular run as your body warms up. Don't rush it—you've got plenty of time to get in a good rhythm for the second half of the run.

- *Strides:* Short (100 meters or so) bouts of fast running at around mile race pace, usually done either after an easy run or before a hard workout or race. Concentrate on maintaining good running form and staying relaxed while running fast. Strides should feel good and be fun; you'll usually feel better after doing them than you did before. Do strides on a flat, level surface with reliable footing.

Lessons From Coach Coogan's Quick Transitions

I ran the Pan American Games Marathon in March 1995. I thought it would be a good idea to run because, if I wanted to run the Olympic Marathon in the heat of Atlanta the following year, this race in Argentina would be good practice. Also, it would be only my second marathon; I needed more experience at the distance before the U.S. marathon trials in February 1996. With the Pan Am race being held 11 months before the trials, I would have plenty of time to recover and wouldn't need to do a marathon in the fall of 1995.

I came in second in Argentina. I was pumped. I was also fine physically. After I got back home to Boulder, I set my focus on the 5,000 meters at the U.S. championships in June. I didn't want to train for a 10K that spring because doing so would be too similar to marathon training. I still did long runs, but they were in the 16- to 18-mile range, not 20 miles or longer. I knew I would be marathon training all fall and winter, so this was a good break for me.

All the endurance strength I gained from marathon training translated right into the spring track season. I set personal records for the 2-mile (8:21) and 5,000 meters (13:23). The marathon training allowed me to hold these fast paces. A 13:20 5K is 64 seconds per 400-meter lap. A lot of people can run a 64-second lap. Not many people can run 12.5 laps at that pace with no breaks. It wasn't that I was super fast, but I was strong from marathon training, and I could handle the 64s. Just three months after winning the Pan Am marathon silver, I was able to finish second in the U.S. championships at 5K. That experience convinced me that if you feel physically fine and mentally sharp after a marathon or long race, you can put your training for those races to great use soon afterward in much shorter events.

Now I'd like to talk about lessons from other runners' transitions from longer to shorter races.

When I was coaching collegiately, soon after cross-country season there would be an indoor track meet at Boston University. The meet was for people to get a fast time and hopefully qualify for the indoor NCAA championships before they took a break from cross-country season.

In this early December meet, many people wound up running faster than they did the rest of the indoor season. They would say, "I can't believe I ran this fast! I haven't done any speed workouts yet." They left the meet thinking, "Just wait until I start to sharpen up later in the indoor season; then I'll really run fast." But they often didn't. Why not?

My take is that the runners lost the endurance they gained from cross-country training, so they struggled to hold the faster pace of shorter indoor races for the second half of those races. They mostly stopped doing the long runs and tempo runs that got them so strong during cross-country season. Instead, they did a lot of short, fast interval workouts. By the heart of the indoor season, they might have been faster for 400 meters, but at the expense of the aerobic strength they needed to hold a strong pace for 3,000 or 5,000 meters.

As you transition from a longer race to shorter ones, remember what has made you successful. For most distance runners, it's keeping your mileage up a bit and not skipping long runs. In my career, I often ran well when I was doing marathon-type training. My best races were often after a long buildup period of mileage (usually my fall base phase) and not when I was doing intense track workouts two or three times a week.

The schedules in this chapter reflect these observations. You'll still be doing weekly long runs and tempo runs, even if you're targeting the mile. In chapter 1, I explained why aerobic strength is key to doing your best in any distance race. I showed you via three months of her training how 1,500-meter Olympian and national champion Heather MacLean implements this principle. If now, at the end of this book, I've convinced you of this idea, then I've done my job.

8-Week Marathon-to-5K Schedule: Up to 45 Miles per Week

	Sunday	Monday	Tuesday	Wednesday	Thursday	Friday	Saturday	Week's mileage
Week 1	Easy run: 3-4 miles	Easy run: 3-4 miles	Easy run: 3-4 miles	Easy run: 4-6 miles	Easy run: 3-4 miles	Easy run: 3-4 miles	Easy run: 2-4 miles OR Day off	19-30
Week 2	Regular run: 6-8 miles	Easy run: 3-5 miles	Easy intervals: 2-mile warm-up; 6-8 × 400 meters at 5K pace with 200-meter jog between; 1-mile cool-down	Easy run: 4-6 miles	Regular run: 4-5 miles	Tempo run: 2-mile warm-up; 2-3 miles continuous at 25-30 seconds per mile slower than 10K pace; 1-mile cool-down	Easy run: 2-4 miles	31-42
Week 3	Long run: 8-10 miles	Easy run: 3-5 miles, then 6 × 100-meter strides	Intervals: 2-mile warm-up; 3 × 1,000 meters at 5K pace with 400-meter jog between; 1-mile cool-down	Easy run: 6-8 miles	Regular run: 4-5 miles, then 6 × 100-meter strides	Tempo run: 2-mile warm-up; 3 miles continuous at 25-30 seconds per mile slower than 10K pace; 1-mile cool-down	Day off	33-40
Week 4	Long run: 8-10 miles	Easy run: 3-5 miles, then 6 × 100-meter strides	Intervals: 2-mile warm-up; 2 × set of 800 meters, 400 meters, 400 meters, with 800s at 5K pace and 400s at mile pace; 400-meter jog between all sets; 1-mile cool-down	Easy run: 6-8 miles	Regular run: 4-5 miles, then 6 × 100-meter strides	Progression run: 2-mile warm-up; 3 miles continuous, starting at 30 seconds per mile slower than 10K pace and increasing pace 5-10 seconds per mile after each mile; 1-mile cool-down	Easy to regular run: 3-4 miles	36-44

(continued)

8-Week Marathon-to-5K Schedule: Up to 45 Miles per Week (continued)

	Sunday	Monday	Tuesday	Wednesday	Thursday	Friday	Saturday	Week's mileage
Week 5	Long run: 8-10 miles	Easy run: 3-5 miles, then 6 × 100-meter strides	Intervals: 2-mile warm-up; 2 × 400 meters at mile pace with 200-meter jog after each; 2 × 800 meters at 5K pace with 400-meter jog after each; 2 × 400 meters at mile pace with 200-meter jog after each; 1-mile cool-down	Easy run: 6-8 miles	Regular run: 4-5 miles, then 6 × 100-meter strides	Intervals and tempo run: 2-mile warm-up; 3 × 600 meters at 5K pace with 400-meter jog after each; 2 miles continuous at 25 seconds per mile slower than 10K pace; 2 × 400 meters at mile pace with 200-meter jog between; 1-mile cool-down	Easy run: 3-4 miles OR Day off	34-45
Week 6	Long run: 8-10 miles	Easy run: 3-5 miles, then 6 × 100-meter strides	Intervals: 2-mile warm-up; 8 × 400 meters at 5K pace with 200-meter jog between; 1-mile cool-down	Easy run: 6-8 miles	Regular run: 4-5 miles, then 6 × 100-meter strides	Tempo run: 2-mile warm-up; 3 miles continuous at 25-30 seconds per mile slower than 10K pace; 1-mile cool-down	Easy run: 3-4 miles	36-44
Week 7	Long run: 6-8 miles	Easy run: 1-3 miles OR Day off	Intervals: 2-mile warm-up; 1,200 meters at 5K pace; 4 × 400 meters at mile pace; 400-meter jog between all intervals; 1-mile cool-down	Easy run: 4-6 miles	Regular run: 3-5 miles, then 6 × 100-meter strides	Tempo work: 2-mile warm-up; 2-3 miles continuous at 15-20 seconds per mile slower than 10K pace; 800-meter jog; 4 × 300 meters at mile pace with 100-meter walk between; 1-mile cool-down	Easy run: 3-4 miles OR Day off	24-39
Week 8	Long run: 5-7 miles	Easy run: 3 miles	Intervals: 2-mile warm-up; 6-8 × 300 meters at 5K pace with 200-meter jog between; 1-mile cool-down	Easy run: 2-4 miles OR Day off	Easy run: 3 miles, then 6 × 100-meter strides	Easy run: 2-3 miles, then 4-6 × 100-meter strides	Race 5K	19-26 (not including race)

The marathon-to-5K schedules assume one week off from running between your marathon and the first week of the schedule. If you like to do a little jogging during that week, that's up to you.

8-Week Marathon-to-5K Schedule: 25-55 Miles per Week

	Sunday	Monday	Tuesday	Wednesday	Thursday	Friday	Saturday	Week's mileage
Week 1	Easy run: 4-5 miles	Easy run: 4-5 miles	Easy run: 4-5 miles	Easy run: 4-6 miles	Easy run: 4-5 miles	Easy run: 4-5 miles	Easy run: 4-5 miles OR Day off	24-36
Week 2	Regular run: 7-10 miles	Easy run: 4-5 miles	Intervals: 2-mile warm-up; 8 × 400 meters at 5K pace with 200-meter jog between; 1-mile cool-down	Easy run: 6-8 miles	Regular run: 4-6 miles	Tempo run: 2-mile warm-up; 3 miles continuous at 25-30 seconds per mile slower than 10K pace; 1-mile cool-down	Easy run: 4-6 miles	37-47
Week 3	Long run: 8-12 miles	Easy run: 4-6 miles, then 6 × 100-meter strides	Intervals: 2-mile warm-up; 4 × 1,000 meters at 5K pace with 400-meter jog between; 1-mile cool-down	Easy run: 6-8 miles	Regular run: 5-8 miles, then 8 × 100-meter strides	Tempo run: 2-mile warm-up; 3 miles continuous at 25-30 seconds per mile slower than 10K pace; 1-mile cool-down	Easy run: 4-6 miles OR Day off	36-53
Week 4	Long run: 8-12 miles	Easy run: 4-6 miles, then 6 × 100-meter strides	Intervals: 2-mile warm-up; 3 × set of 800 meters, 400 meters, 400 meters, with 800s at 5K pace and 400s at mile pace; 400-meter jog between all repeats; 1-mile cool-down	Easy run: 6-9 miles	Regular run: 6-8 miles, then 8 × 100-meter strides	Progression run: 2-mile warm-up; 3-4 miles continuous, starting at 30 seconds per mile slower than 10K pace and increasing pace 5-10 seconds per mile after each mile; 1-mile cool-down	Easy run: 4-6 miles	40-54

(continued)

8-Week Marathon-to-5K Schedule: 25-55 Miles per Week (continued)

	Sunday	Monday	Tuesday	Wednesday	Thursday	Friday	Saturday	Week's mileage
Week 5	Long run: 8-12 miles	Easy run: 4-6 miles, then 6 × 100-meter strides	Intervals: 2-mile warm-up; 3 × 400 meters at mile pace with 200-meter jog after each; 2 × 800 meters at 5K pace with 400-meter jog after each; 3 × 400 meters at mile pace with 200-meter jog after each; 1-mile cool-down	Easy run: 8-9 miles	Regular run: 5-8 miles, then 8 × 100-meter strides	Intervals and tempo run: 2-mile warm-up; 3 × 600 meters at 5K pace with 400-meter jog after each; 2 miles continuous at 25 seconds per mile slower than 10K pace; 400-meter jog; 2 × 400 meters at mile pace with 200-meter jog between; 1-mile cool-down	Easy run: 4-6 miles	43-55
Week 6	Long run: 8-12 miles	Easy run: 4-6 miles, then 6 × 100-meter strides	Intervals: 2-mile warm-up; 8 × 400 meters at 5K pace with 200-meter jog between; 1-mile cool-down	Easy run: 6-8 miles	Regular run: 5-8 miles, then 6 × 100-meter strides	Tempo run: 2-mile warm-up; 3 miles continuous at 25-30 seconds per mile slower than 10K pace; 1-mile cool-down	Easy run: 1-4 miles OR Day off	35-50
Week 7	Long run: 6-8 miles	Easy run: 3-4 miles, then 6 × 100-meter strides	Intervals: 2-mile warm-up; 1 mile at 5K pace or a few seconds slower; 4 × 400 meters at mile pace; 1 mile at 5K pace or a few seconds slower; 400-meter jog between all intervals; 1-mile cool-down	Easy run: 4-6 miles	Regular run: 4-6 miles, then 6 × 100-meter strides	Tempo work: 2-mile warm-up; 2-3 miles continuous at 15-20 seconds slower than 10K pace; 800-meter jog; 4 × 300 meters at mile pace with 100-meter walk between; 1-mile cool-down	Easy run: 3-4 miles	33-41
Week 8	Long run: 6-8 miles	Easy run: 4 miles, then 6 × 100-meter strides	Intervals: 2-mile warm-up; 8 × 300 meters at 5K pace with 200-meter jog between; 1-mile cool-down	Easy run; 3-4 miles OR Day off	Easy run: 3-4 miles, then 6 × 100-meter strides OR Day off	Easy run: 2-3 miles, then 4-6 × 100-meter strides	Race 5K	20-28 (not including race)

The marathon-to-5K schedules assume one week off from running between your marathon and the first week of the schedule. If you like to do a little jogging during that week, that's up to you.

8-Week Marathon-to-5K Schedule: 35+ Miles per Week

	Sunday	Monday	Tuesday	Wednesday	Thursday	Friday	Saturday	Week's mileage
Week 1	Easy run: 4-5 miles	Easy run: 4-5 miles	Easy run: 4-5 miles	Easy run: 4-6 miles	Easy run: 4-5 miles	Easy run: 4-5 miles	Easy run: 4-5 miles OR Day off	24-36
Week 2	Regular run: 8-10 miles	Easy run: 4-5 miles	Easy intervals: 2- to 3-mile warm-up; 8-10 × 400 meters at 5K pace with 200-meter jog between; 1- to 2-mile cool-down	Easy run: 6-8 miles	Regular run: 4-6 miles	Tempo run: 2- to 3-mile warm-up; 3 miles continuous at 25-30 seconds per mile slower than 10K pace; 1- to 2-mile cool-down	Easy run: 4-6 miles	38-51
Week 3	Long run: 10-14 miles	Easy run: 7-9 miles, then 8 × 100-meter strides	Intervals: 2- to 3-mile warm-up; 6 × 1,000 meters at 5K pace with 400-meter jog between; 1- to 2-mile cool-down	Easy run: 7-10 miles	Regular run: 7-9 miles, then 8 × 100-meter strides	Tempo run: 2- to 3-mile warm-up; 3-4 miles continuous at 25-30 seconds per mile slower than 10K pace; 1- to 2-mile cool-down	Easy run: 4-6 miles	48-65
Week 4	Long run: 10-14 miles	Easy run: 7-9 miles, then 8 × 100-meter strides	Intervals: 2- to 3-mile warm-up; 4 × set of 800 meters, 400 meters, 400 meters, with 800s at 5K pace and 400s at mile pace; 400-meter jog between all repeats; 1- to 2-mile cool-down	Easy run: 7-10 miles	Regular run: 7-9 miles, then 8 × 100-meter strides	Progression run: 2- to 3-mile warm-up; 3-4 miles continuous, starting at 30 seconds per mile slower than 10K pace and increasing pace 5-10 seconds per mile after each mile; 1- to 2-mile cool-down	Easy to regular run: 4-6 miles	50-68

(continued)

8-Week Marathon-to-5K Schedule: 35+ Miles per Week (continued)

	Sunday	Monday	Tuesday	Wednesday	Thursday	Friday	Saturday	Week's mileage
Week 5	Long run: 10-14 miles	Easy run: 1-4 miles OR Day off	Intervals: 2- to 3-mile warm-up; 4 × 400 meters at mile pace with 200-meter jog after each; 2 × 800 meters at 5K pace with 400-meter jog after each; 4 × 400 meters at mile pace with 200-meter jog after each; 1- to 2-mile cool-down	Easy run: 7-10 miles	Regular run: 7-9 miles, then 8 × 100-meter strides	Intervals and tempo run: 2- to 3-mile warm-up; 3 × 600 meters at 5K pace with 400-meter jog after each; 2 miles continuous at 25 seconds per mile slower than 10K pace; 400-meter jog; 2 × 400 meters at mile pace with 200-meter jog between; 1- to 2-mile cool-down	Easy run: 4-6 miles	43-62
Week 6	Long run: 10-14 miles	Easy run: 6-8 miles, then 8 × 100-meter strides	Intervals: 2- to 3-mile warm-up; 8 × 400 meters at 5K pace with 200-meter jog between; 1- to 2-mile cool-down	Easy run: 7-10 miles	Regular run: 7-9 miles, then 8 × 100-meter strides	Tempo run: 2- to 3-mile warm-up; 3-4 miles continuous at 25-30 seconds per mile slower than 10K pace; 1- to 2-mile cool-down	Easy run: 4-6 miles	46-63
Week 7	Long run: 10-12 miles	Day off (preferred) OR Easy run: 3 miles, then 8 × 100-meter strides	Intervals: 2- to 3-mile warm-up; 1 mile at 5K pace; 4 × 400 meters at mile pace; 1 mile at 5K pace or a few seconds slower; 400-meter jog between all intervals; 1- to 2-mile cool-down	Easy run: 6-8 miles	Regular run: 5-8 miles, then 6 × 100-meter strides	Tempo work: 2- to 3-mile warm-up; 2-3 miles continuous at 15-20 seconds slower than 10K pace; 800-meter jog; 4 × 300 meters at mile pace with 100-meter walk between; 1- to 2-mile cool-down	Easy run: 3-4 miles	37-50
Week 8	Long run: 6-8 miles	Easy run: 4 miles	Intervals: 2- to 3-mile warm-up; 8 × 300 meters at 5K pace with 200-meter jog between; 1- to 2-mile cool-down	Easy run: 4-5 miles	Easy run: 3-4 miles, then 8 × 100-meter strides	Easy run: 2-3 miles, then 4-6 × 100-meter strides	Race 5K	24-31 (not including race)

The marathon-to-5K schedules assume one week off from running between your marathon and the first week of the schedule. If you like to do a little jogging during that week, that's up to you.

8-Week Marathon-to-10K Schedule: Up to 45 Miles per Week

	Sunday	Monday	Tuesday	Wednesday	Thursday	Friday	Saturday	Week's mileage
Week 1	Day off (rest from marathon)	Day off (rest from marathon)	Day off (rest from marathon)	Day off (rest from marathon)	Easy run: 4 miles	Easy run: 4 miles	Easy run: 2-4 miles	10-12
Week 2	Long run: 5-8 miles	Easy run: 3-5 miles	Easy run: 3-5 miles	Easy run: 3-6 miles	Easy run: 3-6 miles	Intervals: 2-mile warm-up; 6-8 × 400 meters at 10K pace with 200-meter jog between; 1-mile cool-down	Day off	22-36
Week 3	Long run: 8-10 miles	Easy run: 3-5 miles, then 6 × 100-meter strides	Intervals: 2-mile warm-up; 3 × 1 mile at 5-10 seconds per mile faster than 10K pace with 400-meter jog between; 1-mile cool-down	Easy run: 6 miles	Regular run: 3-5 miles, then 6 × 100-meter strides	Tempo run: 2-mile warm-up; 3-4 miles continuous at 25-30 seconds per mile slower than 10K pace; 1-mile cool-down	Day off	32-39
Week 4	Long run: 10-12 miles	Easy run: 3-5 miles, then 6 × 100-meter strides	Intervals: 2-mile warm-up; 6 × 800 meters at 10-20 seconds per mile faster than 10K pace with 400-meter jog between; 1-mile cool-down	Easy run: 6-8 miles	Regular run: 4-5 miles, then 6 × 100-meter strides	Progression run: 2-mile warm-up; 3 miles continuous, starting at 30 seconds per mile slower than 10K pace and increasing pace 5-10 seconds per mile after each mile; 1-mile cool-down	Easy to regular run: 3-4 miles	39-47

(continued)

8-Week Marathon-to-10K Schedule: Up to 45 Miles per Week (continued)

	Sunday	Monday	Tuesday	Wednesday	Thursday	Friday	Saturday	Week's mileage
Week 5	Long run: 10-12 miles	Easy run: 3-5 miles, then 6 × 100-meter strides	Intervals: 2-mile warm-up; 2 × 1,200 meters at 10K pace; 2 × 800 meters at 5K pace; 2 × 400 meters at mile pace; 400-meter jog after all intervals; 1-mile cool-down	Easy run: 6-8 miles	Regular run: 3-5 miles, then 6 × 100-meter strides	Intervals and tempo run: 2-mile warm-up; 2 × 800 meters at 10K pace with 400-meter jog after each; 2 miles continuous at 25 seconds per mile slower than 10K pace; 400-meter jog; 2 × 400 meters at mile pace with 200-meter jog between; 1-mile cool-down	Easy run: 1-3 miles OR Day off	37-48
Week 6	Long run: 10-12 miles	Easy run: 3-5 miles, then 6 × 100-meter strides	Intervals: 2-mile warm-up; 8 × 400 meters at 5K pace with 200-meter jog between; 1- to 2-mile cool-down	Easy run: 6-8 miles	Regular run: 3-5 miles, then 6 × 100-meter strides	Tempo run: 2-mile warm-up; 3-4 miles continuous at 25-30 seconds per mile slower than 10K pace (see if you can go a bit faster than 3 weeks ago at the same effort); 1-mile cool-down	Easy run: 3-4 miles	37-46
Week 7	Long run: 10-12 miles	Easy run: 1-3 miles OR Day off	Intervals: 2-mile warm-up; 6 × 800 meters at 20 seconds per mile faster than 10K pace with 400-meter jog between; 1-mile cool-down	Easy run: 6-8 miles	Regular run: 3-5 miles, then 6 × 100-meter strides	Race pace work: 2-mile warm-up; 3 × 1 mile at 10K pace with 400-meter jog between; 1-mile cool-down	Easy run: 2-4 miles	35-46
Week 8	Long run: 6-8 miles	Easy run: 3 miles	Intervals: 2-mile warm-up; 8 × 400 meters at 5K pace with 200-meter jog between; 1-mile cool-down	Day off	Easy run: 3 miles, then 6 × 100-meter strides OR Day off	Easy run: 3 miles, then a few 100-meter strides	Race 10K	18-23 (not including race)

The marathon-to-10K schedules assume one week off from running between your marathon and the first week of the schedule. That continues one or more days into the first week of these schedules.

8-Week Marathon-to-10K Schedule: 30-55 Miles per Week

	Sunday	Monday	Tuesday	Wednesday	Thursday	Friday	Saturday	Week's mileage
Week 1	Day off (rest from marathon)	Easy run: 2-4 miles	Easy run: 4 miles	Easy run: 4 miles	Easy run: 4-6 miles	Easy run: 4-6 miles	Easy run: 2-4 miles	20-28
Week 2	Long run: 6-10 miles	Easy run: 5-7 miles	Easy run: 5-7 miles	Easy run: 5-7 miles	Easy run: 5-7 miles	Intervals: 2-mile warm-up; 6-8 × 400 meters at 10K pace with 200-meter jog between; 1-mile cool-down	Easy run: 3-4 miles	34-48
Week 3	Long run: 10-12 miles	Easy run: 5-7 miles, then 6 × 100-meter strides	Intervals: 2-mile warm-up; 3-4 × 1 mile at 5-10 seconds per mile faster than 10K pace with 400-meter jog between; 1-mile cool-down	Easy run: 7-9 miles	Regular run: 5-7 miles, then 6 × 100-meter strides	Tempo run: 2-mile warm-up; 3-5 miles continuous at 25-30 seconds per mile slower than 10K pace; 1-mile cool-down	Day off	40-51
Week 4	Long run: 10-14 miles	Easy run: 5-7 miles, then 6 × 100-meter strides	Intervals: 2-mile warm-up; 6 × 800 meters at 10-20 seconds per mile faster than 10K pace with 400-meter jog between; 1-mile cool-down	Easy run: 7-9 miles	Regular run: 5-7 miles, then 6 × 100-meter strides	Progression run: 2-mile warm-up; 4 miles continuous, starting at 30 seconds per mile slower than 10K pace and increasing pace 5-10 seconds per mile after each mile; 1-mile cool-down	Easy to regular run: 3-5 miles	44-56

(continued)

8-Week Marathon-to-10K Schedule: 30-55 Miles per Week (continued)

	Sunday	Monday	Tuesday	Wednesday	Thursday	Friday	Saturday	Week's mileage
Week 5	Long run: 12-14 miles	Easy run: 5-7 miles, then 6 × 100-meter strides	Intervals: 2-mile warm-up; 2 × 1,200 meters at 10K pace; 2 × 800 meters at 5K pace; 2 × 400 meters at mile pace; 400-meter jog after all intervals; 1-mile cool-down	Easy run: 7-9 miles	Regular run: 5-7 miles, then 6 × 100-meter strides	Intervals and tempo run: 2-mile warm-up; 2 × 800 meters at 10K pace with 400-meter jog after each; 2 miles continuous at 25 seconds per mile slower than 10K pace; 400-meter jog; 2 × 400 meters at mile pace with 200-meter jog between; 1-mile cool-down	Easy run: 2-3 miles OR Day off	45-56
Week 6	Long run: 10-13 miles	Easy run: 5-7 miles, then 6 × 100-meter strides	Intervals: 2-mile warm-up; 8 × 400 meters at 5K pace with 200-meter jog between; 1-mile cool-down	Easy run: 6-8 miles	Regular run: 5-7 miles, then 6 × 100-meter strides	Tempo run: 2-mile warm-up; 3-5 miles continuous at 25-30 seconds per mile slower than 10K pace (see if you can go a bit faster than 3 weeks ago at the same effort); 1-mile cool-down	Easy run: 3-5 miles	41-52
Week 7	Long run: 10-12 miles	Easy run: 3-4 miles	Intervals: 2-mile warm-up; 6 × 800 meters at 20 seconds per mile faster than 10K pace with 400-meter jog between; 1-mile cool-down	Easy run: 6-8 miles	Regular run: 4-6 miles, then 6 × 100-meter strides	Race pace work: 2-mile warm-up; 3 × 1 mile at 10K pace with 400-meter jog between; 1-mile cool-down	Easy run: 3-4 miles	40-48
Week 8	Long run: 6-10 miles	Easy run: 3-4 miles	Intervals: 2-mile warm-up; 8 × 400 meters at 5K pace with 200-meter jog between; 1-mile cool-down	Day off	Easy run: 3 miles, then 6 × 100-meter strides	Easy run: 3 miles, then a few 100-meter strides	Race 10K	21-26 (not including race)

The marathon-to-10K schedules assume one week off from running between your marathon and the first week of the schedule. That continues one or more days into the first week of these schedules.

8-Week Marathon-to-10K Schedule: 30+ Miles per Week

	Sunday	Monday	Tuesday	Wednesday	Thursday	Friday	Saturday	Week's mileage
Week 1	Day off (rest from marathon)	Easy run: 2-4 miles	Easy run: 4 miles	Easy run: 4 miles	Easy run: 4-6 miles	Easy run: 4-6 miles	Easy run: 2-4 miles	20-28
Week 2	Long run: 6-10 miles	Easy run: 6-8 miles	Easy run: 6-8 miles	Easy run: 6-9 miles	Easy run: 6-8 miles	Intervals: 2- to 3-mile warm-up; 6-8 × 400 meters at 10K pace with 200-meter jog between intervals; 1- to 2-mile cool-down	Easy run: 4-6 miles	39-57
Week 3	Long run: 10-14 miles	Easy run: 6-8 miles, then 8 × 100-meter strides	Intervals: 2- to 3-mile warm-up; 4-5 × 1 mile at 5-10 seconds per mile faster than 10K pace with 400-meter jog between; 1- to 2-mile cool-down	Easy run: 7-9 miles	Regular run: 6-8 miles, then 8 × 100-meter strides	Tempo run: 2- to 3-mile warm-up; 3-5 miles continuous at 25-30 seconds per mile slower than 10K pace; 1- to 2-mile cool-down	Easy run: 4-6 miles	47-64
Week 4	Long run: 12-15 miles	Easy run: 6-8 miles, then 8 × 100-meter strides	Intervals: 2- to 3-mile warm-up; 6-8 × 800 meters at 10-20 seconds per mile faster than 10K pace with 400-meter jog between; 1- to 2-mile cool-down	Easy run: 7-10 miles	Regular run: 6-8 miles, then 8 × 100-meter strides	Progression run: 2- to 3-mile warm-up; 4-5 miles continuous, starting at 30 seconds per mile slower than 10K pace and increasing pace 5-10 seconds per mile after each mile; 1- to 2-mile cool-down	Easy to regular run: 4-6 miles	49-65

(continued)

8-Week Marathon-to-10K Schedule: 30+ Miles per Week (continued)

	Sunday	Monday	Tuesday	Wednesday	Thursday	Friday	Saturday	Week's mileage
Week 5	Long run: 12-15 miles	Easy run: 6-8 miles, then 8 × 100-meter strides	Intervals: 2- to 3-mile warm-up; 2 × 1,200 meters at 10K pace; 2 × 800 meters at 5K pace; 2 × 400 meters at mile pace; 400-meter jog after all intervals; 1- to 2-mile cool-down	Easy run: 7-10 miles	Regular run: 6-8 miles, then 8 × 100-meter strides	Intervals and tempo run: 2- to 3-mile warm-up; 2 × 800 meters at 10K pace with 400-meter jog after each; 3 miles continuous at 25 seconds per mile slower than 10K pace; 400-meter jog; 2 × 400 meters at mile pace with 200-meter jog between; 1- to 2-mile cool-down	Easy run: 4-6 miles OR Day off	47-67
Week 6	Long run: 10-14 miles	Easy run: 6-8 miles, then 6 × 100-meter strides	Intervals: 2- to 3-mile warm-up; 8-10 × 400 meters at 5K pace with 200-meter jog between; 1- to 2-mile cool-down	Easy run: 7-9 miles	Regular run: 6-8 miles, then 6 × 100-meter strides	Tempo run: 2- to 3-mile warm-up; 4-5 miles continuous at 25-30 seconds per mile slower than 10K pace (see if you can go a bit faster than 3 weeks ago at the same effort); 1- to 2-mile cool-down	Easy run: 4-6 miles	46-64
Week 7	Long run: 10-13 miles	Easy run: 4-6 miles	Intervals: 2- to 3-mile warm-up; 8 × 800 meters at 20 seconds per mile faster than 10K pace with 400-meter jog between; 1- to 2-mile cool-down	Easy run: 7-9 miles	Regular run: 4-6 miles, then 8 × 100-meter strides	Race pace work: 2- to 3-mile warm-up; 3-4 × 1 mile at 10K pace with 400-meter jog between; 1- to 2-mile cool-down	Easy run: 3-4 miles	43-59
Week 8	Long run: 6-10 miles	Easy run: 3-4 miles	Intervals: 2- to 3-mile warm-up; 8 × 400 meters at 5K pace with 200-meter jog between; 1- to 2-mile cool-down	Easy run: 3-4 miles OR Day off	Easy run: 3 miles, then 8 × 100-meter strides	Easy run: 3-4 miles, then a few 100-meter strides	Race 10K	21-33 (not including race)

The marathon-to-10K schedules assume one week off from running between your marathon and the first week of the schedule. That continues one or more days into the first week of these schedules.

8-Week 15K–Half-Marathon-to-Mile-or-5K Schedule: Up to 45 Miles per Week

	Sunday	Monday	Tuesday	Wednesday	Thursday	Friday	Saturday	Week's mileage
Week 1	Easy run: 6-8 miles	Easy run: 3-4 miles	Easy run: 3-4 miles	Easy run: 4-6 miles	Easy run: 3-4 miles	Easy run: 3-4 miles	Easy run: 2-4 miles OR Day off	22-34
Week 2	Regular run: 6-8 miles	Easy run: 3-5 miles	Easy intervals: 2-mile warm-up; 12 × 200 meters at 5K pace with 200-meter jog between; 1-mile cool-down	Easy run: 4-6 miles	Regular run: 4-5 miles	Tempo run: 2-mile warm-up; 2-3 miles continuous at 25-30 seconds per mile slower than 10K pace; 1-mile cool-down	Easy run: 2-4 miles	30-40
Week 3	Long run: 8-10 miles	Easy run: 3-5 miles, then 6 × 100-meter strides	Intervals: 2-mile warm-up; 3 × 1,000 meters at 5K pace with 400-meter jog between; 1-mile cool-down	Easy run: 6-8 miles	Regular run: 4-5 miles, then 6 × 100-meter strides	Tempo run: 2-mile warm-up; 2-3 miles continuous at 25-30 seconds per mile slower than 10K pace; 1-mile cool-down	Day off	32-40
Week 4	Long run: 8-10 miles	Easy run: 3-5 miles, then 6 × 100-meter strides	Intervals: 2-mile warm-up; 2 × set of 800 meters, 400 meters, 400 meters, with 800s at 5K pace, 400s at mile pace; 400-meter jog between all repeats; 1-mile cool-down	Easy run: 6-8 miles	Regular run: 4-5 miles, then 6 × 100-meter strides	Progression run: 2-mile warm-up; 3 miles continuous, starting at 30 seconds per mile slower than 10K pace and increasing pace 5-10 seconds per mile after each mile; 1-mile cool-down	Easy run: 3-4 miles	35-43

(continued)

8-Week 15K–Half-Marathon-to-Mile-or-5K Schedule: Up to 45 Miles per Week (continued)

	Sunday	Monday	Tuesday	Wednesday	Thursday	Friday	Saturday	Week's mileage
Week 5	Long run: 8-10 miles	Easy run: 3-5 miles, then 6 × 100-meter strides	Intervals: 2-mile warm-up; 400 meters at mile pace with 400-meter jog after; 2 × 800 meters at mile pace with 400-meter jog after each; 400 meters at mile pace; 1-mile cool-down	Easy run: 6-8 miles	Regular run: 4-5 miles, then 6 × 100-meter strides	Intervals and tempo run: 2-mile warm-up; 2 × 600 meters at mile pace with 400-meter jog after each; 2 miles continuous at 25 seconds per mile slower than 10K pace; 400-meter jog; 2 × 400 meters at mile pace with 200-meter jog between; 1-mile cool-down	Easy run: 3-4 miles OR Day off	33-44
Week 6	Long run: 8-10 miles	Easy run: 3-5 miles, then 6 × 100-meter strides	Intervals: 2-mile warm-up; 6 × 400 meters at 5K pace; 4 × 200 meters at mile pace; 200-meter jog between all repeats; 1-mile cool-down	Easy run: 6-8 miles	Regular run: 4-5 miles, then 6 × 100-meter strides	Tempo run: 2-mile warm-up; 2-3 miles continuous at 20-30 seconds per mile slower than 10K pace; 800-meter jog; 4 × 200 meters at mile pace with 200-meter jog between; 1-mile cool-down	Easy run: 3-4 miles	36-45
Week 7	Long run: 6-8 miles	Easy run: 1-3 miles OR Day off	Intervals: 2-mile warm-up; 1,200 meters at 5K pace; 4 × 400 meters at mile pace; 400-meter jog between all intervals; 1-mile cool-down	Easy run: 4-6 miles	Regular run: 3-5 miles, then 6 × 100-meter strides	Tempo work: 2-mile warm-up; 2 miles continuous at 10K pace; 800-meter jog; 4 × 300 meters at mile pace with 100-meter walk between; 1-mile cool-down	Easy run: 3-4 miles OR Day off	25-38
Week 8	Long run: 5-7 miles	Easy run: 3 miles	Intervals: 2-mile warm-up; 6 × 300 meters at mile pace with 200-meter jog between; 1-mile cool-down	Easy run: 2-4 miles OR Day off	Easy run: 3 miles, then 6 × 100-meter strides	Easy run: 2-3 miles, then 4-6 × 100-meter strides	Race 5K or 1 mile	18-25 (not including race)

8-Week 15K–Half-Marathon-to-Mile-or-5K Schedule: 25-50 Miles per Week

	Sunday	Monday	Tuesday	Wednesday	Thursday	Friday	Saturday	Week's mileage
Week 1	Easy run: 6-8 miles	Easy run: 3-4 miles	Easy run: 3-4 miles	Easy run: 4-6 miles	Easy run: 4-6 miles	Easy run: 4-6 miles	Easy run: 3-4 miles OR Day off	24-36
Week 2	Regular run: 8-10 miles	Easy run: 4-6 miles	Easy intervals: 2-mile warm-up; 12 × 200 meters at 5K pace with 200-meter jog between; 1-mile cool-down	Easy run: 6-8 miles	Regular run: 5-7 miles	Tempo run: 2-mile warm-up; 3 miles continuous at 25-30 seconds per mile slower than 10K pace; 1-mile cool-down	Easy run: 3-4 miles	38-47
Week 3	Long run: 8-12 miles	Easy run: 4-6 miles, then 6 × 100-meter strides	Intervals: 2-mile warm-up; 3 × 1,000 meters at 5K pace with 400-meter jog between; 1-mile cool-down	Easy run: 6-8 miles	Regular run: 5-7 miles, then 6 × 100-meter strides	Tempo run: 2-mile warm-up; 3 miles continuous at 25-30 seconds per mile slower than 10K pace; 1-mile cool-down	Easy run: 3-4 miles OR Day off	35-49
Week 4	Long run: 8-12 miles	Easy run: 4-6 miles, then 6 × 100-meter strides	Intervals: 2-mile warm-up; 3-4 × sets of 800 meters, 400 meters, 400 meters, with 800s at 5K pace and 400s at mile pace; 400-meter jog between all repeats; 1-mile cool-down	Easy run: 6-8 miles	Regular run: 5-7 miles, then 6 × 100-meter strides	Progression run: 2-mile warm-up; 3-4 miles continuous, starting at 30 seconds per mile slower than 10K pace and increasing pace 5-10 seconds per mile after each mile; 1-mile cool-down	Easy run: 3-4 miles	39-49

(continued)

8-Week 15K–Half-Marathon-to-Mile-or-5K Schedule: 25-50 Miles per Week (continued)

	Sunday	Monday	Tuesday	Wednesday	Thursday	Friday	Saturday	Week's mileage
Week 5	Long run: 8-12 miles	Easy run: 4-6 miles, then 6 × 100-meter strides	Intervals: 2-mile warm-up: 400 meters at mile pace with 400-meter jog after; 2 × 800 meters at mile pace with 400-meter jog after each; 400 meters at mile pace; 1-mile cool-down	Easy run: 6-8 miles	Regular run: 5-7 miles, then 6 × 100-meter strides	Intervals and tempo run: 2-mile warm-up; 3 × 600 meters at mile pace with 400-meter jog after each; 2 miles continuous at 25 seconds per mile slower than 10K pace; 400-meter jog; 2 × 400 meters at mile pace with 200-meter jog between; 1-mile cool-down	Easy run: 3-4 miles OR Day off	36-48
Week 6	Long run: 8-12 miles	Easy run: 4-6 miles, then 6 × 100-meter strides	Intervals: 2-mile warm-up; 6-8 × 400 meters at 5K pace; 4 × 200 meters at mile pace; 200-meter jog between all repeats; 1-mile cool-down	Easy run: 6-8 miles	Regular run: 5-7 miles, then 6 × 100-meter strides	Tempo run: 2-mile warm-up; 2-3 miles continuous at 20-30 seconds per mile slower than 10K pace; 800-meter jog; 4 × 200 meters at mile pace with 200-meter jog between; 1-mile cool-down	Easy run: 3-4 miles	36-56
Week 7	Long run: 6-8 miles	Easy run: 3-4 miles	Intervals: 2-mile warm-up; 1,200 meters at 5K pace; 4 × 400 meters at mile pace; 400-meter jog between all intervals; 1-mile cool-down	Easy run: 4-6 miles	Regular run: 4-6 miles, then 6 × 100-meter strides	Tempo work: 2-mile warm-up; 2 miles continuous at 10K pace; 800-meter jog; 4 × 300 meters at mile pace with 100-meter walk between; 1-mile cool-down	Easy run: 3-4 miles OR Day off	29-41
Week 8	Long run: 5-7 miles	Easy run: 3-4 miles	Intervals: 2-mile warm-up; 6 × 300 meters at mile pace with 200-meter jog between; 1-mile cool-down	Easy run: 2-4 miles OR Day off	Easy run: 3-4 miles, then 6 × 100-meter strides	Easy run: 2-3 miles, then 4-6 × 100-meter strides	Race 5K or 1 mile	18-27 (not including race)

8-Week 15K–Half-Marathon-to-Mile-or-5K Schedule: 30+ Miles per Week

	Sunday	Monday	Tuesday	Wednesday	Thursday	Friday	Saturday	Week's mileage
Week 1	Easy run: 6-8 miles	Easy run: 3-4 miles	Easy run: 4-6 miles	Easy run: 5-6 miles	Easy run: 4-6 miles	Easy run: 4-6 miles	Easy run: 3-4 miles OR Day off	26-40
Week 2	Regular run: 8-10 miles	Easy run: 5-7 miles	Intervals: 2- to 3-mile warm-up; 12 × 200 meters at 5K pace with 200-meter jog between; 1- to 2-mile cool-down	Easy run: 7-8 miles	Regular run: 6-8 miles	Tempo run: 2- to 3-mile warm-up; 3-4 miles continuous at 25-30 seconds per mile slower than 10K pace; 1- to 2-mile cool-down	Easy run: 4-6 miles	42-55
Week 3	Long run: 10-13 miles	Easy run: 5-7 miles, then 6 × 100-meter strides	Intervals: 2- to 3-mile warm-up; 3-4 × 1,000 meters at 5K pace with 400-meter jog between; 1- to 2-mile cool-down	Easy run: 7-8 miles	Regular run: 6-8 miles, then 6 × 100-meter strides	Tempo run: 2- to 3-mile warm-up; 3-4 miles continuous at 25-30 seconds per mile slower than 10K pace; 1- to 2-mile cool-down	Easy run: 4-6 miles OR Day off	40-60
Week 4	Long run: 10-13 miles	Easy run: 5-7 miles, then 6 × 100-meter strides	Intervals: 2- to 3-mile warm-up; 3-4 × set of 800 meters, 400 meters, 400 meters, with 800s at 5K pace and 400s at mile pace; 400-meter jog between all repeats; 1- to 2-mile cool-down	Easy run: 7-8 miles	Regular run: 6-8 miles, then 6 × 100-meter strides	Progression run: 2- to 3-mile warm-up; 3-4 miles continuous, starting at 30 seconds per mile slower than 10K pace and increasing pace 5-10 seconds per mile after each mile; 1- to 2-mile cool-down	Easy run: 4-6 miles	45-61

(continued)

8-Week 15K–Half-Marathon-to-Mile-or-5K Schedule: 30+ Miles per Week *(continued)*

	Sunday	Monday	Tuesday	Wednesday	Thursday	Friday	Saturday	Week's mileage
Week 5	Long run: 10-13 miles	Easy run: 5-7 miles, then 6 × 100-meter strides	Intervals: 2- to 3-mile warm-up; 400 meters at mile pace with 400-meter jog after; 2 × 800 meters at mile pace with 400-meter jog after each; 400 meters at mile pace; 1- to 2-mile cool-down	Easy run: 7-8 miles	Regular run: 6-8 miles, then 6 × 100-meter strides	Intervals and tempo run: 2- to 3-mile warm-up; 4 × 600 meters at mile pace with 400-meter jog after each; 2 miles continuous at 20-25 seconds per mile slower than 10K pace; 400-meter jog; 4 × 400 meters at mile pace with 200-meter jog between; 1- to 2-mile cool-down	Easy run: 4-6 miles OR Day off	41-59
Week 6	Long run: 10-13 miles	Easy run: 5-7 miles, then 6 × 100-meter strides	Intervals: 2- to 3-mile warm-up; 8 × 400 meters at 5K pace; 4 × 200 meters at mile pace; 200-meter jog between all repeats; 1- to 2-mile cool-down	Easy run: 7-8 miles	Regular run: 6-8 miles, then 6 × 100-meter strides	Tempo run: 2- to 3-mile warm-up; 3-4 miles continuous at 20-30 seconds per mile slower than 10K pace; 800-meter jog; 4 × 200 meters at mile pace with 200-meter jog between; 1- to 2-mile cool-down	Easy run: 4-6 miles	46-60
Week 7	Long run: 6-8 miles	Easy run: 4-6 miles	Intervals: 2- to 3-mile warm-up; 1,200 meters at 5K pace; 4 × 400 meters at mile pace; 400-meter jog between all intervals; 1- to 2-mile cool-down	Easy run: 4-6 miles	Regular run: 6-8 miles, then 6 × 100-meter strides	Tempo work: 2- to 3-mile warm-up; 2 miles continuous at 10K pace; 4 × 300 meters at mile pace with 100-meter walk between; 1- to 2-mile cool-down	Easy run: 4-6 miles OR Day off	32-50
Week 8	Long run: 5-7 miles	Easy run: 3-4 miles	Intervals: 2- to 3-mile warm-up; 6 × 300 meters at mile pace with 200-meter jog between; 1- to 2-mile cool-down	Easy run: 2-4 miles OR Day off	Easy run: 3-4 miles, then 6 × 100-meter strides	Easy run: 2-3 miles, then 4-6 × 100-meter strides	Race 5K or 1 mile	18-29 (not including race)

INDEX

ABOUT THE AUTHORS

Mark Coogan (@mark_coogan) is the coach of Team New Balance Boston (@teamnbboston), an elite distance running team that sent three athletes to the 2021 Olympics. He was previously the distance running coach at Dartmouth College and also coached at Tufts University, Massachusetts Institute of Technology, and Phillips Exeter Academy. Among the athletes Coogan has coached are Olympians Elle St. Pierre, who holds the U.S. indoor records for the 1-mile and 2-mile races and is a world championship silver medalist; Heather MacLean, the 2022 U.S. indoor 1,500-meter champion; and Abbey D'Agostino Cooper, whose seven NCAA titles make her the most decorated distance runner in Ivy League history. Before becoming an elite coach, Coogan was a professional runner from 1988 to 2004. He was on the 1996 U.S. Olympic marathon team, won the silver medal in the marathon at the 1995 Pan American Games, represented the United States in the 5,000-meter race in the 1995 World Track and Field Championships, and ran in seven World Cross Country Championships. He had unique range, ranking in the top 10 in the United States in the mile, steeplechase, 5K, 10K, and marathon during his career. He was also the first Massachusetts native to run a mile in less than 4 minutes. He lives in Newburyport, Massachusetts.

Scott Douglas (@mescottdouglas) is a contributing writer for *Runner's World* and the author or coauthor of several well-known running books, including *Advanced Marathoning*, *Running Is My Therapy*, and the New York Times best sellers *Meb for Mortals* and *26 Marathons*. His writing on fitness and health has appeared in *The Atlantic*, *Washington Post*, *Slate*, and *Outside*. He lives in North Yarmouth, Maine.

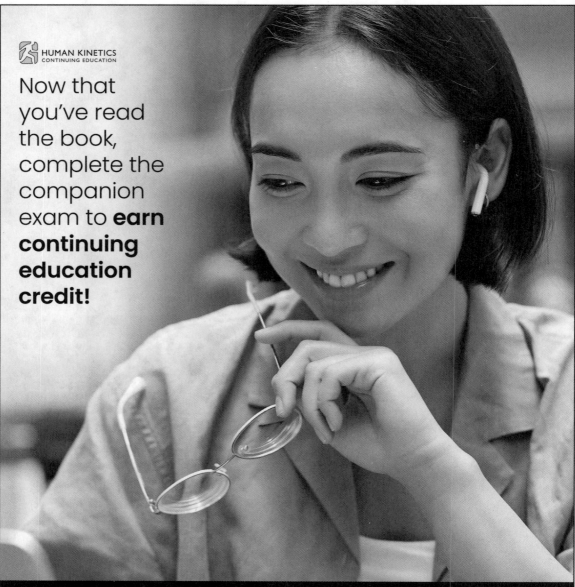